The Political Use of Racial Narratives

The Political Use of Racial Narratives

School Desegregation in
Mobile, Alabama, 1954–97

RICHARD A. PRIDE

University of Illinois Press
URBANA AND CHICAGO

∞ This book is printed on acid-free paper.

Library of Congress Cataloging-in-Publication Data
Pride, Richard A. (Richard Alan), 1942–
The political use of racial narratives : school desegregation
in Mobile, Alabama, 1954–97 / Richard A. Pride.
p.   cm.
Includes bibliographical references (p.   ) and index.
ISBN 0-252-02766-3 (cloth : alk. paper)
1. African Americans—Education—Alabama—Mobile.
2. Politics and education—Alabama—Mobile.
3. School integration—Alabama—Mobile.
I. Title.
LC2803.M63P75   2002
379.2'63'0976122—dc21   2002002823

For Dick and Nadine Pride

Contents

Acknowledgments

I WISH TO THANK staff members of the Mobile County public school system for their help in gathering material for this book. They are too numerous to name here, but I had unfailingly good and productive relationships with them all. Similarly, I thank Michael Marshall, managing editor of the *Mobile Register;* his predecessor, Thomas Taylor; and others there for timely access to the clipping files and electronic library. I could not have negotiated federal court records without the kind and determined guidance of Larry Strahan, deputy clerk of the U.S. District Court in Mobile.

I extend a special thanks to two people. Vaughan May served as my research assistant and intellectual companion as both graduate student and faculty peer; his continuing interest has been a source of strength for me. And, more recently, Mary Helen Clarke's trenchant editorial comment made itself felt, and without her skill and encouragement I could not have so easily and readily completed this book.

While others assisted the book's progress, I alone am responsible for its perspective and argument, as well as any errors in fact or judgment.

Two parts of this book were published previously, and both are reprinted here with permission. The epilogue to *The Confession of Dorothy Danner: Telling a Life* (Nashville, Tenn.: Vanderbilt University Press, 1995) appears here as the opening pages of chapter 1. Chapter 10 is a revised version of a paper that first appeared as "Redefining the Problem of Racial Inequality," *Political Communication* 16 (1999): 147–67.

Introduction

School board member Dan Alexander waved a note given to him by a distressed white parent. A teacher, he said, had sent the note home, and the mother read it, was horrified, and complained to him. It read: "Scott is dropping in his studies he acts as if he don't care. Scott want pass in his assignment at all, he a had a poem to learn and he fell to do it. Mrs. [Name] I feel that you should know this."

Alexander said that this ungrammatical communication was unacceptable, that teachers who spoke and wrote like this ought to be removed from teaching in the Mobile public schools. The board's responsibility was to make that happen. The board needed to establish competency tests for teachers so that inadequate teachers could be purged from the schools.

Alexander told this story first at a press conference in March 1978 and later to the school board and the whole country—indeed, a photograph of him waving the note at a school board meeting appeared in *Time* magazine. His story changed everything. With it he shifted the focus of the race problem from white discrimination against blacks to the failure of African American individuals to live up to the reasonable expectations of a competitive world.

Politics is, at its most basic level, a contest to establish the meaning of events, because whoever constructs the public meaning of happenings sets the agenda for our collective lives. Stories make meaning of life. The stories we tell each other, and particularly the stories we insist others learn, not only contain knowledge of our selves and our past but they intend a distinct future. Hence, telling a story is an elemental political act.

In this book I examine the narrative undercurrents of racial politics and cultural change. My central proposition here is that stories affect our perceptions of the world and that these alterations in turn affect our individual and collective behaviors. By definition, whenever perceptions and behaviors of most people in an area are significantly reconfigured, the culture of a place changes. In order to demonstrate the connection between narrative contest and cultural change, I am laying bare the record of one metropolitan area, Mobile, Alabama.

Mobile is one of the American South's oldest and best places. It sits on the shores of a great natural harbor about thirty miles from the Gulf of Mexico. It has a long history of surprising racial and ethnic diversity, but its roots followed the rivers north into the heart of the black belt of Mississippi and Alabama, where cotton and timber grew abundantly, and planters, rednecks, and blacks marked all the society that people acknowledged. The city had its face turned toward the world, but it nevertheless grew out of the Old South.

Mobile has been governed under six national flags. The French established the city in 1702 and ceded it to the English in 1763. In 1780 it was captured by Spain, then by the United States in 1813. In 1861 Alabama seceded from the Union and formed the Republic of Alabama before becoming part of the Confederate States of America. During the Civil War the city played a prominent role in the Confederate war effort and surrendered only in the last days of the war.[1]

Today Mobile is a city of 200,000 in a metropolitan area of more than 500,000. The city is about 45 percent black, the metropolitan area about 25 percent.

The South and Cultural Change

The federal government sought to change the culture of the South following the Civil War and again during and after the civil rights movement. The first period of Reconstruction lasted from 1865 to about 1877. The federal government tried a second reconstruction from the 1950s to 1970s, certainly, and arguably into the 1990s. On both occasions the U.S. government tried to destroy a racially hierarchical culture and replace it with a culture of individual merit. People were to be judged by their characters and achievements, not by the color of their skin.

The first Reconstruction of the South by the federal government sought to establish voting rights and equality before the law for all individuals and to create a free market in labor in order to totally transform the southern way of life. Thaddeus Stevens, a Radical Republican leader in the U.S. House of Representatives, made it plain in a speech in 1865: "The whole fabric of southern society must be changed and never can it be done if this opportunity is lost. . . . It never has been a true republic. Heretofore, it had more the features of aristocracy than of democracy. The Southern States have been despotisms, not government of the people. It is impossible that any practical equality of rights can exist where a few thousand men monopolize the whole landed property. The larger the number of small proprietors the more safe and stable the government. If the South is ever to be made a safe republic let her lands be cultivated by the toil of the owners or the free labor of intelligent citizens."[2]

Stevens was clear: Reconstruction was intended to transform the hierarchy of the Old South into the individualized culture of liberal America. But, in the event, the effort failed.

Radically segregationist southern whites recaptured political power in the 1870s, particularly after the withdrawal of federal troops in 1877. Some in the South called the period "the Redemption" because native white men were once again able to govern, and in the years that followed they diminished the status of blacks and separated the races by law.

Ohio-born Albion W. Tourgee became prominent in North Carolina politics during Reconstruction. He was what many called a carpetbagger, and after Redemption he wrote a novel in which The Fool expressed the author's feelings: "We tried to superimpose the civilization, the idea of the North, upon the South at a moment's warning. We presumed that, by the suppression of rebellion, the Southern white man had become identical with the Caucasian of the North in thought and sentiment; and that the slave, by emancipation, had become a saint and a Solomon at once. We tried to build up communities there which would be identical in thought, sentiment, growth, and development with those of the North. It was A Fool's Errand."[3]

By the time the southern radicals lost their political dominance, in about 1915, they had put in place Jim Crow laws that defined separation of the races in all aspects of life. The separate-but-unequal regime of Jim Crow lasted until the 1950s. Arguably, the second reconstruction of the South began with the U.S. Supreme Court's ruling in *Brown v. Board of Education* in 1954 and finally ended with the ascendence of the southerner-led Republican Party in Congress in 1994. During the second reconstruction black political representation, in voting rights and electoral redistricting, and affirmative action, in education as well as employment, were the policies chosen to end the racial discrimination and sociopolitical hierarchy in the South.

The goal of both reconstructions was cultural change, and both required southerners to take a stand on the goals and instruments of change. Joel Williamson lays out the responses of southern whites in *The Crucible of Race* (1984) in which he identifies three "mentalities" in the culture of the South during the last century and a half—radicals, conservatives, and liberals.[4] Each position had a political agenda and embraced different public narratives and underlying metanarratives. The most pessimistic were the radicals. The radical white mentality, forged during Reconstruction, emerged most dramatically in 1889 through a burst of interracial lynchings and held sway until 1915. Radicals held that Negroes freed from the tight control of slavery would retrogress rapidly toward their natural state of savagery. Metanarratives of providential will and Darwinian selection lay behind their rhetoric, and they assumed that black people could have no legitimate place in the United States. The conservatives were the second, less extreme, force. They too assumed black inferiority but sought to find a suitable, permanent place for blacks within the social fabric. Conservatives sought to specify the nature of Negro inferiority and to create institutions that accommodated that inferiority naturally. Where radicals would expel blacks, conservatives accepted social separation and economic hierarchy as natural and benign. "Conservativism" as a mentality came into full flower before the Civil War but persisted throughout the years. Indeed, Williamson sees radicals and liberals as children of an older, established conservative ideology. The "liberal" mind-set was strongest in the 1880s; liberals were impressed with the progress of the Negro race under northern leadership during Reconstruction. Southern liberals argued that if the environment could be changed, blacks could prosper. Liberalism was assimilative. It argued that blacks could learn white culture. It was a matter of teaching certain values, like discipline and hard work, and providing employment opportunity. Liberals insisted that the race problem resulted from white oppression and continuing discrimination but could be ended with the enculturation of the black race.

White liberals of recent decades in the South trace their lineage to their nineteenth century roots, and they allied themselves with blacks, northern liberals, and the federal government to bring about the second reconstruction, just as they did the first.

Critical Concepts in Cultural Change

Public education was central to the public agenda of each ideological perspective, because everyone knew that social and civic values were inculcated right along with facts and figures. In the twenty-first century the primary question, for scholars and attentive citizens alike, is this: Did the second reconstruction of the South through federally imposed school desegregation succeed in changing southern culture and, if so, how?

The central claim of this book is, yes, the culture of Mobile and the South has changed in important ways and that this change was brought about when a new and more robust narrative came to justify any continuing racial inequality. But before I can proceed with this inquiry, I must make clear my concepts and perspectives. What is a story? What is political power? What is a culture? How do they fit together?

A story is simply an account that arranges people and events through time and space. Narrative discourse differs from other forms, like legal briefs, formal essays, or the "inverted pyramid" of newspaper reports. Story is both more primitive and causally prior to any of these modes. If the narrative form is not innate to humans, it is nearly so. Before writers write, they have a story in mind. Before readers understand, a story provides the lens through which they see.

In an analytical essay arguing the centrality of the story for political science, Molly Patterson and Kristen Monroe distinguish between story and other forms of discourse in human affairs.[5] First, they point out, a story generally requires human agency. Disembodied forces may work in history, but human beings must play a role, even a decisive role, in the unfolding of events in the world, even if that role is only that of the keen observer or suffering servant. Humans are assumed to organize information and act in the world in the pursuit of goals. Second, the word *narrative* implies that the speaker's view is canonical. The speaker is matter-of-fact about what is normal. It is the unusual that the speaker notes. Otherwise, why tell the story? We do not tell stories about the habits of lives but about the departures from habit. Social surprise, ironic twist, impending threat—these are the stuff of stories. Third, a narrative requires an ordering of events in time, but the events may be real or fabricated. The ordering is what reveals the speaker's mind, not the fidelity to facts. And finally, narrative discourse requires the narrator to have perspective. The account cannot be without a point of view; it is not a recitation of merely random data. A story shows how the teller organizes the world and her place in it.[6]

Margaret R. Somers and Gloria D. Gibson usefully distinguish among four types of stories: personal, public, conceptual, and metanarrative (or, as it is sometimes called, the metastory or master narrative).[7] Personal narratives are our own particular constructions; they place us within space and time and within a nexus of social relationships. The stories that we tell family, friends, and new acquaintances, however, depend on other, deeper stories. Metanarratives are fundamental texts from which individual life stories and collective history emerge. Metanarratives always serve as context—they are foundational, even mythic, stories that frame the running accounts that people give about the happenings of their time and place. Metanarratives give precedence to certain ungrounded values: individuals over collectives, freedom over duty, order over disorder, or vice versa.[8]

In Mobile, Alabama, a prominent white woman "adopted" the daughter of her black maid and delighted in telling others of the child's intellectual accomplishments. Every time she had Caroline speak her newly acquired French, the matron implicitly countered the older, deeper metanarrative of blacks' innate inferiority. Intuitively, everyone listening to the personal story knew this. As in this case, personal narrative is often the signal of broader cultural shifts. But because intimates, the news media, or scholars do not often record personal stories, we usually miss and neglect their place in cultural change.

Between personal and metanarratives are two other types. Public narrative involves the stories that institutions and social movements advance. Social forces collide in the stories that groups and institutions explicitly or implicitly tell as they wrestle over our collective destiny. This is the world of symbolic politics, the kind of thing covered by newspapers and therefore available to all of us. For instance, some whites today celebrate the Confederate battle flag as a sign of their distinctive cultural heritage; they claim that it represents the appeal of rooted community, of home and family, and honor of the valiant dead; they say they do not wave the flag out of personal bigotry or the ideology of racial superiority. Many other people, however, claim that the flag stands for white supremacy, and defiant racists display it today. Across the South public controversy erupts whenever anyone displays this flag. Stories are told and countered in the public war about the meaning of this old banner. The stakes are high: Newspaper reporters, textbook authors, and the legal system incorporate in their writings the worldview of the victor. People know this.

Intellectuals construct the fourth type of narrative, the conceptual narrative; intellectuals define terms and posit causal patterns in a manner amenable to formal logic and scientific explanation. Scholars embrace this form of narrative. In fact, this book represents a conceptual narrative of cultural change: First, there were old stories, then some storytellers used both old and new stories to shape the imagination of other people, and the newly recast images not only held people's attention but got them to live in a new way. The better storytellers won the contest and got the prize.

Perhaps the most important conceptual story that influenced families in Mobile and other communities was the one that James Coleman and other sociologists told in the 1960s. Research by Coleman and others showed that black students' academic achievement went up when they attended school with middle-class whites.[9] This finding was generalized into a scientific story of racial assimilation called the "contact theory" of racial integration, and it led ultimately to busing for racial balance in the public schools.[10]

Clearly, whatever the generic type of story—personal, public, conceptual, or meta—they are all connected. In the telling and retelling, in the acting out or alluding to, each type of narrative responds to and acts upon the others. In examining events and narratives embedded in racial conflict about the racial desegregation of public schools in Mobile, we want to see who benefits and who pays when different stories are told and become accepted as true. School board meetings, street demonstrations, courts of law, newspaper staffs and their printed pages, and civic forums are the public venues where citizens act out underlying narratives.

Because stories are portrayed as much as told, we may regard public events as performances, as stages set for narrative conflict; we may regard leaders as actors. The task for us, then, is to note the underlying stories that they are acting out or alluding to and to infer why they are using these stories in specific settings and to what effect. In this process readers of this book are participants too, and I implicitly invite them to develop a story of their own from the record of dramatic events presented here.

Metanarratives about Race

Race has always been a problem in the United States, and over time different metanarratives have "explained" obvious inequalities between whites and blacks in different ways. Some definitions of "the race problem" have risen to prominence and affected public policy. Others were offered, discussed briefly perhaps, then cast aside, where they lingered persistently in some subcultures but made no mark on policy or polity. No one has assembled a catalog of all the definitions of the race problem in American public life, but a large and old literature gives guidance and assigns blame.[11] Attributing blame for racial inequality depends on the metanarrative used:

1. Sometimes people say that God established the inequalities between blacks and whites for some divine reason. Clearly, this definition of the problem subsumes all others. If blacks simply do not try hard enough, that could be God's will. If God ordained inequality, what could government do about it? The response to such a view could only be numbing fatalism or prayerful petition to God, and in any case the policy derived from it would likely be paternalism in some form. In recent decades the historical record in Mobile finds little of this rhetoric in public, but survey data show that many people, both black and white, accept some notion of the hand of Providence in racial matters.

2. Another metanarrative invokes a kind of pseudoscientific Darwinism. Throughout the slave period in the South whites thought that blacks were biologically inferior, incapable of critical thinking. Many southern whites approached the American "race problem" by arguing about how to deal with a genetically inferior people. This definition of the problem favored an official attitude of paternalism and a public policy of separate and *un*equal public schools. That explanation, while eclipsed in recent decades nearly everywhere, was voiced in Mobile until the 1960s as part of the official defense of school segregation. Recently, after decades of suppression the biological argument reemerged in the public arena. *The Bell Curve* (1994), by Richard Herrnstein and Charles Murray, again raised the biological basis for persistent inequalities, and their argument provoked widespread attention—*Newsweek*, the *New Republic*, and many other media gave it significant play.[12] A special issue of the multidisciplinary journal *Intelligence* supported aspects of Herrnstein and Murray's argument.[13]

If not God or biology, perhaps blacks themselves are to blame for their persistent socioeconomic inequality. Two related narrative tracks signal a subcultural critique in U.S. culture:

3. Many blacks have self-destructive cultural values and behaviors. To people who take this perspective, it accounts, for example, for bad choices (early pregnancy, drug and alcohol abuse, and criminal acts) by those who should know better and could do better. If black culture is flawed, one appropriate public policy might be to assimilate blacks into another, more functional (read "white"), culture. In *The Unheavenly City* (1970) Edward Banfield singles out "present orientation" as a symptom of the dysfunction of ghetto subcultures.[14] Banfield argues that the pursuit of immediate gratification is a dysfunctional and self-defeating family trait that has been passed along for generations in the ghetto. Its presence legitimizes a wholesale reconstruction of urban life. But scholars like Banfield were not alone in making this claim. The black Muslim leader Louis Farrakhan and the Million Man March in 1995 emphasized the costs to black people of inappropriate attitudes and behavior.[15]

4. The absence of individual effort and responsibility as a subcultural value is central to another variant of the culturalist critique. In *Race and Economics* (1975) Thomas Sowell argues that black Americans could be compared to recent immigrants who must make a choice about strategies for getting ahead.[16] If blacks choose rightly—individual and collective discipline, education, and the intergenerational transfer of wealth—they will succeed just as other immigrant groups have. If they choose wrongly, according to Sowell, and make an issue of their social status, they will not. In another seminal book, *Losing Ground* (1984), Charles Murray uses the notion of a dysfunctional in-

ner-city (black) culture to denigrate liberal social welfare programs because, he says, they subvert self-reliance, the very trait that blacks need most in order to succeed in American life.[17] In any case, a public policy of benign neglect might follow from this definition of the problem of race in the United States. From this perspective African Americans alone can change their future.

5. Other definitions of the race problem see blacks as victims of a pattern of historical and continuing discrimination by whites. One definition of the problem sees blacks as victims of white oppression on a grand scale. This view emphasizes the control of society by wealthy and powerful whites who conspire to keep blacks down. The pervasive racism of the whole Eurocentric culture finds its point in specific, concerted race-conscious exclusions. Generations of militant leaders, men like Malcolm X, Asa Hilliard, and Leonard Jeffries, spoke out of this narrative tradition.[18] The folklorist Patricia A. Turner recorded urban legends among contemporary African Americans and found that many of their stories play out the themes of white oppression: that the Klan owns a fried chicken chain that systematically poisons black males to make them sterile; that the killing of twenty-eight blacks in Atlanta attributed to a serial killer was instead genocide; that government scientists developed the AIDS virus and tested it in Africa because they viewed blacks as expendable; and so on.[19] Stories like these, told in the black community, bear witness to an internalized metanarrative about white oppression.

6. Still another view sees blacks not actively oppressed so much as freighted by the losses suffered during slavery and Jim Crow segregation. Historical discrimination and accumulated burdens make blacks unable to compete and succeed as other ethnic groups have done. Andrew Hacker takes this view in *Two Nations* (1995): "It is white America that has made being black so disconsolate an estate. Legal slavery may be in the past, but segregation and subordination have been allowed to persist. Even today, America imposes a stigma on every black child at birth."[20]

If either of the latter two views prevails and redress is sought, government will have to remedy present inequalities by whatever means necessary, including affirmative action employment policies, multicultural education, and even direct financial reparations. Restructuring of political power may also be warranted, including guaranteed racial representation in legislative bodies.

During the struggle over school desegregation in Mobile, these six explanations were all "in play," offered as fundamental sources of human action. When black citizens protested and school board members resisted, each group saw itself as acting in continuity with one of the metanarratives and wanted to be seen as doing so. At issue politically, then and now, is which stories to advance, contest, and accept as "true," because what the majority of citizens believes becomes legitimized through unchallenged repetition and is confirmed by public policy.

Stories may reinforce or change cultures. Storytellers build popular expectations by assigning meanings to events. If individuals or whole peoples fail and fall, storytellers can ascribe their demise to a whim of fate (or God), innate ineptitude, a failure of character, or oppression by evildoers—that is, political actors assign the problem, the agency, and the blame through culturally available metanarratives. As Williamson shows in *The Crucible of Race,* southern social movements—radicals, conservatives, and liberals—used public narratives about race that grew out of and used metanarratives about racial difference.

Culture and Politics

Culture consists of both shared values and beliefs, on the one hand, and patterns of interpersonal relations on the other.[21] Culture is a way of living. Stories, example, and experience teach culture. Culture persists through traditional socialization, but it changes in significant ways with time and circumstances.

The United States has many subcultures, just as it has many people with viable ways of living life. In *Cultural Theory* Michael Thompson, Richard Ellis, and Aaron Wildavsky aggregate subcultures into five general types: The main ones are hierarchical, egalitarian, fatalistic, and individualistic, but what they call "hermitude" is also possible.[22] They distinguish these cultural types by the interaction of two dimensions—the degree to which social structures favor individual autonomy as opposed to social control of human behavior, and the degree to which individuals are embedded within or separated from social groups. According to this theory, all five cultural patterns are present in every nation at all times, but one form may predominate and characterize the society as a whole.

Speaking broadly, the American South was a hierarchical culture right from the start, although embedded in the dominant pattern were some elements of all cultural types. In cultures that are hierarchical to whatever degree, individuals occupy relatively fixed positions within a matrix of institutions, groups, and places, and society expects individuals to act out the roles assigned to those positions. In the Old South individuals knew their station and were socially constrained to behave in a proper manner, regardless of whether they were masters, overseers, or slaves. Richard Ellis uses this perspective in examining American history in his book *American Political Cultures* (1993).[23] Ellis portrays the subculture of slaves as fatalistic, set within the hierarchical culture of southern planters.

In individualistic cultures, on the other hand, individuals float freely and are largely unconstrained by outside expectations. While the industrial culture of the North certainly included inequalities, the free market in labor and capital permitted, even encouraged, a socioeconomic flux, the mythic American dream of merited ascendency by individuals and groups. Moreover, popular accounts, such as the stories of Horatio Alger, not only held out personal hope to individuals but gave legitimacy to the whole system.

The cultural types involve ways of seeing and living. Typically, people in individualistic cultures see nature as a cornucopia of opportunities and human beings as endlessly and rightly self-interested. On the other hand, people in hierarchical cultures see the world as offering limited opportunity and believe that people can do only so much without causing frightening social instability. Hierarchists believe that humankind needs definite limits but that proper authorities can guide people to be better individuals. In the South conservatives were hierarchists who clearly saw themselves as guardians of the racial and class status quo.

Narrative, Power, and Politics

Generally speaking, politics has been defined as "who gets what, where, when, and how" in the struggle over our collective destiny, when someone invokes or threatens the ultimate power of government. The "what" could be material goods or social status. The "where" could be intimate communal relations or marketplace associations. The "when" could be now or much later. The "how," in racial politics, could be the process of cultural assimilation or subcultural separation.[24]

When American political scientists talk about politics, they most often refer to a contemporary contest involving material goods distributed through government policy among contending interest groups. They assume that rational self-interest takes priority as people try to maximize their benefits. This perspective frames the current debate about Medicare or Social Security or school vouchers as a cost or benefit, pitting age groups and social classes against each other.

The prevailing behavioral approach in political science wrongly minimizes the power of stories and storytellers, arguably the real vessels of knowledge and meaning in political life. Political science has all too often neglected the effects of culture on political life because of the discipline's narrow foci—on rational decision making, formal institutions, and legal arenas, using supposedly scientific methods and discourse. But, most of all, the discipline's failure to study the formation and effects of values has limited its appeal and scope.[25] In particular, the dominant school has neglected stories and story-tellers' influence on political behavior.

Since the early 1990s a group of social scientists has moved an interpretivist critique forward. They have insisted that symbolic representation, including language itself, is inherently political, and they have given a theoretical basis for a new, nonbehavioral postpositivistic scholarship of political communication. Frederick Dolan and Thomas Dumm edited a set of essays called *Rhetorical Republic* (1993) in this new tradition.[26] They claim that "ours is a republic of words, which also means, necessarily, a republic of fantasies and images." Clearly, stories convey fantasies and images, so other scholars have looked specifically at the use of narrative in reframing social problems and public policy: Donald Schon and Martin Rein in *Frame Reflection* (1994); Sanford Schram and Philip Neisser, eds., in *Tales of the State: Narrative in Contemporary U.S. Politics and Public Policy* (1997), and Emery Roe in *Narrative Policy Analysis* (1994), to name just a few.[27]

In political science Murray Edelman was the godfather of symbolic politics.[28] Richard Merelman, also of the University of Wisconsin, has noticeably extended Edelman's work. Merelman's *Representing Black Culture* (1995) defines cultural projection as "the conscious or unconscious effort by a social group and its allies to place new images of itself before other social groups, and before the general public."[29] When blacks and whites argue about new images of each other in an effort to gain or hold social respect, they engage in cultural politics. Stories and storytellers are central to this process.

In sociology Herbert Blumer, an icon of symbolic interactionist theory, argues that racial prejudice is more a "sense of group position" than an attitude. What matters is how the "color line" is moved, and that process involves the restructuring of meaning.[30] Laurel Richardson and David R. Maines each have purposed that sociology is properly an interpretive rather than hypothesis-testing science.[31] Maines, in *The Faultline of Consciousness* (2001), shows how stories and narrative structures affect the making of meaning.[32] Narrative structures are cultural frames and ideologies that are frequently reduced to ideographic metaphors, such as "white flight." Maines says, "These phrases are not stories, but they are understood as a history of events, values, struggles, and beliefs that together constitute a collective story with an implotted point. In short, they perform a common cultural function of coding particular events into categories of meaning by including those events inside the parameter of a narrative structure."[33]

In *Power and Powerlessness* (1980) John Gaventa makes one of the best efforts to link sociopolitical dominance with the play of underlying narratives.[34] Gaventa asked why poor coal miners, who were a numerical majority in their communities, nonetheless allowed themselves to be oppressed by absentee mine owners and their hired managers. To answer the question he looked at the basis for and distribution of political power in the coalfields. Gaventa maintains that political power has three aspects. He argues that money, knowledge, and organization are resources that can be successfully mobilized for political purposes.Resources, then, are the "first face" of political power. The "second face" of power is the "mobilization of bias," an invisible boundary against the acknowledgment of new grievances brought by powerless people. Those already active in the political arena, of whatever political faction, share an automatic response that blocks the voices and claims of those on the margins of the political arena. Just as men as a group thoughtlessly denigrated the claims of women, so too did cosmopolitans put aside the petitions of miners from the Appalachian mountains. In this way, not making a decision is a form of power.

The "third face" of power, however, is the most pervasive. It is the capacity of the powerful to get the powerless to internalize the values of the powerful and thereby to "voluntarily" act in a manner that benefits the powerful but not the powerless. When owners touted and mountaineers accepted the idea that "progress" was better than tradition, and that competition was the engine of progress, the miners "competed" themselves into poverty while the managers and owners reaped the profits. The metanarrative of progress—that individuals who work hard in a competitive business climate will win more and better goods and that all will be better off tomorrow than today—was a myth that controlled the imaginations of those who labored for others' profits and their own impoverishment.[35] Gaventa shows that a particular metanarrative about humankind's nature and destiny captured the hearts and minds of a people who were consequently seduced into sociopolitical impotence.

In old Mobile myths of family, race, and class circumscribed opportunity. People from good families could be trusted, but those from the lower orders, poor whites and blacks, could not. This, of course, became a self-fulfilling prophecy. The bourbon elite controlled both work and play, both commerce and Mardi Gras, and it elected to public office people who sided with its interests. In this era interpersonal guardedness was a ubiquitous social convention, and both the good manners and the poor access to power by those who wanted significant change deflected personal and public grievances.

Gaventa argues that the escalation toward oppression is sequential: First one group uses its resources to obtain government power, then it habitually excludes and dismisses the voices of others, and finally it gets the weaker members of society to adopt the self-serving values of the new elite group. A kind of colonization occurs, a cultural hegemony. And the stories—personal, public, and meta—contain the images and values that legitimize or delegitimize social and economic arrangements. Stories, particularly mythological stories, are powerful instruments of social dynamics.

In Mobile, and in the South generally, white radicalism required a special kind of metaphor to mobilize fearful whites, stories of the menacing black male. In the twentieth century, when that image was diminished in white minds, radicalism shriveled as a political force, leaving the field to the genteel and more subtle language of bourbon conservatism.[36] White liberals required a different kind of metaphoric sustenance. For them it was the perfectibility of humankind. Williamson reminds us that during the first Reconstruction liberals saw "education, guided by whites, [as] the key to achieving a brotherhood of black and white."[37] This was true during the second reconstruction as well.

Whether education leads to harmony is still an open question, but stories are the force for change one way or the other, and people tell each other stories every day. When one mother tells another that a public schoolteacher is neglecting her bright daughter in order to pull up the slower children, she is not only telling a story but performing a political act.

Stories about welfare queens, black criminals, teacher insensitivity, or whatever else are not just a feature of our common lives but actually constitute politics, whether voiced unconsciously in conversation or intentionally offered as malicious rumor, because they give shape and meaning to events and actors alike.[38] As Sanford Schram and Philip Neisser write, "[Stories] are 'already there' in the sense that they are not so much an artifact of a preexisting actual reality as they are constitutive of it and even written into it. It is this 'already-there-ness' that makes such stories so potent—i.e., they are not as dependent upon facts as perhaps we often would like to assume. Stories therefore are arguably 'foundational,' preexisting facts and living beyond them, often surviving empirical refutation, in not just popular culture but everything else including politics and public policy-making. That is why 'counterstories' that offer alternative narratives as to why things are as they are can be an important political resource."[39]

Narrative Contest: Logic and Prediction

Walter Fisher lays out the basis of a narrative logic in *Human Communication as Narration* (1987).[40] A narrative logic lies behind and empowers all other discourse, including argument by exposition.[41] "No matter how strictly a case is argued—scientifically, philosophically, or legally—it will always be a story, an interpretation of some aspect of the world that is historically and culturally grounded and shaped by human personality," Fisher writes.[42] Reason is not "logic" alone; reason may include the logic of story, a "logos/mythos" conception of rationality.[43] Fisher quotes Carol C. Arnold: "We interpret and evaluate new stories against older stories acquired through experience. We search new accounts for their faithfulness to what we know, or think we know, and for their internal and external coherence. Later we *learn* more sophisticated criteria and standards for assessing a story's fidelity and coherence, but constructing, interpreting, and evaluating discourse as 'story' remains our primary, innate, species-specific 'logic.'"[44] We experience and comprehend life as a series of ongoing narratives, as conflicts, characters, beginnings, middles, and ends. Thus we may regard the various modes of communication—all forms of symbolic action— as stories, interpretations of things in sequence.[45]

The hearer assesses stories according to whether they make sense. Stories make sense if they cohere in terms of structure, material, and character and if they seem truthful. According to Fisher, then, coherence and fidelity form the basis of narrative logic. "We naturally and without formal instruction ask about any account of any sort whatever whether or not it 'holds together' and adds up to a reliable claim to reality," Fisher says. "We ask whether or not an account is faithful to related accounts we already know and believe."[46] He continues: "On these terms we *identify* with an account (and its author) or we treat it as mistaken. We identify with stories or accounts when we find that they offer 'good reasons' for being accepted. Good reasons are elements in human discourse or performance that we take as warrants for belief or action. Reasons are good when they are perceived as (1) true to and consistent with what we think we know and what we value, (2) appropriate to whatever decision is pending, (3) promising in effects for ourselves and others, and (4) consistent with what we believe is an ideal basis for conduct."[47]

Explicitly or implicitly, stories forecast. They say, "If you behave this way, then this will happen." People told many stories during Mobile's struggles over school desegregation. White resisters often claimed that outside agitators were the only people who wanted change, that they just stirred up trouble. Often, the leaders of the radicals told about the communist influence in the federal government and the civil rights movement. As long as they told these stories, their conspiratorial notions were hard to refute. But when they extrapolated into the future, their claims subverted themselves, as happened when they said, "Whites won't take it anymore: they will . . ." In the second reconstruction of Mobile whites resisted, but not en masse or violently, and when whites failed to rise up, the failure undercut the radical leaders.

Narratives and Social Problems

Explanations for racial inequality vary considerably, and have varied through time. These metanarratives shape and impel the personal and public narratives that people tell each other day by day about racial conflict and about the sources of inequality because that is simply how meaning is conveyed. Moreover, implicitly or explicitly, stories tell us what is wrong. Stories precipitate what we call social problems. Social problems are the problems that affect so many people so directly that we all agree that something is afflicting us and we feel compelled to give it a name: the race problem, the environmental problem, the crime problem, and so on.

Whenever a social problem is defined for the first time, or redefined later, we need to know whether the shift is the result of changing conditions in the real world or whether it is mostly "spin." This is an important and disputed question within political science and sociology.[48] Here's a case. When someone asks, "What is wrong with the public schools today?" educational activists and ordinary people throw out story upon story, competing with each other to define "the problem" of public education. In so doing, some will imply that too little disciplined learning takes place, while others will say that society heaps too many extravagant expectations on the schools.

The competitive nature of political life, rather than objective conditions, largely determines whether one definition of the problem of racial inequality supplants another. Both individuals and sociopolitical institutions have limited ability to make sense of the contending claims about what is or is not a social problem that requires a public solution. Because the attention of the elite and of the public is a scarce resource, whoever manages to define "the problem" also uses that advantage to shape the response.[49] Hypothetically, for example, if a social movement captures everyone's attention with the view that poor nutrition causes racial inequality, the movement probably would also tell us how to gain better nutrition.

Many factors affect whether contending claims capture enough attention to become full-blown "social problems"; among these are (1) the way we use stories to frame issues, and (2) whether those stories attract media and public interest, especially through a dramatic presentation of culturally mythic themes, the number of other problems raised at the same time, the material and social resources of institutions, and which social movement organizations are involved in the contest.

Critical Events

Public events activate storytellers, whether in the mass media or across the family dinner table. Something happens, say, parents boycott or picket a school. For a moment, because of the shared attention to the new phenomenon, minds are concentrated, attention is focused. People want interpretation. Especially when they are stimulated by events erupting in the objective world, activist citizens participate in the collective definition of social problems by articulating particular public narratives.

The collective definition of social problems is accelerated more by critical events than by incremental performance trends because critical events are more likely to stimulate competition among civic activists, politicians, and the mass media, nationally and locally, about the meaning to be given to newly problematic aspects of our collective lives.[50] Critical events are eruptions. Unlike routine occurrences, they are radical discontinuities in the real world that attract attention.[51]

Events drive politics "insofar as critical events alter *expectations and perceptions of threats,* focusing or distracting the attention of movement constituents and other important actors on or away from movement issues," writes Suzanne Staggenborg.[52] She says that events in themselves do not cause political change; instead, "actors' interpretations and organizational structures intervene between events and their outcomes."[53]

Members of the mass media and social and political activists frequently frame problems for publics, but whether these interpretations are congruent with objective indicators of system performance and how media and/or a political activist's perspectives may come to dominate an issue arena is always open to question. In Mobile the question of whether black and white children had similar educational resources was not defined empirically so much as rhetorically, because the real world was messier than the imagined one.

The Question of Assimilation

Assimilation is a process in which groups with different cultures, occupying the same geographical areas, come to have a common culture.[54] Politics and public policy can make this happen through either the absorption of one people by another or by fusion of all into something new. In the United States during the eighteenth and nineteenth centuries, absorption demanded the complete renunciation of the immigrant's ancestral culture in favor of the behavior and values of the Anglo-Saxon core group. Alternatively, assimilation can occur when two cultures of whatever size and scope fuse into a third, hybrid way of living.[55]

School desegregation, and particularly busing for racial balance, was an assimilationist policy.[56] Following the 1954 *Brown* decision, blacks were supposed to have access to white schools. Simple access, desegregation, was but the first step in the assimilationist enterprise. When it began, scholars and, later, activists saw busing for racial balance as a strong attempt to absorb blacks into the prevailing white culture. Over time, as politicized blacks saw absorption as culturally hegemonic, schools adopted a culturally fusionist policy. The schools were to blend together elements of both black and white cultures. In the South this meant that schools had to set aside nicknames and fight songs, like "Rebels" and "Dixie," in favor of generic new symbols and slogans. Cheerleading squads had to be integrated, even if doing so meant setting aside the usual rules of selection. Publishers had to reformulate U.S. history textbooks to give greater play to the minority experience. Some whites, though, believed that busing threatened to make dysfunctional black culture ascendant, and they rejected it on that ground.[57]

Separation is the process by which groups with different cultures preserve their distinctive values and behaviors, and multiculturalism is a bundle of government policies designed to sustain those separate lifestyles. Separate-but-unequal schools, mandated by Jim Crow laws in the South, was a bicultural policy. Arguably, vouchers that allow families to pay private school tuition from public funds is a contemporary example of a culturally separatist public policy because, if given the choice, parents are likely to place their children in culturally homogeneous settings, schools that socialize the young with parental or subcultural values, not civic values.

Central Questions

School desegregation was a policy central to the second reconstruction of the American South. I will use the historical record of the struggle to desegregate the public schools of Mobile, Alabama, to show the personal and public narratives that were presented, and I will seek out the metanarratives that animated and gave meaning to the actions of political leaders, movement activists, and ordinary citizens. I will show that over time white people in Mobile changed the story of racial inequality from biology to white discrimination and, later, to a failed black work ethic.

I also need to adduce the cause of that change: Was it the result of political leadership, media reframing, or lived experience? Moreover, did one dominant story replace another because of critical events in the empirical world or because of incremental evolutionary trends? Were the public policies adopted by the courts or by the school board linked in some direct way to the metanarrative contest? Finally, I ask whether the South, as measured by school desegregation in Mobile, has been culturally reconstructed—whether it has moved away from hierarchy and toward individualism.

The approach that I take here differs in certain respects from straight academic history. I will tell the story of Mobile predominantly through contemporaneous primary rather than subsequent secondary sources. I present to readers information that an attentive citizen of Mobile might have had as the events unfolded. This technique allows readers to continuously update their assessment and perhaps change it as new events prompt new stories. I will note various stories in their immediate contexts and provide stories with different perspectives on unfolding events in order to illustrate the contest for meaning that propels our political lives. I shall make clear my own analysis from time to time, mainly in the discussion section at the end of each chapter and in part 3. I invite readers to participate in this process as well and to judge for themselves which story has more power.

The process of narrative politics is endless, so we shall drop into the stream in 1955, just after the Supreme Court ordered school desegregation to proceed in the South "with all deliberate speed," because that was the first challenge to Mobile's pattern of separate schooling. Thereafter, I shall stick to a detailed, chronological account, inviting interpretation from events and documents available to attentive citizens at that time.

Theory-derived Propositions

Certain propositions guide my attempt to use the perspective of narrative politics to answer critical questions about cultural change:

1. The real world matters, but the interpretations made by storytellers are decisive because they establish the meanings that guide our lives. Stories, whether personal, public, or metanarrative, are perceptual filters that we use to make sense of an otherwise chaotic world. This is not to say that the real world is irrelevant. Empirical reality does discipline narrative accounts, but all too often the real world is ambiguous, and that is the situation in which interpretation matters most. Political leadership involves imagination. Political leaders and followers could tell or act out many stories, but they must decide which one is best.

2. Political leaders are likely to fail when the narratives that they tell their audiences fail to predict. Prediction is the biggest gamble for a politicized story. If the story makes sense and correctly anticipates unfolding events, its

interpretation of unfolding events is strongly enhanced, and the leader's claim to special status is justified. But, similarly, if the political leader tells a story that predicts and the prediction fails, both the story and the leader lose standing. For instance, in Mobile, when white radicals predicted that racial integration would lead to interracial violence, and significant violence did not occur, their stories of injury, injustice, and protest were impeached; they were not seen as telling the truth according to what people knew to be the case, and the radicals' erstwhile leaders faded from the stage. Accuracy in prediction, then, is one major factor in the ascendency of one story over another in the narrative contest, but there are others.

3. Narrative logic also requires coherence but not syllogistic reasoning. Instead, a prominent feature of narrative coherence is the degree to which cultural values are ordered and ordered in a way that is congruent with the foundational myths of a people. American public life bundles civic values together: personal liberty, equality, individualism, democracy, and the rule of law under a constitution.[58] The role of the political leaders is to interpret unfolding events in terms of these values. They are successful to the extent that they can define public issues as violations of one or another of these fundamental public values. American values are not rank-ordered but are instead cross-cutting.[59] Nevertheless, liberty stands out because our founding documents, particularly the Declaration of Independence, trumpet its place.[60] Arguably, then, a leader who frames public policy in terms of personal liberty will have an advantage in the rhetorical contest over those touting equality or even justice under law. We will see that leader's stories as more faithful to our origins.

4. Repetition itself is probably a useful tactic in narrative politics. Simple restatement, again and again, seems to play a strong part in political suasion, perhaps as much as in commercial advertising, particularly if conditions in the real world are neither directly felt nor onerous. The stories repeated by political contestants in Mobile worked partly because so few people knew firsthand what really happened in schools.

5. In politics narratives are the basis for contests within as well as between socioeconomic constellations. Within the black or white community, then, different leaders assumed and articulated different stories of the problems faced by their races, and they did so independent of facts because the facts were ambiguous. In Mobile, for instance, African American leaders told stories of recalcitrant white officials or of blacks' poor choices in an effort to account for the lower-than-average test scores of black children. The interpretations made, and the stories told in order to frame the debate, affected who would win and who would lose status within the black community, and that process also shaped the legal struggle for racial equity.

* * *

Mobile's struggle with race has been endless, but the narrative account presented here begins in 1955 with the story of one white liberal's quest to desegregate the public schools of her home city. From that point I ask readers to suspend privileged, after-the-fact knowledge and judgment and to live within the flow of events of that time, to take the perspective of an attentive citizen of that day. Only then can we take seriously the claims of the competing actors and critically examine their political moves.

PART 1

Protest and Resistance

1. Breaking the Color Line

THE LETTER, dated September 3, 1956, was addressed to Kenneth W. Reed, president of the Mobile County Board of School Commissioners. "Dear Mr. Reed," it began, "I am asking you as president of our school board for individual placement of my foster-daughter, a little Negro girl. This child is named Carrie Mae McCants. She is twelve years old and has been educated in various schools in Europe for the past two years."[1] This simple request broke a cultural taboo. It was a first attempt to desegregate the Mobile public schools, and it was made by an upper-class white woman. The writer, Dorothy D. DaPonte, then forty, was the only child of a wealthy Mobile businessman, and with this petition she stepped outside the magic circle of southern society.

The U.S. Supreme Court had rendered "separate but equal" schools unconstitutional in 1954, but it had not fixed a specific date for ending dual school systems. Instead, the Court ordered segregated school systems to desegregate "with all deliberate speed." In Alabama, as all across the Deep South, public officials adopted a policy of massive resistance to court-ordered desegregation. Newly enacted state laws and local policies would serve as renewable barricades that protected the norms of the Old South. Lengthy litigation regarding the constitutionality of these laws meant change would come only much later, if ever.[2]

Alabama enacted its pupil placement law in August 1955. It placed final authority for student assignment with local school boards, which were to study the issue and make policies affecting pupil placement that would take into account available space, the effect of new pupils on the established or proposed academic program, the scholastic preparation and ability of the student, the effect of admission upon the prevailing academic standards, the home environment of the student, and the possibility of friction or disorder among students or others, among many other considerations.[3] Although the law was racially neutral on its face, what it intended was never in doubt. In August 1956 Alabama voters amended the state constitution to empower the legislature to abolish public schools if necessary to prevent integration. The amendment also authorized state aid for private schools; the sale or gift of public facilities to private owners, who could operate them as segregated academies; and freedom of choice, which meant that parents could send their children to schools attended only by members of their own race.

* * *

Who was Dorothy DaPonte and why did she challenge the established patterns of southern life?[4] DaPonte was born Dorothy Danner in February 1916 into a conventional and well-to-do Mobile family. Dorothy's mother died when she was thirteen, and Paul Danner, her reserved and sometimes bewildered father, did the best he could to raise his intelligent and strong-willed daughter in the manner of southern women of their station. She attended the best schools and participated in the social seasons of Mobile. Her relatives were queens, maids, and knights at Mardi Gras, honors seldom given to those who did not have the traditions of Mobile and the South near their hearts.[5] But unlike other upper-class southern girls, who would marry and settle down, or sometimes go to Agnes Scott or to Sweetbriar for further education, Dorothy Danner chose to attend Vassar College in New York, where she was graduated in 1939. In the company of a friend, Sarah Harris of Tuscaloosa, Dorothy Danner took off for Greenwich Village, leaving behind her confused and disappointed father. In 1941 she celebrated her twenty-fifth birthday amid her adventures in New York City.

With the outbreak of World War II she returned to Mobile, but she never would fit comfortably into the culture into which she was born. She had become a pacifist and refused to pay her income taxes in protest of war, until the government compelled her to do so. She became a vegetarian and later an animal rights advocate. In 1944 she married a Dutch national, M. Nicolo DaPonte, who proved to be a heavy drinker and killed himself just six months later with a gun given to him for Christmas by her father.

Motherless, childless, and now widowed, Dorothy DaPonte retired to the family cabin on Dog River, just south of Mobile. Perhaps because she felt like a victim of cruel fate herself, she began to support others diminished in life, including blacks. When a bus driver and other white men beat and kicked Marie Gayle when she refused to move to the back of the bus, Dorothy Da-

Ponte paid $1,200 to a Birmingham attorney to prosecute the bus company; the verdict was that no more force had been used than was necessary. This incident fueled her outrage, and she began to use her money and the law to fight for the rights of other black people.

In the summer of 1949 she began to pass time with Carrie Mae McCants, the six-year-old daughter of her servant. In time she took Carrie Mae into her home. She wanted to show, her friends later said, that culture and graciousness could be brought into being by environment as well as by heredity.[6] The journey was both literal and figurative. Carrie Mae lived with Dorothy DaPonte but went to colored schools in Mobile during the early grades, and she excelled. DaPonte then took her ward to Europe and enrolled Carrie Mae in a series of fine private schools there. For eighth grade the peripatetic pair were back in Mobile. Carrie Mae was ready.

Dorothy DaPonte knew what she was doing when she wrote her letter to the school board. She knew the southern way of life, and she knew the law. She wrote, "I have brought up Carrie Mae myself since she was six and a half years old. Her background academically, morally and socially is adequate for her entrance into an integrated school." She continued, "The 'psychological effect' on her would be good as she has attended schools with white pupils for two years now. She would understand the significance of her position and is prepared by personal character, intelligence, and training to conduct herself in such manner as to minimize the possibility of friction and disorder. Such acceptance of her would give the Negro race an opportunity to show what their development can be under favorable circumstances. It would give Alabama a chance to show good faith in a case where there is no danger of large numbers or lowering of standards."

Reed, the school board president, replied for the board. He said that acts of the state legislature and recent revision of the state constitution had yet to be fully studied. In the meantime, planning for the current year had been done "on the basis of a continuation of the segregation status that was maintained during the last term. It is physically and financially impossible to make any change during the current term. There is a pupil-load in this county in excess of 52,000, and a material shortage in physical housing." Reed concluded his letter by saying flatly that "it is not possible . . . to make exceptions of this type."[7]

Denying Carrie Mae an assignment to a white school was not a matter of inadequate space; it was a matter of cultural norms. That a well-prepared black child sponsored by a privileged white woman could not be reassigned was a sign of how slowly the board was prepared to turn away from segregation.

Others in the community made it known that even to have asked was too much. On September 12 the local newspaper printed a small story summarizing DaPonte's petition.[8] On the night of September 12 eighteen cars with about one hundred white-robed men drove into DaPonte's driveway with horns blaring. They erected and ignited a ten-foot cross.[9] After milling about and shouting, the caravan left. "That DaPonte woman" and Carrie Mae were not at home. Days later another cross was burned at the home of a friend with whom they were staying. Reflecting in 1956 on her experience, DaPonte said, "The main reason my friends and relatives are afraid to mix with me is because they are afraid to be burned out."[10]

The burning of crosses was not all that happened. "Obscene calls and letters flooded my home and the homes of my friends and family," DaPonte recalled. Her father, one of her sharpest critics, fled to Mississippi to get away from it all. "Of course I know the rumors that are being circulated by lowlifes and trash," she said. "My friends and some of my family are beginning to believe some of these awful accusations that I'm Carrie Mae's mother." Salacious gossip argued that her husband had committed suicide when he found out the "true circumstances" surrounding Dorothy and Carrie Mae.

The marauding Klan harassed DaPonte, and it signaled to others that they were not to break the color line. Klansmen burned other crosses in the city, paraded at night in full regalia down the main street, ran ads in the local newspaper, and bombed several black homes. The newly organized Mobile Council on Human Relations, an affiliate of the Alabama Council on Human Relations and the Southern Regional Council, petitioned the city commission to pass ordinances curbing violence and intimidation by the Klan. This led to more disturbances and greater efforts to cow white liberals sympathetic to school desegregation. City fathers vowed to keep order but otherwise did not address publicly the underlying issues of race and class.[11]

After DaPonte's letter on behalf of Carrie Mae, school desegregation in Mobile subsided as a focus of concern. Between 1956 and 1963, under the state's pupil placement law, not a single black child was admitted to a white public school.[12] In the years that followed, Dorothy DaPonte and Carrie Mae faded from public life and became increasingly estranged from their roots and from each other. Much later DaPonte would tell her life story in all its complexity.[13] It reflected the hope, naïveté, and arguably the arrogance of the southern liberal's mind.

Culture and Power in Mobile

Culture encompasses both a people's worldview and their patterns of social interaction. Among five theoretically distinct cultural patterns—individualistic, egalitarian, hierarchical, fatalistic, and hermitude—there are regional preponderances. Although individualism prevailed most of the time in most places in the United States in the 1950s, in the South hierarchy was embedded in every public encounter.

In hierarchical cultures people know their places, defer to their betters, and generally fear change. Even the stories they tell each other reinforce the notion that calamities that befall those who defy tradition. Dorothy DaPonte defied tradition and paid a price. She was the quintessential white liberal, and every time she told a personal story of Carrie Mae's academic and social accomplishments, she reiterated the liberal's metanarrative, but it was not a story most others shared. Where she saw hope, others saw disaster.

Public shunning was not the only way to sanction rebels. Institutions of common life protected the status hierarchy in routine ways. Not just courts of law, churches, hospitals, and civic groups but even suffrage and elections—the very levers of power—were racially discriminatory. Whites dominated electoral politics in Mobile as elsewhere across the South. School board members, like county commissioners, were elected by countywide at-large elections in staggered terms, and this practice allowed a plurality of white voters to obtain and keep all power. Because the public schools required the largest share of local property taxes and served as a mechanism of social control, the county's elite institutionalized its control. Throughout the decades an ad hoc, club-centered process selected prominent citizens for service on the school board: The oligarchy informally tapped its own to run for the board. Dorothy's own father, Paul Danner, had served in his day.[14]

The board's watchword was stability. Hierarchical cultures require it. A policy adopted by the board in 1955, immediately following the Supreme Court's decision in *Brown II* and close upon the passage of Alabama's pupil law, showed the board's rationale for resisting federal power: "It must be recognized that integration is not acceptable to the major portion of our people. This is a factor that cannot be ignored, as was recognized by the Supreme Court in its decree implementing its decisions. The accomplishment of a full and complete result; which the bulk of our people feel was imposed on them by a superior power that, as they see it, was without adequate appreciation of the sociological, factual and psychological conditions of our people; may not be had with one blow. The traditions of two centuries can be altered by degrees only."[15]

Board members reacted as others did. They followed the same script because they shared similar biases: In brief, they claimed, the present school system meets the needs of its people, both black and white; outsiders do not know what is best, we do. Superior power may compel change, but we will resist and in the end prevail, just like we did after the first Reconstruction.

The Black Revolt

If Dorothy Danner DaPonte, with her social background, wealth, and willingness to use the law, could not break the color barrier, surely Mobile was secure. The DaPonte incident was, however, only a small squall; elsewhere across Alabama and the South thunderstorms of change erupted. Black people led and supported these civic upheavals.

The black revolt in Alabama came on two fronts. Nationally, the NAACP (National Association for the Advancement of Colored People) and the NAACP Legal Defense and Education Fund favored use of the law and federal courts to overturn segregation practices. They already had won significant battles, most notably in *Brown* in 1954. Alabama had several chapters of the NAACP, and they threatened to bring legal action if their negotiations with officials did not alter dual systems of education and public accommodations. When the NAACP began to support the Montgomery bus boycott financially and legally, state officials acted. In June 1956, in order to thwart the boycott, and especially to break the financial and legal leadership exercised from New York and Washington, D.C., Gov. James E. "Big Jim" Folsom Sr. got a state court order prohibiting NAACP operations in Alabama.[16] Local black leaders simply formed new organizations to continue their long persistent campaign, but they were handicapped by this exercise of state power.

In 1957 the state legislature amended the pupil placement law. The amendments made the local school boards judicial tribunals when they considered transfer requests, with the power to subpoena people and records, with legal immunities from future lawsuits based on statements made in their findings or decisions, and with their legal fees and other costs to be paid by local school funds.[17] The state wanted to give school boards power sufficient to discourage or intimidate black parents and their attorneys.

The second front in the black rebellion against the cultural patterns of Alabama began in 1956 with mass nonviolent protest. This battle was both more direct and more visible. On December 1, 1955, Rosa Parks refused to surrender her seat on a Montgomery bus to a white man. Her arrest sparked an immediate boycott of the buses by Montgomery blacks. Black leaders there formed a new organization, the Montgomery Improvement Association, and selected the twenty-six-year-old Baptist pastor Martin Luther King Jr. to be its leader. The group's initial demands were modest: to establish a more flexible but still segregated pattern of seating on the buses, more respect to be shown to black passengers by drivers, and the employment of some black drivers on city buses. The members thought the bus company and city officials would agree to these terms, and the boycott would end within a week.

But city officials were intransigent. The boycott continued for a year, and with it black demands increased, until the U.S. Supreme Court affirmed a lower court order to end segregation on the city's bus lines in November 1956.[18] During this time the black community demonstrated that it could organize and remain united for a long campaign in the face of Klan violence and hostile local officials. It learned that nonviolent protest was an effective tactic. And it found an uncommon spokesman in King, who could effectively articulate the grievances of black people, demand change, and do this with a spirit of ultimate reconciliation.

Events in Montgomery greatly overshadowed the attempt of a lone white woman and her foster child to desegregate the public schools in Mobile. The tactics and the agenda for the assault on southern segregation were set in Montgomery, not Mobile.

The yearlong boycott in Montgomery became a critical event; it focused national and local attention on the grievances of black people. Others were emboldened during that struggle. Autherine Lucy forced the University of Alabama to enroll her as its first black student. She was later expelled for making supposedly false and outrageous statements to school officials, but her challenge became part of a rising tide.

In the fall of 1957 Arkansas governor Orval Faubus used the national guard to block the admission of six black students to Little Rock's Central High School. President Dwight D. Eisenhower federalized the guard and called in one thousand army paratroopers to break the governor's challenge to federal authority. The second reconstruction began in earnest. Faubus closed the schools for a year rather than integrate. He became a hero to much of the South, and a posture of defiance of the federal government spread throughout the region.

In 1958 in *Cooper v. Aaron,* a case growing out of the Little Rock situation, the Supreme Court said that no state "scheme" would be allowed to prevent integration. Each justice signed the decision individually and nodded assent from the bench to demonstrate the court's unanimity. It became increasingly clear that the judicial branch was determined to pursue racial justice fully and to brook no defiance of judicial power from southern states.

Young blacks would not wait for court orders; they wanted direct action. In February 1960 they began sit-in demonstrations at lunch counters in Greensboro, North Carolina; Nashville, Tennessee; and Tallahassee, Florida. The sit-ins provoked sporadic violence and stimulated media coverage. Because they gained national attention and sympathy, collectively they became significant events in the evolution of public opinion. By late 1961 restaurants in more than ninety cities had been desegregated.

In May 1961 another tactic stimulated more backlash from disgruntled whites. Young blacks and whites challenged Jim Crow in interstate transportation when they rode Greyhound buses into the South and sought to use "whites only" bus terminals. Rednecks responded by attacking the riders, and the television news footage of heads bloodied by white thugs prompted Attorney General Robert Kennedy to respond with federal force. That September ten black children peacefully desegregated four public high schools in Atlanta. In December, Martin Luther King's Southern Christian Leadership Conference (SCLC) launched its Albany, Georgia, campaign against racial segregation in schools, hiring, and public accommodations. After a huge effort it failed because the police chief exercised firm nonviolent counterforce. The federal government did not intervene; local authorities gave the Justice Department no pretext.

In September 1962 James Meredith sought to enter the University of Mississippi. Twice he was blocked physically by the lieutenant governor. When federal marshals were sent to his aid, they were attacked. Two people were killed and scores wounded in an all-night confrontation. Ultimately, thirty thousand federal troops kept order while Meredith enrolled. President John F. Kennedy prohibited racial discrimination in federally financed housing that November.

And in 1963 the tide of racial change rolled ever more strongly across the Jim Crow South. In April the movement began its Birmingham campaign. Confrontations, demonstrations, and boycotts met official intransigence, including police barricades, fire hoses, and dogs. Conflict escalated to the point that President Kennedy put unprecedented pressure on civic leaders to end their intransigence.

In June Gov. George Wallace stood in the schoolhouse door to prevent black students from attending the University of Alabama. In a television address that night President Kennedy pledged that he would seek effective civil rights legislation from Congress. The night after Kennedy's televised speech, Medgar Evers, an NAACP field secretary, was assassinated in Jackson, Mississippi. In August, King delivered his famous "I Have a Dream" speech at the Lincoln Memorial in Washington, D.C., to more than 100,000 black and white people gathered to lobby on behalf of the sweeping civil rights laws that lay before Congress. It was the single largest protest demonstration in U.S. history to that point. Throughout King's public ministry he evoked God's hand in deliverance, first of Israel under Moses and now of blacks in the United States. Whites had held blacks back, but with God's help and constant nonviolent effort, King's children would someday be judged by the content of their characters, not the color of their skin. King argued that the United States had to undergo a cultural transformation: A culture based on individual merit should replace racial hierarchy.

1963: First Steps toward School Desegregation in Mobile

The Board of School Commissioners of Mobile County met on November 14, 1962. In the audience sat John LeFlore, a black mail carrier and leader of the Mobile NAACP (then operating as the Citizens Committee). Clutched in his hand was a formal petition requesting that the board desegregate the public schools. The board conducted its business—the allocation of musical instruments, use of television in schools, problems with the sale of candy and soft drinks, name changes proposed for schools—and when LeFlore attempted to address the board, he was rebuffed. The board president informed him that this was not "delegation day," a once-a-month meeting at which citizens could address the board. LeFlore would have to return at that time.

One wonders what stories were told that night. Members of the board doubtless told their wives and friends about LeFlore's demand and how he had not followed the board's rules. He surely told his friends about how the whites once again used technical details to thwart justice. It was not the first frustration LeFlore had known. In 1945 LeFlore and a friend had brought a complaint to the Interstate Commerce Commission because the Gulf, Mobile, and Ohio railroad had not provided them with Pullman and dining car services. The commission held a hearing, then dismissed the complaint, ruling that the service provided "colored passengers" was not unreasonably prejudicial, but LeFlore's protest led to desegregation of those services on eight railroads. In 1946 Milton Schnell, chairman of the Board of Registrars, accused LeFlore of violating the Hatch Act, which prohibited federal employees from participating in partisan political activities; LeFlore had appeared frequently before the registrars to coach other blacks in meeting voting requirements. The Truman administration investigated, said LeFlore was not working for a particular candidate, and commended him for his community service. In recent years he had helped to desegregate retail stores and the public golf course in Mobile. His persistence and leadership owed in part to character and in part to economic invulnerability—he worked for the U.S. Post Office and not a local white businessman and therefore was somewhat insulated from economic reprisal.[19]

The school system that LeFlore wanted desegregated was Alabama's largest. Its eighty-nine schools had 72,696 students, of whom 27,965—almost 40 percent—were black. Of its eighty-seven administrators, nine (only 10 percent) were black. In the schools themselves, however, 37 percent of the 2,594 principals and teachers were black. Thirty-three percent of the eighty-seven principals were black, as were 35 percent of the twenty-three assistant principals.[20] Staff members with the same certification and years of experience made the same salaries: For example, Sammy F. Gilbert, white, and Frances Daffin, black, were new teachers with the same certificate, and both made $3,654 for the academic year. Dorothy Burns, white, and Fredrick Perry, black, held the same certificate and had thirteen years' experience; both made $4,770.[21] But black faculty, like black students, occupied separate schools from whites.

LeFlore and others turned up on "delegation day," the November 28 meeting of the board. The board they faced was made up of prominent members of the Mobile business community, which had for decades controlled the schools: William B. Crane, Charles E. McNeil, Arthur F. Smith Jr., Jack C. Gallalee, and Kenneth Reed.

The first delegation to speak that evening, black members of the George Washington Carver PTA, complained to the board about overcrowding at their school, which required double sessions to handle all the children, and poor drainage, which made the schoolyard little more than a swamp. The parents' complaints prompted an immediate response from the senior staff about overcrowded conditions throughout the system: Mobile's school enrollment had tripled in twenty-two years, and school construction had not kept pace because tax revenues were inadequate. By implication at least, whites suffered as much as blacks. But implicit in the response was reprise of another story: white paternalism. Black parents simply did not understand the big picture. They needed to be reminded of their place.

John LeFlore addressed the board next. He read his petition, signed by twenty-seven black parents of Mobile, requesting that the board establish a plan within sixty days to eliminate segregation based on race, color, or creed. He reminded the board that the Supreme Court had required this in 1954, 1955, and 1958 and that other southern cities had already begun desegregation of their schools. He continued, "We are not unmindful of the challenge to probity this important question poses in our own state but are confident that citizens of goodwill and all who respect law and order will defend with their moral support a course of action which will bring to our city and county another instance of a high standard in race relations." LeFlore reminded the board that he had first petitioned for an end to segregated schools in 1955 and had no response.[22] The board thanked him and went on with its business. The board manifested the "second face" of political power, "the mobilization of bias," by which people with control of the public agenda more or less unconsciously agree to rule some things out of bounds.

After LeFlore spoke, the board heard a staff report on "communism and the teaching of Americanism" in the schools. This report, unlike LeFlore's petition, prompted considerable discussion among the board members. It seemed that a conspiratorial movement and alien ideas threatened the social fabric of the community.

On January 15, 1963, the board replied to LeFlore. In a letter signed by all five members the commissioners referred to the problems of overcrowding and rundown buildings across the county and expressed the feeling that "it would be ill-advised and not to the best interests of your Negro people for us to attempt to present a formula for integration of the public schools at this time." This answer was another old story: Get back. Mobile had a color line, not drawn in the sand but in the minds of all southerners, that black people could not cross with impunity. The warning was often coded, just as in this case.

The blacks' response was immediate, if indirect. In New York the next day Constance Baker Motley, the associate counsel for the NAACP Legal Defense and Education Fund, announced that "we have been requested by the people who signed the [Mobile] petition to take legal action, and we plan to act on the request."[23] Legal action came more quickly and from a different direction than the board or the NAACP thought. On January 18 the U.S. Department of Justice filed suit in U.S. District Court, contending that racial segregation of children of service members and other federal workers in the public schools violated the Fourteenth Amendment to the U.S. Constitution. Brookley Air Force Base, located on the southern border of Mobile, was one of the country's largest federal installations. Several thousand children would be affected if the suit were successful. The Mobile County school board voted unanimously to resist the suit and on February 8 had papers filed to dismiss the action.

On January 30 four black students supervised by LeFlore attempted to transfer to Baker High, a white school. A few days later three more tried. LeFlore explained that the round-trip from their homes to St. Elmo, the black high school to which they were assigned, was thirty-four miles, but they lived only four miles from Baker.[24] They were not admitted to Baker and were not informed about what action, if any, would be taken on their transfer requests.

LeFlore had done his part; the NAACP lawyers now did theirs, filing *Birdie Mae Davis et al. v. Board of School Commissioners of Mobile County* in U.S. District Court in Mobile on March 27, 1963. The plaintiffs were the parents of twenty black children, and they were represented by two local black attorneys, Vernon Z. Crawford and Clarence E. Moses, acting for Derrick Bell and Constance Baker Motley of the NAACP Legal Defense Fund in New York.

The suit asked Judge Daniel H. Thomas to issue injunctions to prevent school officials from operating a "dual school system . . . based wholly upon the race and color" of students.

Barely a week after the lawsuit was filed, the orderly quest for change in Mobile was upstaged by events in Birmingham, where nonviolent demonstrators led by King and the SCLC confronted officers directed by Police Commissioner Eugene "Bull" Connor. Over the next months the eyes of the American people were riveted on newspaper and television accounts of protest marches broken up by police armed with cattle prods, German shepherds, and fire hoses. The contrast between the tactics of the NAACP and the SCLC could not have been greater as each pressed forward with its demands. The NAACP pursued redress patiently through the courts of law; the SCLC used confrontation and mass action to force immediate change.

Judge Thomas held a hearing in the *Birdie Mae Davis* case on April 25, 1963. Counsel for the parents demanded that the school board be required to submit a desegregation plan within thirty days for implementation in the fall. School officials argued that any major reallocation of students for the 1963–64 school year would disrupt educational goals and procedures, particularly because the student population already greatly exceeded the physical capacity of the schools. Thomas ruled on June 24. He denied the parents' request for immediate relief, but at a November 14 hearing he did order the board to submit a desegregation plan to the court for implementation in the 1964–65 school year. Thomas cited the successful desegregation of the Mobile golf course, bus lines, and airport facilities when, he said, sufficient time had been given to prepare a course of action. Moreover, the court noted that fourteen new schools with more than three hundred classrooms were under construction and scheduled to be opened in 1964.[25] Two days later attorneys for the parents appealed this ruling to the Fifth U.S. Circuit Court of Appeals, which then included Alabama; the NAACP clearly wanted immediate change.

For its part the *Mobile Press* and *Register* editorialized in favor of legal and political resistance to desegregation and supported the board's stand.[26] The *Register* was a morning newspaper, the *Press* an afternoon paper. They were, however, both owned by a local family, kin of Ralph B. Chandler, who began the *Press* in 1929 and bought the *Register* in 1932. The same staff contributed to both papers; their news stories and editorials were similar but not identical. People referred to them indiscriminately as the *Press/Register* even though only the Sunday edition was published jointly. The paper was the dominant voice in south Alabama. The Chandlers clearly shared interests with the commercial elite of Mobile.

A three-judge panel of the Fifth U.S. Circuit Court of Appeals heard the parents' appeal for immediate relief on July 8. Counsel for the school board argued that an attempt to desegregate that fall would place an intolerable burden on the system. Barely twenty-four hours later a divided panel issued a temporary injunction requiring the board to make an immediate start toward desegregation that fall, September 1963. Judges John Minor Wisdom of New Orleans and John R. Brown of Houston sided with the parents—nine years' delay in implementing desegregation was long enough. Judge Griffin Bell of Atlanta sided with the lower court's slower timetable.

The appeals court's order said that a permanent plan for integration should start in the first grade that fall in the city of Mobile and proceed on a stair-step, grade-a-year principle, moving one grade higher each year until all twelve grades were integrated. The appeals court ordered the board to submit a plan for implementing its order to the district court by August 1.[27] The ruling was the first affecting public school systems below the college level in Alabama. Speaking for the NAACP, Constance Baker Motley said that this was "the fastest decision we ever got" and it "certainly should speed up desegregation in the South." Charles E. McNeil, president of the Board of School Commissioners, said, "I am sure I speak for the entire board when I say that we are deeply disappointed by the court's ruling."[28]

Alabama Responds

After studying the court order, Gov. George Wallace seemingly pushed resistance, not defiance: "I think we should make every effort within legislative and judicial bounds to preserve segregation." He suggested separate classrooms within schools.[29]

George Corley Wallace had campaigned for governor with segregationist rhetoric, and as governor he had recently tried outright and dramatic defiance and lost. Vivian Malone, a young black woman from Mobile, had applied for admission to the University of Alabama, and after long litigation the U.S. District Court in Birmingham had ordered her admitted. As a gubernatorial candidate, Wallace had pledged to stand in the schoolhouse door to prevent desegregation, and on June 11, 1963, when the day came for Malone to enter the university, Governor Wallace made good his promise. He mobilized two thousand national guardsmen for emergency duty in Tuscaloosa. Flanked by a personal bodyguard of state troopers, Wallace blocked Malone and James A. Hood of Gadsden from entering, although they were accompanied by the assistant U.S. attorney general, Nicholas deB. Katzenbach, U.S. Attorney Macon Weaver, and U.S. Marshall Peyton Norville. The historic confrontation of state and federal power crystallized yet again as Wallace read a statement justifying the states' right to govern themselves. He issued a proclamation denouncing and forbidding the illegal and unwarranted action by the "central government" in violation of the Tenth Amendment to the Constitution. The governor backed down two hours later when President Kennedy nationalized the guard and called on it to enforce the court order.[30]

The drama of the day was not over. That night President Kennedy addressed the American people on radio and television. He urged the nation to fulfill its promise of equality of opportunity for black people and called for Americans to support him in this quest. Subsequently, Kennedy asked Congress to enact legislation authorizing the attorney general to initiate desegregation suits and giving the federal government power to withhold federal aid from racially segregated programs. These provisions were included in the omnibus civil rights bill that he sent to Congress late in the summer. The bill became law in 1964, after Kennedy's death.

On August 16, 1963, Supreme Court Justice Hugo Black, a former U.S. senator from Alabama and the justice for the circuit that included Mobile, declined to issue a stay of the Fifth Circuit's injunction requiring that the public schools in Mobile be desegregated that September.[31] He said: "The Board argues that to require action for the 1963 school year gives it too little time and could disrupt the school system. But the first *Brown* decision was rendered in 1954—nine years ago. . . . [Yet the] record fails to show that the Mobile Board has made a single move of any kind looking towards a constitutional public school system."[32]

The *Register*'s banner headline proclaimed on Tuesday, August 20: "MOBILE SCHOOL MIXING PLANS WILL AFFECT 12TH GRADE ONLY." The school board's proposed plan was a backward stair step: twelfth grade the first year, then eleventh and twelfth the second year, and so on until all twelve grades were included. The plan was limited to the city of Mobile, not the entire county. As a result only the three white schools with twelfth grades—Murphy, Davidson, and Rain— would be affected. The provisions for transferring to another school were similarly limited. The board announced that it had twenty-nine requests from black students to transfer to previously white schools before July 31, its normal deadline. It would review these applications. But it would accept no new transfer applications for the year. Henceforward, the board said, it would accept applications for transfer each year only between April 1 and 15, an especially narrow window of opportunity. The board would judge all transfer applications by the criteria of the Alabama Pupil Placement Act, which gave many reasons for why school boards could assign individual students to one school or another.

The plan that the board submitted was clearly designed to have a limited effect on the pattern of race-based schooling. The board justified the plan by citing its accelerated building program, which could better accommodate changes later, continual "reshaping" of the residential pattern, and the necessity for making preparations for the school term several months in advance. "The board considers," the statement said, "that any general or arbitrary reassignment of pupils presently in attendance at the 89 existing schools, according to any rigid rule of proximity to school or solely by request on the part of parents of pupils would be impractical and a disservice to the system, to the local schools, and to the pupils transferred. Such transfers would tend to overload some schools and leave other facilities in less than full use and at the same time result in an unbalanced teacher-pupil ratio throughout the system."[33]

That same day, August 20, 1963, the *Register* seemed pleased to announce that some northerners were having second thoughts about racial mixing. Its editorial quoted Fred M. Hechinger, writing in the *New York Times:* "The racial balancing enthusiasm may be followed by disillusionment and heartbreak, if the educational needs of the children concerned are not met. The child of the slums—whether white, Negro or of any other background—starts with a handicap that must be painstakingly erased. To transfer such children, without special preparation, to middle-class schools may court disaster. In the routine course of ability groupings, the likelihood is strong that a substantial number of these children . . . will wind up in segregated sub-sections in their new schools, a disastrous experience." The *Register* predicted "agitation for abandonment of ability tests and groupings simply because they are in conflict with the goal of mixing the races—come what may." With some accuracy the editorial concluded, "Already, the drive is under way to break down residential neighborhood patterns with the view of balancing the races, but here is where the mixers are meeting strongest resistance in the North. This is why the whole racial issue will be dominant in future national elections."[34]

Judge Daniel Thomas approved the board's desegregation plan with a single important emendation. He ruled that students had until August 28 to file applications to transfer. The parents' lawyers appealed Thomas's ruling. Several Mobile ministers formed a group to preach law and order in the face of social change, but popular sentiment seemed beyond their reach.

Barely a week after the judicial axe finally fell, the newly organized white Mobile County Citizens Council held a rally at the Sage Avenue Armory. About one thousand whites turned out to hear Leonard Wilson of Montgomery, executive director of the Alabama organization, and Arthur Hanes, a former mayor of Birmingham. Both preached resistance. Wilson asserted that Alabama law required school boards to provide separate white schools for parents who wished to send their children to such schools, and he predicted that if any Mobile public schools were integrated, the local Citizens Council would call on the board to provide those schools.

It was Hanes, though, who really aroused the group. His speech linked communist influence to the integrationist movement. He attacked the foreign policy of the Kennedy administration as "soft" on communism and said that "with missile bases in Cuba, Mobile is two minutes away from annihilation which can happen at any time. But they will not have to attack. They will accomplish their purpose by havoc and disorder within our own country." He then claimed that Attorney General Robert Kennedy was "the chief perpetrator of organized militant Negro moves in the United States. There are no demonstrations held until clearance is given by the Department of Justice." Hanes accused the communists of "fomenting race war" and seeking to "infiltrate the Negro churches of the South and stir up trouble." "The South," Hanes cried, "is the last bastion of race pride and it is the stronghold of true nationalistic feeling. Accordingly, it is the target of left-wing abuse. They say the Civil War was fought one hundred years ago, but I tell you that the Civil War is just starting."[35]

Making Holes in the Color Line

After school administrators considered the transfer requests, only two black students, Henry Hobdy and Dorothy Davis, were scheduled to attend a white school in Mobile. Elsewhere in Alabama twenty-two other black children were ready to desegregate the public schools: thirteen in Tuskeegee, four in Huntsville, and five in Birmingham.[36]

The fateful day was Monday, September 9, but Governor Wallace had a surprise up his sleeve. Late on Sunday night Wallace issued executive orders prohibiting desegregation of Murphy High School in Mobile, which Hobdy and Davis were to attend, and schools in two other cities. At 5 A.M. a detachment of 125 state troopers, who had gathered clandestinely across Mobile Bay, sped across the causeway into the city and blockaded Murphy. When Hobdy and Davis arrived by car at 7:15, they found the streets cordoned off. Their car, driven by Rev. Calvin E. Houston, pastor of a church that the *Press* listed as "Hillsdale Presbyterian Church (Negro)," was allowed to drive to the school entrance, where city police; the attorneys Vernon Crawford and Clarence Moses; John LeFlore; and Chief Joe Smeller of the highway patrol were gathered. Smeller stepped forward and read the following notice: "The Governor of Alabama has issued three executive orders this morning pertaining to public schools in Birmingham, Mobile and Tuskeegee. All schools will be open today by these executive orders prohibiting integration of any public school in the three cities. Law enforcement officers will be on hand to enforce the orders and preserve order."[37] He handed them a copy of Wallace's Executive Order No. 12 without reading it, and the blacks returned to their car and drove off. That was the first notice anyone had about what was going on.

White students were then admitted to the school for regular first-day activities. Similar events were recorded in Birmingham and Tuskegee. Wallace defied the federal government and sought to get his story out to constituents in Alabama and elsewhere by staging dramatic events. Wallace's order stated that integration of the schools would be "detrimental to the public interest" and that it would have the effect of "totally destroying the educational process." Further, it said, integration would cause an "abridgement of the civil rights of other children attending the public schools" and would "deprive them of the equal protection of the laws."

Wallace was gifted at status politics, the use of dramatic events to symbolize the public contest over cultural values.[38] He had made his point: The federal government had compelled the unwelcome change. He did not have to say, "Just like the last time."

Crawford informed reporters that he intended to "contact authorities in the Justice Department" as soon as he could. LeFlore said, "We did not expect this interference. . . . The governor has forced this upon us, and it is now up to the federal government." School board president McNeil averred, "The Negro students were kept out by the governor, and there was nothing we could do. The situation is now between the governor and federal authorities."[39] McNeil's remark was more significant than anyone knew. He later became one of the last of the prominent members of the board. During World War II he had been a pilot and was shot down and captured. Although not from Mobile, he married a Mobile woman and became successful in the insurance business and active in civic affairs. In 1956 Arthur Delchamps, a leading Mobile citizen who owned a supermarket chain, called McNeil over to his table at the Athens Club and asked him to run for the school board. With this blessing McNeil ran and was elected. That was how it was done in those days.[40]

After McNeil took office he learned how other things were done: The real business of the board did not take place at its public meetings. Instead, a few board members met with the superintendent in private to sort things out. This had been especially true regarding desegregation planning. The players, most notably McNeil, had done their homework. In a 1986 interview he recalled that they thought desegregation was a good thing, it was the law, but they had decided that it had to come slowly if it was to work. "Times were bad," and the board had simply tried to keep a lid on the community. Among other things, the governor had telephoned Mobile school board members to say that he wanted to intervene. The board members thought they had persuaded him to desist. Wallace had acted anyway. The local elite had lost control in its own town. This event signaled the beginning of the end of elite power on the board.

Wallace's claim of states' rights did not impress the federal courts or President Kennedy. Five federal district judges, all Alabamans, ordered Wallace and other state authorities to stop interfering with court-ordered desegregation in Mobile, Tuskeegee, and Birmingham. (Wallace, unaccountably, had done nothing in Huntsville, where black students had attended classes without incident.) Wallace, still guarded by state troopers, stayed in his office all that Monday to prevent federal marshals from serving him with the district court order.[41]

In Washington the president announced that he would take whatever action was necessary to see that the desegregation orders were enforced, but he took no immediate action. Federal agents had scouted for signs of trouble in all four cities before the opening of school, and the Kennedy administration had prepared for several contingencies, but Wallace's maneuver had caught them off guard. Wallace and Kennedy were playing a high-stakes game of politics. Kennedy's people were aware that Wallace wanted "those Kennedys" to be seen taking Alabama by bayonet point, just like the North had done once before, and they did not want that.[42]

Late Monday night Wallace ordered units of the national guard to report to their armories at 4 A.M. Tuesday. He intended to replace the state troopers around the schools with guard units. When the guard reported for duty, Kennedy immediately federalized the entire 17,000-member force, removing it from Wallace's control. In the early morning hours the state troopers withdrew, and when Murphy High School opened that morning, no state or federal forces were present. The people of Mobile missed all the predawn action.

Henry Hobdy and Dorothy Davis entered school that Tuesday morning under the watchful eye of local police and sheriff's deputies. They were met by Principal Raymond B. Taylor, handed their course schedules, and escorted to their homerooms. Ironically, they discovered that their first class was called Problems in Democracy. The demeanor of other students was correct, not friendly. At noon the pair went through the cafeteria lunch lines with other students but sat together to eat their meal. They left school ten minutes early by a side entrance and were driven away by friends. There had been no incidents. Attendance at Murphy that day was 2,777 students, with only 170 absent—about normal. Superintendent Cranford Burns credited the school's principal for the happily uneventful day. He had prepared the white students the week before and had sent letters to their parents repeating his instructions. On Tuesday, September 10, 1963, Davis and Hobdy had broken the color line in the Mobile public schools.[43]

At Tuskeegee, where blacks greatly outnumbered whites, thirteen black students went to school with whites without incident. In Birmingham two schools were desegregated relatively smoothly, but at a third school, West End High School, black students had a different experience. Hundreds of white students gathered outside the school to jeer two black teenagers who entered. They shouted, "Nigger go home!" Adult spectators gathered, and scuffles broke out. Confederate flags flew, and shouting continued until police used their nightsticks to push the crowd back two blocks from the school. Nine white men were arrested when they resisted.[44] That night the Chickasaw City Council, in rural Mobile County, adopted a resolution supporting Governor Wallace's attempt to uphold segregation in the public schools.[45]

The white Citizens Council had said it would block desegregation at Murphy by boycotting the school or by instructing children to make things unpleasant for the black students. The council promised to pay all court costs for the protesters. Tuesday's results seemed to belie the council's influence.

On Wednesday some students chanted outside Murphy while waiting for classes to begin. At that day's school board meeting forty members of the white Mobile County Citizens Council asked the board to carry out provisions of a state law that they said required segregated school facilities for children withdrawn from desegregated schools. The board turned their request over to its attorney for study. The board also reminded parents that they could apply to the schools for permission to transfer their children under the Alabama Pupil Placement Act. Moreover, they could appeal a negative decision to the board. The board also voted unanimously to bar news media from the Murphy campus.[46]

Thursday was a different matter. At about 7 A.M. six white girls began chanting outside Murphy High School. By 7:40 A.M. three hundred students had joined in. The throng, urging other students to join them in boycotting the school, paraded up and down in front of the school; the students marched off campus and into the streets. Police could not contain them and called for reinforcements. By the time police broke up the demonstration, they had detained fifty-four students. The Citizens Council signed the bonds for the students, but not before two city commissioners, Joseph N. Langan and George E. McNally, lectured them about breaking the law.[47]

The white Citizens Council was not alone in its focus on desegregation. Liberals also mobilized. Alabamans Behind Local Education (ABLE) was organized earlier that year to support desegregation and to counter the forces in favor of shutting down the public schools and financing private schools with state funds. The white-led integrated group had two hundred members who were mostly upper middle class. During the summer ABLE had held a two-day workshop at which Paul Anthony, executive director of the Southern Regional Council, and Dr. Robert Coles, the Harvard child psychiatrist, were among the speakers. ABLE published flyers and fact sheets, offered speakers for civic gatherings, and produced a television report in its effort to get Mobile residents to face the necessity of desegregating the schools, that all legal delays had been exhausted, and that the schools should be kept tension free so children could concentrate on learning their lessons. ABLE publicly supported officials who worked to preserve order and free public education, most notably Langan and McNally. For its efforts members of ABLE earned the ire of the white Citizens Council and were subject to vilification in the press by George Wallace.[48]

Sporadic incidents continued at Murphy, but the steam was gone. During the second week of school thirty students paraded but dispersed after being told to do so; attendance was normal.[49] In early October three white boys were disciplined for tripping Hobdy at the lunchroom door.[50] The white radicals' claims about direct white resistance proved largely to be hollow threats.

According to one observer, Albert Foley, a Jesuit priest and professor at Spring Hill College, conservative political groups had been active throughout the summer and fall. The John Birch Society, On Guard, the Christian Laymen's Association, and FOCUS (Freedom Over Communism in the United States) recruited large and influential memberships. These groups, including the white Citizens Councils, brought in speakers like Gov. Ross Barnet of Mississippi, "Bull" Connor from Birmingham, and Myers G. Lowman, a right-wing agitator for the Methodist Circuit Riders whose speech to a large gathering was entitled "Fiddling While Church and Schoolhouse Burn." The National States Rights Party sponsored speeches by Dr. Edward Fields, its national chairman, and by the lawyer Matt Murphy, who was identified as the Birmingham lawyer for the Ku Klux Klan in the Viola Liuzza murder trial. The On Guard group sponsored a recorded telephone message that could be dialed at any hour to learn the latest conservative ideology and target of its wrath.

In the November 1964 election Mobile County voted overwhelmingly for conservative and, for the first time since Reconstruction, Republican candidates at the national level.[51] The great historical reversal of party loyalties had begun in full force, despite Lyndon Johnson's runaway victory over Barry Goldwater.

Discussion

Society in the South, from the Redemption in the 1880s through the 1950s, was distinctly hierarchical despite the leveling policies of Reconstruction. Slavery had been ended, but people, both black and white, knew their place. Planters, merchants, rednecks; preachers, teachers, sharecroppers. Whites; blacks. Stability, order, hierarchy: These were native traits. Violations of accepted norms were first ignored, then punished. Flagrant violations among whites led to ostracism, among blacks to lynching. Dorothy Danner DaPonte was marginalized despite her wealth. By burning a cross in her driveway, the Klan had threatened a lynching. School desegregation challenged the social order. Behind it lay the notion of worth based on individual merit rather than social caste. If it were successful, change would come along other fronts all across the South.

Political power can be manifested by the skillful use of superior resources; when used to influence government policy, money, time, and organizational strength are all clear manifestations of political power. But power is more subtle too. A "second face" of power is the mobilization of bias. When all those who have some share of institutional authority react instinctively to block some claims for redress but not others, that cultural predisposition is a kind of political power. Throughout the Jim Crow South, when white men and women reacted automatically to reassert the social inferiority of blacks, that was a manifestation of power.

The third face of power is deeper still. Some people have power over others when they shape the meaning of events into stories that legitimize their own ascendency. That happened in Alabama throughout the civil rights movement's confrontation with the Old South.

Using Carrie Mae, Dorothy DaPonte wanted to show that blacks' inferiority resulted from environmental factors, and that if conditions changed, blacks' performance would change. Hers was the liberal story of social change writ small: Every time she told others of Caroline's accomplishments, she made a political statement. To the extent that she changed others' worldview, she exercised political power.

George Wallace interpreted things differently. He wanted to construct a story of illegitimate federal hegemony: The North had occupied the South once before, and white people had found redemption through patient, persistent defiance. Wallace seemed to echo an old radical refrain.

The white Citizens Councils told a more sinister story: The South was fine as it was; outsiders brought the specter of chaos. The council claimed that international communism was linked to agents of domestic change. The

Kennedys and their clan were traitors. The *Press/Register* and other conservatives were quick to point out the moral hypocrisy of the North. They claimed that the two-faced North would come to regret its insistence on integration once blacks made the same claims to equality in the North.

The subtext of each story was resistance and revenge. White radicals called for direct action, even in the streets, to throw off the threat to the established social hierarchy. White conservatives advocated legal maneuvers; they wanted the legislature to remove the threat. Both, though, asserted revenge: If you make us do this thing (desegregate our schools), we will pay you back. We will marshal forces against you at the polls on election day.

Significant events—racial confrontations in Montgomery, Birmingham, Mobile, and elsewhere—aroused and mobilized the imagination of millions, and every story they told was a political action. All the marches, bloody heads, chants, and placards were part of a continuing play, performance art whose drama encouraged the restructuring of worldviews. Every time black citizens wrested concessions from established whites, blacks and whites had new stories to tell. Among blacks, the stories were about strength, courage, and the fruits of contest. Among many whites, the stories were about fear, betrayal, and the rage of impotence in the face of an alien power.

Political power lay in the cogency of the story told, because whatever else, the future will come.

2. Freedom of Choice, 1963–68

FROM 1954 TO 1963 the social order of the South suffered a series of severe shocks: the *Brown* decision, the Montgomery bus boycott, lunch-counter sit-ins, freedom rides, and federalized national guard units. For a great many white southerners, local blacks could protest—that was troublesome but could be dealt with locally—but the federal government's intrusion struck at the foundations of the culture of separation and hierarchy built so painstakingly after the first, deeply resented Reconstruction of the South following the Civil War.

Federal courts, school boards, citizen groups, lawyers, experts, and plain people were increasingly drawn into the fray. Everyone intuitively recognized that desegregated schooling meant redistribution of educational benefits and social status throughout the region. It was not just a matter of a few children going to new schools. When black and white children went to the same schools, black children would get the same books, teachers, sports, and clubs as white children; this would mute or end the hierarchies of social distance, and that threatened the social standing of whites among whites.

In 1963 the federal courts were the stage for the first act of Mobile's racial drama. The second act offered politics in the streets as actions by one player leapfrogged the actions of the others. The rapid and disordered unfolding events in that difficult time challenged narrative capacity itself.

Public schools in Mobile were desegregated in September 1963 because of the order from the Fifth U.S. Circuit Court of Appeals. The complete desegregation plan would be made permanent only if justified in already scheduled November hearings.

Notions of biological difference and subcultural deficiency—that blacks were not as intellectually and morally capable as whites—drove the conventional wisdom that separate schools were best for black children. In fact, that was the argument made by attorneys for the Mobile school board in defending racial separation. Even if biology were set aside, however, the school board would argue that racially separate cultures meant that parents preferred and children benefited from racially separate schools. Freedom of choice became the catchphrase of white resistance. Freedom of choice, white southerners claimed, was as American as apple pie.

Although the term was grounded in racist resistance, those using it to rally segregationists couched the issue in terms of personal liberty, a fundamental American value. This signaled the radicals' willingness to use symbols and stories of individualism rather than biological or cultural hierarchy in order to win the support of moderates inside and outside the South. Their goal, however, was to maintain the separate, and in their eyes clearly superior, place of whites in Mobile, and they would not allow blacks alone to claim the mantle of freedom in their political struggle.

* * *

In September 1963 four young black girls died when a bomb exploded at the 16th Street Baptist Church in Birmingham. On November 22 John F. Kennedy was assassinated in Dallas. The country seemed to be coming apart. Lyndon Baines Johnson, the new president, quickly asserted that he would press for national legislation that would protect and extend the constitutional rights of black people. Johnson committed the Democratic Party to racial equality, and he knew Democrats would pay a price, politically, in the South.

The Trial

The trial on the merits of entering a permanent order mandating desegregation of the schools of Mobile County began on November 14, 1963, a week before Kennedy's assassination.[1] The facts were not in dispute so much as the meaning of those facts. Everyone participated in the meaning making, especially lawyers. Palmer Pillans, attorney for the school board, immediately moved to dismiss the case. He argued a lame but novel point: "Education is not a right in Alabama, but a privilege." He reminded the court that Alabama had not made the education of young people mandatory until 1915. In 1956, he continued, the state constitution and many statutes had been revised: Public education in Alabama was now voluntary. When students attended schools on a voluntary basis, they could be subjected to a variety of regulations, such as those specified in the Alabama Pupil Placement Act. He cited a number of cases in which courts had supported this view. Pillans claimed that since 1956 segregation in Mobile had been a matter of custom, not law, and that the [1957] Civil Rights Act and the Fourteenth Amendment therefore did not apply.[2] The federal government had no authority over cultural practices in Mobile, he opined.

Derrick Bell Jr., of the NAACP Legal Defense Fund, representing the parents, argued that the court should issue a permanent order requiring desegregation. He said that the Mobile school board had denied the requests of black students to transfer to white schools and that black parents had therefore come to court to get relief.[3]

Undaunted when Thomas refused to dismiss the case, Pillans tried to show that assigning black children to black schools was educationally sound policy. Toward this end, he moved that the court require administration of nationally recognized tests of mental maturity and achievement in at least four grades. He also moved that the judge admit into evidence the opinions of four psychologists and sociologists in a Savannah desegregation case on the question of "educable differences" between white and black children.[4]

Bell called Dr. Cranford Burns as his only witness. As the long-serving schools superintendent, Burns was a central figure in Mobile's school system. He was from a poor family in Culman County, in north-central Alabama, where he had played football and been an excellent student. Before becoming an assistant superintendent in Mobile, Burns had secretly attended school board meetings there. He saw two things he did not like: that board members often specified which teachers would teach in certain schools; and that while the high standards and traditional curriculum in the system served the children of the elite very well, they also forced a high dropout rate among others. As a thorough-going professional educator, Burns was guided by two beliefs: Professional educators should run the schools, and schools should be "community" institutions, each serving the needs of its clientele.[5]

Burns became assistant superintendent for instruction in 1948 and superintendent in 1952. He became a strong educational leader in difficult times. The local population explosion of the war years had been followed by the baby boom; he had had as many as fourteen thousand schoolchildren on half-day sessions in Mobile County because the school board could not build new facilities fast enough.

During his tenure the board made policy, but he directed the programs and staff of the schools. He and members of the board would meet in "conferences" before the public meetings and decide what they would do; the public meeting then would move along with finesse. Burns and the board used their private meetings to discuss desegregation and its implications.

Throughout the early years of his administration, Burns had worked to make the distribution of resources between white and black schools more equal; the county had equalized pay for teachers and evened out the teaching load and facilities. Outright desegregation of the schools was, however, another matter.[6] Only one of the five school board members, Alfred Delchamps, said after the 1954 *Brown* decision that the board ought to consider desegregating the schools and then only by selected transfers, not by neighborhood zones. There was, however, considerable resistance to this idea on the board, both because of personal feelings and a sense of what the members thought the community would accept. Superintendent Burns was comfortable with this. For him, appropriate educational programs and community schools were more important than race mixing.[7]

For his testimony in court Burns had prepared maps and charts at the NAACP's request. The system had 77,200 students that year, 39 percent of whom were black. Bell sought to demonstrate that the school zones had been drawn in such a manner as to cause segregation in the elementary grades. At junior and senior high school levels, Bell maintained, the board required blacks to go to black schools and whites to white schools. Burns denied this, and under cross-examination he said that to his knowledge only four black students had requested transfers and that these had been denied because of crowded conditions.[8]

The school board's first witness was Floyd Replogle, a psychologist for the Mobile school system. He testified about two nationally used tests, the California Mental Maturity series, which measured intelligence and ability, and the California Achievement series, which determined a student's level of achievement in arithmetic, reading, and language arts. Both tests had been given to black and white children in various grades in Mobile. Bell immediately objected to the reporting of information about test results in open court, saying the findings would needlessly embarrass his clients, but Thomas overruled him. Based on national averages, Replogle said, the tests showed the average black child in the fourth grade was a year and three months behind the average white student in the same grade. By the eleventh grade, he continued, the black student was, on average, three years behind the average white student in the same grade. And, despite Bell's objections, testimony from the Savannah case was read into the court record. It showed that testing of black and white schoolchildren in Georgia had produced similar results.

The school board's second witness was Dr. Clay Sheffield, director of guidance for the Birmingham schools. His testimony supported the evidence from Mobile and Savannah. Bell objected to most of this testimony and said that it showed only that blacks in the South were behind whites in the South, which, he said, could be explained wholly by the policies and practices of Jim Crow segregation. The board's attorney then showed Sheffield a clipping from the *New York Times.* The November 11 story, Sheffield said, reported that New York had used the same tests and that the results were the same as in the three southern cities.[9]

Friday's testimony followed the same line. Dr. Frank C. J. McGurk, professor of psychology at Alabama College, testified that between 1918 and 1950 he had done a study that showed that, despite considerable social and economic change during the period, the gap between white and black scores remained the same for thirty-two years. He found that the gap increased with the age and grade of the students. He claimed that the test rankings of black children of high social and economic backgrounds usually were slightly above those of white students from the lowest socioeconomic class. On cross-examination McGurk answered Bell's questions about research methods and their implications. McGurk acknowledged that he knew of some blacks whom he would consider superior, but he believed that the races were happier if they were segregated.[10]

Dr. Ernest van den Haag, a professor at New York University, was next to take the stand. He said he had written a variety of articles, reports, and books on differences between black and white students. He said his research showed that students preferred to select their own groups from among people visually similar to themselves. Members of each race tended to prefer associating with others of their race. If a person of one race is thrown into a group of another race and experiences an inhospitable reaction, he said, he may well suffer emotional damage. Van den Haag said that whenever the races had been thrown together in integrated schools, the association between the two seldom continued outside school. He had never seen a white student choose a black student for a friend. He averred that two races living together would not bring acceptance. Racial segregation, van den Haag asserted, is universal and dates from biblical times—Jews shunned foreigners—and is true in all nations at all times. He believed, he said, that separate schools for the races are best. Standardized tests given in the United States showed that black high school seniors in the South had scored a grade higher than black seniors in a northern, integrated school. In the North ability grouping consigned black children to separate classrooms.[11]

Bell could not budge van den Haag during cross-examination. Van den Haag said he was opposed to segregation imposed by law but favored segregation if it came by custom or policy of a community. He favored voluntary education, with students attending their school of choice. Under such circumstances he had no doubt that students would choose to attend schools with their own race. "I find it difficult to believe the parents of Negro students actually want their children to go to a white school," he said.[12]

The final witness was Dr. Wesley C. George, a retired professor from the University of North Carolina School of Medicine. He had made extensive studies of the brain and other body parts. He testified that the average white person's brain weighed 100 grams more than the average black person's brain. Only one black in six had a brain the size of the average white, George claimed. He said that the layers of the brain responsible for nerve functioning and intellectual and abstract reasoning are 18 percent thinner in a black person. Derrick Bell asked the doctor on cross-examination if it were true that only 5 to 10 percent of the black population in the United States was of pure African stock. George said he did not know that to be true. Bell asked if George felt that segregated schools were preferable. The doctor replied, "In this country, yes." It was apparent that the school board's lawyers intended to present shorthand versions of old racial texts: Blacks needed separate schools because they were genetically inferior and culturally different and therefore could never catch up.

At the end of two days of testimony Bell asked that the parent-plaintiffs' desegregation plan be entered into the record of the case. The plan would desegregate the schools in three years beginning in the lower grades. Thomas granted the request. He gave no indication of how or when he would rule on the main issue—a permanent injunction against the dual school system—and adjourned the hearing.[13]

Seven months later Thomas still had not ruled on the parent-plaintiffs' request for an end to the dual school system. On June 18, 1964, the Fifth U.S. Circuit Court of Appeals in New Orleans entered the fray once again. Acting on the appeal that the NAACP had filed a year earlier, the appellate court remanded the case with the instruction that desegregation proceed at a swifter pace, along the lines that the court had set down in the case of *Armstrong v. Birmingham*.[14] That meant that the Mobile school board would have to shorten the time for desegregating several grades and abolish altogether all dual school zones, areas, or districts.

On July 31 Judge Thomas accepted with little modification a new plan proposed by the board. The plan became known as the "freedom-of-choice" plan, because a student could choose to attend either the black or white school in her or his zone. Transfers could be obtained by following the Alabama Pupil Placement Act. In addition, the court agreed with the school board that "the close personal relationship that must exist between teacher, pupil and parents for maximum educational effect would be adversely affected by any efforts toward teacher and staff desegregation at this time."[15]

Despite appeals from the parent-plaintiffs and some marginal modifications, the county's schools operated under this plan until 1968.[16] Sure enough, under freedom of choice relatively few blacks and whites shared schools.

Discussion

Courts are places of reasoned argument, but behind the argument lie big, deep stories that guide the selection of facts. During the hearing on whether to make the injunction permanent, advocates for each side presented facts that fit their understanding of the problem of racial inequality. The school board's lawyers essentially gave two reasons for the necessity of separate schools: biology and separate racial cultures. In either case, the inescapable conclusion would be the same. If the court accepted a biological basis for inequality, separate schools were necessary. If the court accepted the cultural differences argument, separate schools were preferable.

The NAACP offered no testimony on behalf of the parents beyond the superintendent's recitation about separation in practice and in plans. But Bell's questions during cross-examination elicited the information that differences in educational performance between blacks and whites were the *result* of discriminatory Jim Crow separation, not the *cause*. Black children were victims of white power, and equity required that black children be given full and equal access to educational opportunities so that they might rise to the highest fulfillment of their nature.

Judges respond to the stories they already know as well as to those presented to them in legal proceedings. In Mobile the federal judge was faced with competing stories from competing worldviews: If he saw the school board members as scofflaws, his decision would focus upon the numbers of children involved and the board's defiance, and he would hammer the school system for its inaction. On the other hand, if he saw the federal law as interfering with individual freedom and local social norms, he would treat the board as leniently as he could. When he ruled in favor of the board's freedom-of-choice plan on July 31, Thomas sided with racial conservatives in the community and on the board. He seemed to be saying that change is necessary because of the law, but Mobile will proceed slowly and protect individual freedom.

Results of Freedom of Choice

As the opening of schools neared in September 1964, the *Mobile Press* and the *Register* attacked the concentration of power in the federal government, particularly power controlled by "left-wingers" in Washington. An editorial that ran in both papers supported Governor Wallace's call for a constitutional amendment to vest power over schools in state government.[17]

Schools opened that fall without incident. Seven of fifteen black students requesting transfers were permitted to enroll in three previously all-white schools. Birmingham, Tuskegee, and Huntsville also began their second year of desegregation quietly. Montgomery and Gadsden enrolled black students (nine and fifteen, respectively) at formerly all-white schools for the first time.

A year later only thirty-two of the approximately thirty-one thousand African American pupils in Mobile County attended nine formerly white schools. In May 1966 the U.S. Department of Health, Education, and Welfare (HEW) announced that it would withhold federal school aid from districts that had not met the department's desegregation guidelines. Governor Wallace found it shocking that a federal agency "should employ totalitarian methods in the form of threats to deny benefits of educational programs from innocent parties in order to accomplish an illegal purpose."[18] In August, under the headline "WALLACE MAY ASK DESEGREGATION SHOWDOWN," the *Register* reported that the governor wanted the state legislature to give money to any school district that faced HEW cutbacks for resisting desegregation.[19]

On August 16, 1966, the Fifth U.S. Circuit Court of Appeals reversed Judge Thomas and required him to modify the 1964 plan. The appellate judges said the attendance zones drawn by the board and approved by Thomas, purportedly to eliminate the former dual school zones, were "readily distinguishable as 'white' and 'Negro.'" The appeals court also said that the board was operating a racially segregated "feeder" pattern. It required that the school board develop a plan for full desegregation of all grades by the beginning of the 1967–68 school year. At that time, it asserted, "there be an end [put] to the present policy of hiring and assigning teachers according to race."[20]

Three weeks later the *Register* reported in a headline: "NO INCIDENTS AS SCHOOLS OPEN DOORS." The Mobile County school system, the paper reported, had approved the transfer of 147 black students to white schools, and Birmingham had approved three hundred such transfers, up from fifty the previous year.[21] In Montgomery, George Wallace Jr., the governor's son, attended Bellingrath Junior High School, where sixteen black students were enrolled for the first time.

The ease and peace with which self-selected blacks now entered previously all-white schools confirmed a shift in cultural norms only to some limited extent. Separation by law was gone, but separation by choice continued. Everyone chose, but the overwhelming number apparently chose that which they knew best. Would that suffice?

The answer was not long in coming. The courts continued to force assimilation. In December 30, 1966, in a consolidated case involving three school districts in Alabama and four in Louisiana, a panel of the Fifth U.S. Circuit Court of Appeals declared, "The clock has ticked the last tick for tokenism and delay." The court specified no racial proportion for schools but said that, according to HEW guidelines, 15 to 18 percent of students should have selected desegregated schools after two years of freedom of choice.[22]

Back on October 19 the Mobile board had filed a new school attendance plan. Six months after that, on April 18, 1967, the NAACP filed a motion for the parents in the *Birdie Mae Davis* case that opposed the school board's plan and sought additional relief similar to that proposed in the Fifth Circuit's *Jefferson County* decision.

In June the U.S. Department of Justice filed a motion to intervene in the Mobile case, and it was granted immediately. The Justice Department said the board's plan failed to assign students on a nonracial basis; did not provide for affirmative action to eliminate the effects of a state-enforced system of segregation; did not eliminate dual or overlapping bus routes; did not specify school locations that would maximize desegregation; did not establish equivalency of physical facilities, courses of instruction, or closing of facilities; did not provide remedial programs designed to aid black children; and did not establish regular reporting of individual transfer requests to the court.[23]

In July, Judge Thomas held hearings on motions for additional relief from the NAACP and the Justice Department. In August he issued an interim order that made some changes in the freedom-of-choice plan. In October he entered findings of fact, conclusions of law, and a decree generally supporting the board's latest limited desegregation plan. He denied the motions for additional relief. Both the NAACP and the Justice Department filed appeals.

In September 1967, 692 black students in Mobile attended twenty-eight "white" schools; the students were assigned to schools by residence.[24] Eight black teachers transferred to "white" schools, and one white music teacher taught at a "colored" school.[25] Across Alabama 16,800 African American pupils enrolled in formerly white schools. Eighty black schools were closed, affecting four thousand children. Statewide, 364 white teachers now taught in "colored" schools, and 564 black teachers taught in formerly white schools.[26]

Rhetorical Battles

Meanwhile, an editorial in the *Mobile Press* said that HEW's civil rights director, Peter Libassi, had confirmed "that the school integration scheme was politically conceived, designed and driven into law to single out the South as its victim. . . . Having struck the blow with his integration blackjack, LBJ now is playing the people of the South for a short-minded, stupid set. How well he succeeds will be answered at the polls in November next year."[27] For its part, the newspaper left little doubt that southern voters would repudiate Johnson. It was payback time.

In December 1967 the Supreme Court refused to reconsider the Fifth Circuit's decision in *Jefferson County,* letting stand the appellate court's impatience with "tokenism and delay" and its desegregation targets. George C. Wallace could not serve another term as governor, so his wife, Lurleen, ran in his stead. In that role she blasted the court ruling, calling it "a part of a master plan being pushed and sponsored by enemies of our Constitution to nationalize our schools." Lurleen Wallace predicted that Americans "are not going to put up with the continued interference with the tender lives and impressionable minds of their children."[28]

In an apparent attempt to keep black teachers from presiding over predominantly white classrooms, in 1967 the Alabama legislature passed a "teacher choice law," which allowed parents to pick the race of their children's teacher. A federal court quickly struck that law down.[29]

Clearly, for many white southerners the federal government was the enemy more than were pesky indigenous blacks. The practice of freedom of choice confirmed their understanding of things: that blacks and whites preferred to remain in racially separate schools. The underlying interpretation made by both racial radicals and conservatives was the same: The problem was that outsiders stirred up trouble; the demon was the federal government under the control of northern liberals.

In the 1968 presidential campaign George Wallace, running on the American Independent Party line, told the story of excessive federal power over and over again. That November Wallace carried Alabama and other southern states. The Democratic candidate, Vice President Hubert Humphrey, ran third behind Richard Nixon and Wallace. The South, the Democrats' erstwhile stronghold, had moved decisively away from the party in a second straight presidential election. Revenge was visited upon the Democrats: Richard Nixon became president.

The End of Freedom of Choice

Many Mobile residents were struck dumb on the morning of March 13, 1968, when the *Register* announced, "FREEDOM-OF-CHOICE OUT FOR MOBILE SCHOOLS." After months of silence the Fifth Circuit had reversed Thomas and issued its own decree to the Mobile school board.[30] The appeals court rejected the board's argument that its plan was acceptable because it had met HEW guidelines by having 15 to 18 percent of its student population in desegregated schools in the 1967–68 academic year. Quoting from *United States v. Jefferson County,* the court said, "'School desegregation can first be measured quantitatively, using percentages as a rough rule of thumb, but ultimately must be measured qualitatively, judging whether schools are still identifiable as white or Negro.'" The opinion of the three-judge panel, written by Homer Thornberry of Austin, Texas, said, "The percentage of total students in biracial schools is superficially acceptable, but beneath the surface the picture is not good. . . . Two-thirds of the schools remain totally segregated and unquestionably identifiable as Negro or white. . . . The number of Negro children in school with white children is so far out of line with the ratio of Negro school children to white school children in the system as to make inescapable the inference that discrimination yet exists." "Freedom-of-choice," the court continued, "is not a goal in itself, but one of many approaches available to school boards. . . . If it does not work, another method must be tried." The court would not accept racial separation, even by choice.

Its sweeping nine-page decree governed student assignments, school construction, and faculty and staff assignments, as well as services, facilities, activities, and programs.[31] It ordered "a new effort to draw zone lines on a non-racial basis so that the attendance-area plan will promote desegregation rather than perpetuate segregation." In addition, the appellate court ruled that the school board had to submit its plans for school construction to the federal district court for review and approval in order to effect desegregation.

The reason for lack of progress in faculty desegregation, the court said, "is that the board has not yet shouldered the burden. . . . It seems apparent that the policy of hiring and assigning teachers according to race still exists. In a system having approximately 2,700 teachers, the surface of the problem of faculty desegregation is hardly scratched by the transfer of 15 teachers to schools of the opposite race." In the new plan each student in the urban area would have to attend the school serving his attendance zone unless there was some compelling nonracial reason for his transfer. The appellate court gave the board until June 1 to draft the new attendance zones, which were to go into effect in the fall. Students in the rural areas of the county could continue to exercise freedom of choice, but all other aspects of the decree applied to the rural areas too.[32]

Less than a month later, on April 4, 1968, Martin Luther King was gunned down in Memphis. Across the country anger spilled into the streets even before people could fully feel their grief. In Mobile a new radical black leadership emerged and transformed a small moribund organization, Neighborhood Organized Workers, or NOW, as it was soon called, into a vehicle for black power. NOW had been organized in 1966 to promote grassroots political education and voter registration. David L. Jacobs, a schoolteacher, was its first president.

On the Sunday after King's assassination a memorial march organized by NOW proceeded from the North Side black community down to the business district and to the Municipal Auditorium. It was the first mass demonstration of its kind in Mobile, and both black and white community leaders participated, but King's death and the success of the march seemed to radicalize NOW. On May 15 marchers organized by NOW walked from the center of the black community to city hall to protest job discrimination and school segregation. NOW continued its meetings and demonstrations throughout the summer, culminating in a mass meeting addressed by Stokely Carmichael in late July.[33]

NOW leaders gained both confidence and a public following by their militance. In appearances before the school board they articulated their demands to the established political authority and mobilized black students for systematic picketing of traditionally black schools in order to reach broader audiences. In April 1969 NOW began picketing at Dunbar Junior High; twenty-three pickets marched outside Booker T. Washington Junior High in Toulminville and later at Central High School. Trinity Gardens and Mobile County Training School, Blount High and Toulminville High: All were picketed. The messages on the signs were clear: "MOBILE COUNTY SCHOOL BOARD IS RACIST"; "GIVE US BETTER SCHOOLS OR ELSE"; "BLACK STUDENTS DEMAND BLACK HISTORY"; "BLACK SCHOOLS ARE JUNK YARDS, CHEAP RAGGED PRISONS"; "WE WANT MORE TEACHER RESPECT"; "SCHOOL BOARD SAYS IT'S ALRIGHT TO USE 'NIGGER'."[34]

The school board sought an injunction that would end the picketing by NOW and other organizations cooperating with it, principally the American Friends Service Committee (AFSC). The board alleged that the picketing was distracting students from academic work and drew some students from the campus to the picket line. Large numbers of students, three hundred to five hundred more than usual, were truant during these demonstrations. NOW countered that it was not encouraging truancy but was protesting the denial of equal educational opportunities to black students. NOW and the other organizations criticized the inferiority of black schools, the absence of meaningful black education, and the token integration of black central office personnel. They argued that the demonstrations at the schools were part of a campaign of speeches, leaflets, mass meetings, and picketing that they had mounted to seek redress of their grievances, an action protected by the Constitution.[35] The FBI and the Justice Department confirmed the peacefulness of the picketing process, but on May 16 Judge Thomas nonetheless enjoined the organizations from picketing schools.[36]

For many white southerners the South was fine as it was. If protest occurred, it had to be because outsiders were agitating local people. That was the theme in Mobile that spring: The American Friends Service Committee—the Quakers—were behind the local uprising. Southerners reminded each other that the Quakers had sent emissaries to the enemy in Vietnam, and this surely meant they were communists or communist sympathizers. So too was NOW.

* * *

Until the Fifth Circuit issued its decree in March 1968, the schools operated under a modified freedom-of-choice arrangement. This one allowed students to attend the school in their zone or the nearest formerly white or formerly black school outside their attendance zone.

On May 17, 1968, the school board published its proposals for mandatory attendance zones in the morning and afternoon newspapers. People looked at the maps with relief or alarm.

On the evening of May 20 the school board met at the Municipal Theater to hear from citizens and decide whether to go forward with its proposed plan. Nearly one thousand people showed up, mostly angry white parents whose children were to be assigned to black schools. The board's plan called for fourteen hundred white students to attend formerly black schools and twenty-five hundred black students to attend formerly white schools. Included were five hundred whites now required to attend the formerly all-black Williamson High School, located in the Maysville area of Mobile. Parents of these students were particularly vociferous that night as they complained about the continual crime and lawlessness in the area. P. D. Betancourt told of hearing gunfire, police sirens, and screams of agony from the Maysville area many weekend nights. It was incredible, he said, that anyone would assign white students to that school. Behind his emotional speech lurked the story of the black "beast," that age-old image of the wild black male that inhabited the white person's unconscious mind. W. B. "Bill" Westbrook complained that the price that the federal government asked white parents to pay was "too great, and the burden is too heavy"—and by "burden" he meant that white children would bear the brunt of enculturating blacks. He asserted that white parents would find some way to ensure that their children would not be educated under "jungle-like" conditions.[37]

Thirty-one people expressed opinions about the board's plan, among them four black leaders. About one-quarter of the white audience left the theater when Jerry Pogue, the director of NOW, and Jacqueline Jacobs appeared at

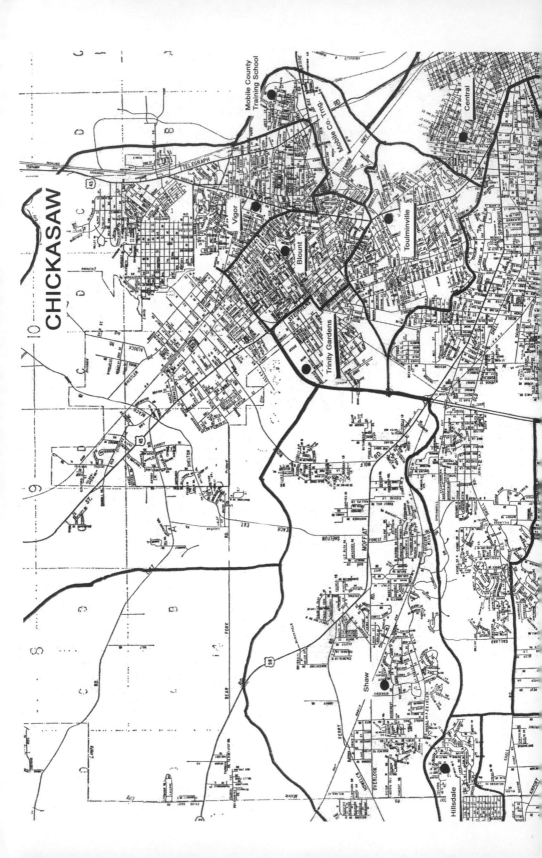

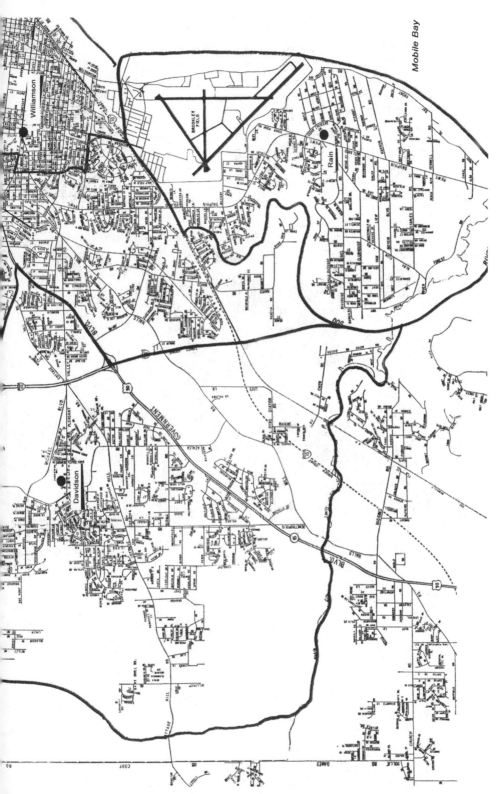

Map 1. Proposed High School Zones, 1968. (*Mobile Press and Register*, May 17, 1968)

the microphone to speak. Jacobs was particularly upset that the whites were leaving and accused them of denying her her right to be heard. She conceded that crime was rampant at Williamson but added that segregation had forced her own children to go there for years and said that white children should be treated no better than blacks. Pogue, a big man with a big voice, attacked the all-white composition of the school board. He said that, given the racial makeup of the community, two of its five members should be black. He also maintained that the schools should teach "black culture" and "black self-determination." John LeFlore, the head of Mobile's NAACP chapter, called for peace and harmony between the races, drawing catcalls and boos from some in the audience. He said that rather than criticize the board, whites should pay its members homage for working so diligently to prevent desegregation. He warned that if he found evidence of gerrymandering in the new zones, he would personally ask the federal judiciary to correct the situation. Another black spokesman, Jesse Thomas, vigorously defended the Williamson and Maysville schools. He said that they were not situated in "a jungle" and pointed out that black sections have no monopoly of crime, dope, and prostitution. Lawlessness exists in many white areas too, he noted.[38]

Rev. Leon Hill, pastor of Our Mother of Mercy Church and the representative of the Plateau–Magazine Point Community Council, argued that whites should accept total integration of the schools immediately. "If we're going to cut off the dog's tail, then let's do it all at once," he said with a grin. He called for law and order during the present crisis and begged whites to swallow the bitter pill. As he left the microphone, someone yelled out, "How many kids do you have, Father?"[39]

In approving the attendance zones after the three-hour meeting, the board stressed that it had no choice. But this position was unacceptable to many people in the white community. They formed a new organization, STAND, the acronym for Stand Together and Never Divide. It drew ten thousand Mobile residents to the Sage Avenue Armory that Friday night. There, frustration and anger animated the audience and speakers alike. Many white people were afraid: afraid of blacks, afraid of their own powerlessness. Something had to be done, but what? That question was deferred.

On Monday, May 26, the U.S. Supreme Court ruled in *New Kent County,* a Virginia case involving three school districts. It found that freedom-of-choice plans were unconstitutional. In response James Allen, a Democrat running for the Senate from Alabama, reiterated the southern lament, saying the ruling "illustrates that our most sacred possession, our children, are being made pawns of bureaucrats in Washington who are attempting to regiment every aspect of our daily lives."[40]

In Mobile an attorney for STAND, state senator Pierre Pelham, petitioned the federal district court for intervenor status and argued that the court should drop its rezoning requirement because white students would be unsafe in black schools and neighborhoods. To support his argument Pelham reviewed in great detail the race riots, mob violence, and civil disorders that had occurred throughout the United States in recent years. He stated that black people, "in reaction to incidents which on many occasions have been insubstantial in nature, have engaged in mob violence and in various unlawful acts causing the destruction of property and life." He also noted the emergence of "such national Negro spokesman as Rap Brown and Stokely Carmichael and others who advocate a philosophy of hostility and hatred toward white people and a course of violence against white people."[41] The court accepted Pelham's petition, and STAND was given official standing in court.

Meanwhile, in Washington, D.C., HEW released a report showing that in the South only 14 percent of students attended desegregated schools in the 1967–68 academic year, up from 3.2 percent in 1964, 6.5 percent in 1965, and 12.5 percent in 1966. In Alabama 5.4 percent of students attended desegregated schools in 1967–68.[42]

Liberals had made school desegregation into a moral crusade, and attentive southern conservatives developed a fine sense of moral outrage themselves. An editorial in the *Mobile Press* and *Register* attacked HEW for not presenting the data on the percentage of blacks in predominantly white schools in the North and once again cited the high level of white flight in the Washington, D.C., school system as evidence of northern hypocrisy. It continued: "The Great Society has never been equaled in political false pretense-of-interest in Negro betterment, educationally and otherwise. Gearing its desperate hope of political survival to the Negro vote, a last resort hope, the Great Society has ruthlessly assaulted the constitutional rights of American citizens in education and other vital respects under the pretense of having Negro aid as its goal. Playing politics . . . to entrap votes from the misled and gullible can be a dangerous game in any nation."[43]

Hearing for a New Plan

On June 12, 1968, the school board filed a motion asking the federal district court to disapprove its desegregation proposal and instead place the entire school system under a freedom-of-choice plan. Newly elected governor Albert Brewer said he wanted to keep on using freedom-of-choice plans despite the federal government's position. He claimed that the abolition of freedom of choice would seriously jeopardize public support for education in Alabama.[44] Judge Thomas scheduled trial for Wednesday, July 17, and citizens mobilized in a vain attempt to influence the outcome.

On Monday night, June 24, a STAND rally at Hartwell Field attracted seventy-five hundred anxious critics of the mandatory attendance zones. The organization planned to hold a rally at the federal courthouse to protest fixed attendance zones. Speakers demanded local control of local schools.[45] The next night Dr. Robert W. Gilliard, a black dentist who then was president of the Mobile NAACP chapter and an ally of LeFlore's, urged a cheering throng at the Greater Union Baptist Church to get to the courtroom before members of STAND could occupy the 182 observers' seats. The purpose of this action, he said, was to demonstrate that black people supported the fixed attendance zones mandated by the Fifth Circuit. He cautioned the group to obey police officers and be peaceful and law abiding, but "if the police ask some black people to go home, they'd better ask some white people to go home, too. If any elbows are rubbed, we want both the white and black elbows arrested."

Other speakers wanted desegregation as simple access, but one person wanted more than that. Joe Reed, executive secretary of the Alabama State Teachers Association and chairman of the NAACP Committee on Education, spoke in opposition to both freedom of choice and fixed zoning approaches because both meant de facto segregation of the races. He advocated fostering full-scale cultural assimilation by requiring racial balance in every school. Because blacks comprised about 40 percent of the population in Mobile, every public school should contain that percentage of black children, he said. It was the only way to ensure that black people could receive an equal education. His position was so radical that no one knew quite what to make of it.

After Reed spoke, a man named Arthur Whitfield and several students protested that whites' allegations of drug dealing, violence, and prostitution in the Williamson neighborhood and school were malicious and false.[46] Blacks were not the "beasts" of white folklore, they implied, and used a string of facts to counter the myths.

Judge Thomas convened his court once again on Wednesday, July 17, at 9:30 A.M. to consider desegregation of Mobile's schools. He had before him the board's plan mandated by the Fifth Circuit and another plan developed by the board itself in opposition to the Fifth Circuit's ruling. The parent-plaintiffs and the Justice Department had also filed plans; notably, both used busing to increase desegregation. Federal marshals and FBI agents stood guard outside the courthouse because, at its Monday night rally, STAND had called for thirty thousand demonstrators to attend. However, only about six hundred people stood on the street as the court met. Westbrook, who now was a STAND leader, told the protesters to leave because they had served their purpose. As if embarrassed by the small showing, Lamar Payne, STAND's chairman, said that the group's attorney had advised white people not to appear and said that alone had diminished the turnout. There were no incidents.

Inside, Superintendent Cranford Burns testified that in his opinion integration of the schools could best be achieved through a freedom-of-choice plan rather than a rigid system that used arbitrarily drawn lines, because the people of Mobile would accept the former but not the latter. He drew a distinction between desegregation and integration; desegregation was simple access to schools on a nonracial basis, whereas integration was the melding of cultures. Government-imposed integration was dangerous for the community, he implied. He claimed that real integration could come about only through the willingness of ethnic groups to accept a voluntary mixing plan. "We could win the battle of desegregation today and lose the war for integration tomorrow," he said plaintively. Burns and Bobby Clardy, the administrative assistant for pupil personnel, testified at length about the new zone lines, but they clearly preferred the board's freedom-of-choice plan to the fixed zone system ordered by the appeals court.[47]

The next day Charles H. Jones Jr., a lawyer with the NAACP Legal Defense Fund, and Frank M. Dunbaugh, a lawyer from the Justice Department, cross-examined Clardy, trying to get him to acknowledge that school officials had used racial factors in drawing the new fixed attendance zones. Clardy stoutly maintained that no one had applied racial considerations. Attorney Pelham, representing STAND, asked Clardy only one question: "Did you consider the safety of white school children in drawing those lines?" "No, sir," replied Clardy.

To close out the second full day of the slow-moving trial, a school board attorney, Abe Philips, called a white parent to the stand. Barbara Macon testified that she preferred freedom of choice because that was "the American way." "I object to outsiders telling us where our children must attend school," she said. "The Federal government has no right to tell us how to run our school system." Macon said she had no objections to black students attending the same school as her children under a freedom-of-choice plan. The visitors' gallery had many empty seats that afternoon because the witnesses' accounts were neither new nor surprising.[48]

On Friday the government called to the stand Dr. Fred Venditti, head of the Educational Opportunities Center at the University of Tennessee, to bolster support for its nonracial zoning plan. Venditti's job was to testify to the physical inadequacies of black schools. At the first opportunity Philips and Pelham attacked Venditti's credibility and forced what they believed would be damaging admissions. Venditti acknowledged, for example, that he was a member of the American Civil Liberties Union and had volunteered to help the government in the Mobile desegregation case and other cases. The two lawyers sought to portray him to the world as a meddlesome outsider, but in court they said only that he was a biased witness. Venditti testified that his children attended a desegregated high school in Knoxville, but he did not know the number of black students in the school. Philips told him: only three. The implication was that Venditti was a hypocrite. He had visited Mobile on three occasions for a total of five days and had inspected only black schools selected by the Justice Department. He had made no survey of the whole system or of white schools. He conceded that he knew nothing about the Mobile County school budget, about land prices or the availability of building sites, and that he had not visited the central office to obtain data. The implicit conclusion was that he was inadequately prepared. The lawyers also reaffirmed their worldview. The witness was an outside agitator or, worse, like one of those southerners who cooperated so fully with the Union forces occupying the South during Reconstruction that they lost their honor.

Philips put three more parents on the stand on Friday to testify in favor of freedom of choice as "the American way." Two vowed that they would not send their children to the presently all-black schools to which they would be assigned in the strict zoning plan. He then rested his case.[49]

On Monday the NAACP produced another expert witness, Dr. Myron Lieberman, a professor of education at Rhode Island College who had been hired by the NAACP Legal Defense Fund.[50] Lieberman testified that he favored racial balance in the schools and that the plan developed by the NAACP had this as its goal. He explained that a computer had been programmed to achieve a 60-40 black-white ratio in schools in predominantly black neighborhoods. The results were subsequently adapted to take into consideration such things as natural barriers and traffic hazards.[51]

Lieberman also testified that he was convinced that the school board had drawn up some of its attendance lines on a racial basis, in contravention of the Fifth Circuit's order. For example, he said, school officials did not use Broad Street consistently as a zone divider: Only where blacks lived on one side and whites the other did school officials use it as a zone line; when a white neighborhood or a black neighborhood straddled Broad Street, the school board had not used the street as the zone line, thereby limiting desegregation.

Philips cross-examined Lieberman, asking, "Do you think Negroes should be forced to go to attend schools with white pupils?" His answer was swift and direct: "Yes, I do." "And vice versa?" Again, yes. Lieberman said he would permit no freedom of choice; instead, he advocated busing students from neighborhoods that had no previous connection. Lieberman acknowledged that he had visited only two schools; he said he had driven past thirty-one others. Philips loosed a barrage of critical questions about the computerized method of assigning students to schools under his plan, but Lieberman was firm in his support for the NAACP's goal of racial balance in the schools.[52]

Another attorney representing STAND, Ralph Kennamer, did no better. When Kennamer asked Lieberman about the "hate whitey" philosophy of the black militants Stokely Carmichael and H. "Rap" Brown, Lieberman said he had never met them and therefore could not form a conclusion. The attorney asserted that all-black Blount High School was a bastion of crime. He asked, "Do you believe white children should be forced to go to an unsafe school?" Lieberman replied, "If the school is unsafe, no children, including Negroes, should be allowed to attend it. I think it is possible to make the schools of Mobile safe for anyone." Kennamer referred to NOW as he probed the witness. Lieberman said he knew of no organization in Mobile County that advocated the "urban guerrilla war" alleged by Kennamer. That was the best the lawyer could get.[53] Kennamer did not say so explicitly, but those reading the newspaper knew who Lieberman was: He was a carpetbagger, one of those detestable men who came from the North during Reconstruction to profit from southern travail.

When Kennamer and Pelham sought to present STAND's case, they were immediately thwarted by rulings from the bench. The lawyer for the parents objected to a paragraph in STAND's motion that contended that it would be dangerous for white students to attend predominantly black schools because of a national pattern of racial unrest transmitted through the media and existing in Mobile. The paragraph went into detail about the use of troops to quell race riots and the hatred-of-whites philosophy voiced by militant black leaders. When Judge Thomas sustained the objection, STAND's lawyers were nonplussed. The court would not let them present evidence about a culturally powerful story—whites' fear of black reprisals, which was itself set into the old radical story of the "black beast" lurking behind the seemingly friendly face.

In an effort to show that white children would be unsafe if forced to attend schools in black neighborhoods, Pelham and Kennamer called Police Chief Dan Davis on the stand. He testified about the emergence of NOW in Prichard, a small racially polarized city bordering Mobile. He said that the group had placed an ad in a newspaper, the *Southern Courier,* about a training school for guerrilla warfare. Davis also testified that unnamed agitators had visited all-black Blount High School in Prichard in an effort to recruit students to a school that would show them how to manufacture "Molotov cocktails." The plaintiffs' lawyers and the government objected to this testimony, saying that these events and the issues before the court had no connection. Thomas sustained this objection. Pelham caused a stir in the courtroom by angrily accusing Thomas of denying the white intervenors their rights. "It's obvious to me, your Honor, that we are not going to be allowed to present our case," he said. "I respectfully submit the court has denied my intervenors their day in court, and so I rest my case." "I respectfully disagree," replied the judge.[54] In fact, he had ruled that the radicals' narrative account was legally out of bounds, and the implicit message was that they would have to invent another approach if ever they wanted to win.

Pelham's outburst was not the only emotional confrontation of the day. While the court met, another animated discussion began in the corridor outside. A woman wearing a Wallace-for-President button, and supported by a small group of other white women, accosted Robert Breecker, a University of California law student who had worked as a clerk during the summer for Vernon Z. Crawford, the local attorney hired by the NAACP to represent the parents. The women were angry about comments that Breecker, who sported an enormous red walrus mustache, had made on a local radio show. They made it plain that Breecker was an "outside agitator" who knew nothing of the South. After a marshal broke up the disturbance, Breecker complained caustically to reporters about the inadequacy of "Southern justice."[55] The Register's account of this incident made it plain to southern eyes that racial stereotyping was wrong but that this northern boy thought that slandering a whole region and its people was fine. More hypocrisy.

Inside the courtroom the school board had called James McPherson, the associate schools superintendent, as a rebuttal witness. McPherson said, "The NAACP plan is the most ridiculous zoning system I've ever seen. It requires massive and expensive busing." He estimated it would cost $200,000 to buy additional buses for the elementary and junior high grades, money the schools just did not have. He also criticized the government's plan. It cost too much for busing, and it ignored natural barriers and traffic hazards. McPherson said the school board's zoning plan was feasible, but a freedom-of-choice plan would be most acceptable for Mobile. The trial had wound down. Now it was up to Judge Thomas. He promised his ruling the next week.[56]

The court hearings caused uncertainty in the schools. Superintendent Burns announced that he was having difficulty getting teachers to sign contracts for the coming year: "Because of the uncertainty of litigation . . . some have gone elsewhere." He sent a letter to principals advising them that instructors might have to pull double duty because of the teacher shortage.[57]

Stokely Carmichael addressed a mass meeting in Mobile on July 26, under the auspices of NOW. Carmichael praised the demonstration of black power manifested in the urban riots across the country during the previous three summers. He had once been chairman of the Student Non-Violent Coordinating Committee, but he showed that his attitudes had changed when he quoted with approval the Maoist saying, "Political power grows out of the barrel of a gun." He said that the only way for blacks to gain equality in the United States was through armed insurrection.[58]

Stories told by extremists on both sides gained currency. Such bald statements chilled any whites, confirming their worst fears. Among blacks, such a naked display of rhetorical power animated ambition. If Stokely could say such things and remain unpunished, then perhaps they could too.

Judge Thomas entered his opinion and decree on July 29. He began by saying, "If there is any one thing on which plaintiffs, plaintiff-intervenor, defendants, and defendant-intervenors agree, it is that no party likes the other parties' suggested zones." The court, accordingly, drew up its own plan for the 1968–69 school year. In the urban area the plan consisted of neighborhood zones for the elementary and junior high grades and freedom of choice for the senior high years. Any student zoned into a school where he was in a 5 percent racial minority could transfer to the school of his choice that was nearest his home and served his grade level. The court acknowledged that its neighborhood zoning plan "due to concentration of races in certain areas . . . will leave some schools with 100 percent white attendance and some with 100 percent Negro attendance."[59] Freedom of choice would continue for all grades in the rural parts of the county. The plan fell far short of the standards requested by the Justice Department and the NAACP Legal Defense and Education Fund.[60]

Within weeks the plaintiffs, government, defendants, and defendant-intervenors all filed notices of appeal from Thomas's latest order. Perhaps as the lesser evil, the *Mobile Press* and *Register* supported Thomas's "solid, practical approach to a very thorny problem." The Justice Department and the NAACP "should beware of the folly" of trying to overturn Thomas's decision, said the editorial, because it "represents the only prospective means administratively possible between now and September to establish a foundation for an orderly transition to fuller integration for the school system." Practicalities aside, the editorial board made clear its anger and its hoped-for revenge:

> We are thoroughly in agreement with the school board witnesses who testified during the trial of the integration case that "freedom-of-choice" school attendance plans represent the "American way" and "the democratic way." . . . The 5th U.S. Circuit and the Supreme Court, aided and abetted by the Justice Department and the NAACP Legal Defense and Education Fund, Inc., of New York, are applying dictatorial means to achieve school integration more rapidly. The court rulings, applying a geographical zone plan to accomplish that end, regardless of the cost, amounts to nothing more nor less than judicial despotism. The selection of the Mobile, Prichard, and Chickasaw city schools

by the Justice Department . . . for extraordinary legal attention is again evidence of the fact that the Deep South is the planned target of legal discrimination in the realm of forced school integration. . . . Fortunately, time and elections have a way of rectifying such matters. Even now the forces of a democratic people are at work to undo the havoc to the American way of life caused by leftist liberals too long in power.[61]

The Fifth Circuit had ordered the desegregation of faculty and specified that the faculty should be 60 percent white and 40 percent black to conform to the racial makeup of the county. Ironically, at that time only 52 percent of the faculty was white. This meant that all new teachers hired by the schools would have to be white until the court-mandated 60-40 ratio was obtained. A large number of black teachers were not hired that fall.[62] Many whites surely sighed and said, "I told you so," when they read those facts in the paper. "The federal government just doesn't know what it's doing."

Discussion

Observers, then and now, can agree on what happened in Mobile but not on the meaning of what happened. Everyone could see that blacks and white lived largely separate lives, that blacks as a race had accumulated less and achieved less than whites, and that black people resented that disparity and wanted it to end. The words and deeds of leaders for both sides explained the reasons for this manifest inequality in public narratives that embodied still deeper myths. People lived by the stories they believed to be true.

What can we make of the actions of white southern leaders? They resisted desegregation, and in so doing they used language that kept traditional stories alive. For some whites and most blacks the story was quite simple: White officials acted out their own personal racism, a racism predicated on notions of white biological and cultural superiority. But other whites saw southern leaders as reacting out of peculiar notions of honor: Fight the good fight for the South, not because you are personally prejudiced but because you want to defend a southern way of life once again against the northern oppressor. A Darwinian metanarrative underpins the first position and a heroic saga the second.

Mobile's school board decided to resist desegregation, and its lawyers used biological and cultural differences to explain the need for separate schools. The governor of Alabama dramatically tried to block the entry of even a few token black students into formerly all-white schools. Surely, these leaders knew that they must lose, that the federal government would triumph in the end. But, imaginatively, white leaders played out their losing struggles against a background of the stories of the Civil War. In the South how one fought and died meant everything. The heroes of the Old South lost the war, but they retained honor and came back during Redemption to recapture the South.

For many white southerners, then, the story of resistance to federal power and northern carpetbaggers was really a hopeful story portending triumph. The conservatives' story contained a clear forecast: Without the South, and by that they meant southern whites, the Democrats would never retain national power. The *Mobile Press* and *Register* beat this drum continually. Southerners would use elections to reassert their way of life, and the presidential elections of 1964 and 1968 gave credence to their claims, as southern whites came increasingly to vote for conservative Republicans. Many in the South took perverse pleasure in seeing Lyndon Johnson's northern liberal vice president, Hubert Humphrey, run a distant third at the polls across the region in 1968.

When the white South finally and reluctantly accepted freedom of choice rather than Jim Crow separation for public schools, it claimed the ascendency of personal liberty, a core value of American political culture. When the federal government, both the Justice Department and the courts speaking independently, said that freedom of choice was not enough and compelled even greater change, the resentment of a second reconstruction became ever deeper among a broad range of white people.

Blacks knew these stories but did not appreciate them; they had their own. Among blacks, Sambo was out, and so was Step 'n' Fetchit. The stories told by national leaders—Malcolm X's great narrative of separation and black power and W. E. B. Du Bois's old but ceaseless demand for racial equality—competed for allegiance in Mobile as Jerry Pogue and John LeFlore gave voice to each perspective. Notably, Martin Luther King's insistent admonition for Christian brotherhood and reconciliation found no forceful voice among the public narratives during the desegregation struggle.

By the summer of 1968 Stokely Carmichael's claim that black power grew out of the barrel of a gun resonated with many black Mobilians, and radical whites tried to tell a story about how blacks' hatred of whites would lead to race war. Across the country blacks rioted in big cities, and in Mobile white radicals claimed that blacks had established a guerrilla-training school. Attorney Pelham could not get this story into the court record, but the Mobile newspapers brought it to every home.

Contrast the vigor and persistence of radical white leaders with the silence of liberals. Few local whites spoke out at public gatherings on behalf of integration in Mobile. Perhaps they were content to let the federal government and the national television news carry the load, but in plain fact the liberals did not advance their story locally in public discourse.

3. Assimilation

IN THE MIDDLE OF the twentieth century southern blacks and whites lived in different subcultures within the overall hierarchy of values and behaviors established by the radicals during the Redemption. Jim Crow laws had mandated physical separation, and separation had meant social and political inequality. Southerners of both races and all classes were schooled in the nuances of difference.

Successfully desegregating the schools would open everything else in society to change, and change itself was threatening to those who believed the abyss sucked down everyone caught on its slippery slope. Public schools socialize children into the public culture, so the terms of assimilation became contested once the federal government compelled the South to desegregate its schools. Stories of mythic evil and debasement, most notably of a black corruption of the white race, shaped the perceptions of the desegregated future for many white southerners. To those whites at the top of the social order, desegregation of schools as much as restaurants meant little because they could control the nature of their social interactions in any case. And some others, to be sure, welcomed desegregation as part of the moral destiny of the United States.

Cultures and subcultures can exist side by side in relative separation, but when they start to move toward each other, however slowly, the terms of the melding become important. Assimilation is the process of developing a common culture, and researchers have found three general patterns—absorption, fusion, and cultural pluralism—by which the process can be negotiated. One scholar, Milton Gordon, describes the American experience this way: "We may say that the 'Anglo-conformity' theory demanded the complete renunciation of the immigrant's ancestral culture in favor of the behavior and values of the Anglo-Saxon core group; the 'melting pot' idea envisaged a biological merger of the Anglo-Saxon peoples with other immigrant groups and a blending of their respective cultures into a new indigenous American type; and 'cultural pluralism' postulated the preservation of the communal life and significant portions of the culture of the later immigrant groups with the context of American citizenship and political and economic integration into American society."[1]

The nation had long dealt with the assimilation of immigrants. During the eighteenth and early nineteenth centuries most foreigners had melted into the dominant Anglo culture. But as the sheer numbers and diversity of immigrants increased in the latter decades of the nineteenth century, public policies, like truancy laws and civics classes in public schooling, signaled "Americanization." Absorption of minority cultures into a dominant culture gave way to the fusion of all cultures into something new and better; some cultural traits were unappreciated and set aside, while others were accepted, admired, and retained by the new.

First slavery and then Jim Crow blocked assimilation of blacks into the wider culture. As school desegregation proceeded, the question became this: Would desegregation function as the absorption of blacks into the dominant white culture, the fusion of black and white cultures into a new third culture, or what? When blacks and whites mixed together, whose stories would prevail? The continual cry of "freedom of choice" from the white community signaled the prevailing sentiment about assimilation. Whites would accept blacks into their schools only so long as white norms were dominant. Anything more than that was too much.

Mobile Responds to Desegregation

When schools opened in September 1968, the desegregation of faculty brought the first strife. About thirty white parents gathered at all-white Tanner-Williams Elementary School in rural Mobile County to protest the arrival of two black teachers. On the third day tempers flared, someone threw a pop bottle at a car carrying a black teacher, and police arrested four whites. Cranford Burns, the superintendent, urged patience and cooperation.[2] Police escorted the teachers to school, and the disturbance dissipated.[3] Across the county school districts assigned 202 teachers to schools where the opposite race was dominant.[4]

Trouble erupted at Vigor High School during the second week. Vigor had enrolled 1,674 students; 105 blacks (6 percent of the total) had chosen to attend. Of the sixty-nine faculty, three were black. When a white student was suspended for fighting with two black students, more than a hundred white students and adults picketed the school to protest integration. At a meeting in the school auditorium, though, they were scolded by the school's chaplain, a minister from the First Baptist Church. He told them that their act of rejection was self-defeating and that it required courage and understanding to accept integration. "Do unto others," he admonished them.[5] Protest dissipated thereafter.

Confrontation began at Shaw High School somewhat later and lasted longer, and by October 1 three police officers were assigned to patrol the school. A white father swore out an arrest warrant against a black student after she and his daughter got into a fight. The white girl had been injured. The black girl was suspended.[6]

In November, Shaw's principal summoned police when fifty black students refused to return to classes or to leave the school grounds. The defiance centered on three demands: that the school's nickname (the Rebels) be eliminated, that "Dixie" no longer be played at school games, and that the school form an Afro-American Club to enable students to study the contributions of black Americans.[7] Implicitly, blacks decided they would not be absorbed by "Anglo conformity." The principal temporized, the school board did not compel changes at Shaw, and these issues festered throughout the year.[8]

The students were not alone in their protests concerning history and culture. All along they had adult allies, most prominently John LeFlore, who tried and failed to get the school board to act on the students' demands. Also involved in the issues of black history were David L. Jacobs, the black leader of NOW and director of the Mobile Education Project of the American Friends Service Committee, and his white adjutant, Bill Rosser.

At the January 1969 delegation meeting Jacobs and Rosser criticized the school board directly to its face for failing to deal fairly and resourcefully with black history. In their comments they amplified on ideas contained in letters sent to the schools superintendent days earlier. They cited scholarship that said that the textbooks used in Mobile to teach U.S. history made black people invisible. In addition, Jacobs and Rosser said, the texts used in the elementary and junior high schools to teach Alabama history needed to be replaced because they treated history "from the point of view of plantation owners." They wanted a new, more accurate story told, one that showed that blacks were the victims of white oppression, not the cheerful beneficiaries of white largesse. "Throughout, these texts glorify slavery as a system where 'most of them were treated kindly,' where the white man was 'the best friend the Negro ever had and they knew it.' The Klan is referred to as an organization which 'struck fear into the hearts of lawless men.' . . . Slavery is referred to as 'the earliest form of social security in the U.S.'"[9] The two men urged the school board to create black history courses, hire teachers especially trained to teach them, and purchase new classroom and library materials on black history and culture for every teacher.[10] Doing these things could change black self-esteem and respect of whites for blacks.

W. B. Westbrook, who rose to speak after Rosser had presented his view, claimed to represent the white parents and students at Shaw. Westbrook told the board that the organization that Rosser (and Jacobs) represented, the American Friends Service Committee, was the same one that had sent blood to the North Vietnamese and that had met in communist capitals around the world, including Moscow in April. Westbrook made reference to firebombings that had occurred in Mobile and said, "Our friend from the American Service Committee was very closely related to the group which is promoting these activities." (Westbrook was referring to NOW.) Westbrook read a letter to the board in which he complained that the introduction of black students from the now-closed Hillsdale High had almost wrecked the educational program and community at Shaw. The people at Shaw wanted to know whether the board was going to require that Shaw change because of the blacks' demands.

Westbrook also said that it was "a shame and disgrace" that the court order meant that the black children of the Toulminville area would not be getting a new high school simply because it would serve mostly black children. "This is," he said, "discrimination in the rawest and most atrocious forms."[11] Here he implicitly supported the notion that black people preferred new facilities of their own over forced integration.

William B. Crane, the school board chair, responded directly by saying that the board having taken no action on the black students' requests for changes at Shaw constituted denial of the appeal. The board supported the current procedures and practices for treating black history and culture.

On February 13 the *Register*'s headline on its story about the previous evening's school board meeting read "SHAW RACIAL SITUATION SAID EASING, SDS LITERATURE CONFISCATION OKAYED." By this time, of course, the national media had portrayed the Students for a Democratic Society (SDS) as a subversive, if not terrorist, organization. (SDS, formed in 1960, had become the New Left's most prominent radical and visible group by the mid-1960s as it challenged established authority in support of civil rights, public welfare, and peace.) So, once again, the local newspaper implied that outside agitators had insinuated themselves into and disrupted the otherwise tranquil world of southern schools. Superintendent Burns, the paper reported, had announced that racial problems at Shaw had "been reduced to normal." In a report to the board he said that Shaw High School clearly had adopted symbols and established practices and procedures that were based on southern traditions and that some blacks interpreted these as an effort to reestablish and perpetuate segregation and to remind black people that they were subservient to white people. The decisions made did not violate the law, he said, and although he personally felt the school had made some mistakes, "it would be inadvisable to impose the views of people outside the school and the community." Burns also said that two other issues had been satisfactorily resolved at Shaw: The protesting students' demand for representation on the student council had been granted, but they had been denied the use of a school assembly to feature black history.

In other action that night Associate Superintendent James A. McPherson told the board that literature from the SDS had been confiscated at Murphy and another school. "Our principals are taking every precaution and strong steps to stamp out this movement before it can take hold." Board member Homer Smith was alarmed and said, "We should be looking for the people who are passing this stuff out."[12]

The continuing theme was that outside agitators, probably communist-inspired, were undermining American society, and as if to confirm nativist suspicion, Rosser and Jacobs came before the school board again at its April 23 meeting. They assured Crane that they would address separate issues, in keeping with the board's new policy of permitting only one speaker from each delegation unless additional speakers addressed different issues. Then they both admonished the board. Bill Rosser spoke first, and he spared nothing: "Gentlemen, I am here to speak to you tonight about racism. About the racism of the School Board and the Central Administrative Staff. The result of racism, which has been rampant in this school system, has been a brutal dehumanization of human beings. The School Board, unfortunately, has the tendency to view racial problems in terms of disorder rather than injustice. . . . The Board has refused continually to make the schools equal."[13]

Rosser listed his specific charges in a two-page diatribe. The board, he said, had resisted the court-ordered desegregation of the schools. Freedom of choice violated the court order, the school zones were consciously gerrymandered by race, and the school system wasted money on resistance that could be better spent on the schools. He further charged that various schools principals and teachers were permitted to use the word *nigger* to address students and teachers, that they allowed children to go hungry, used racist textbooks, treated unfairly any black students who protested, and sought to build a high school at Toulminville, even though it would obviously be an all-black school in violation of the court order. Finally, he said, the school board had blessed the suspension of students at Murphy for possessing certain literature, while board member Sidney Phillips passed out John Birch Society literature after every board meeting.

After presenting his litany of damning charges, Rosser made several recommendations on behalf of the American Friends Service Committee. The first was that the whole school board should resign. The second was that the whole central administrative staff should resign. Rosser concluded: "We want the schools desegregated. We want it NOW! . . . It's incredible that forty percent of the population of this city is black and you have not one black person on the Board. It's incredible that forty percent of the city is black and you have not one black man on the central administrative staff." Failing mass resignation, Rosser said, "We would like for you to explore a new way of electing a school board so that the black community has a chance to be heard and be represented."[14]

David Jacobs offered a different tone, a lamentation on white oppression, but he came to the same conclusion about the solution: power for blacks, one way or the other. "Black folks in Mobile are tired," Jacobs said. ". . . White schools have the money. They have the facilities. They have the equipment. The white folks in the suburbs have the good teachers whether they are black or white. And they rob the black community of their best teachers to put them in white schools. And this is a fact. And things are not going to get any better here in Mobile. If anything they are going to get worse. There is going to be more conflict. There is going to be more disruption. There might be violence right here in Mobile because people just don't care. . . . If there isn't going to be meaningful desegregation here in Mobile, I am going to appeal to the black community to have 'community control.'"[15]

Black people wanted political power. That was the bottom line. The struggle was no longer about equal access to schools. It had become a battle about political power—power to set the agenda, to offer alternative policies, to shape the minds of children, and to tax and to spend.

The next person to speak was Westbrook, who persistently stated the radical white position. He was just as angry as the militant blacks. He thanked the board for its service to Mobile. He accused Rosser of fomenting a recent walkout by black students at Dunbar Junior High, and he branded Rosser an outside agitator. "Now he says there are going to be problems in Mobile, and certainly I can readily agree. As long as we allow people of his caliber to disrupt or to continue the disruption of the students in the Mobile public school system. He has no children here. He has no interest as far as education is concerned, or any member of his family," Westbrook said. "He was imported here from Denver, Colorado. He attended the University of Colorado. He was on a Ford Foundation grant. He is a member of the American Friends Service Committee that's sending blood, food, and clothing to the North Vietnamese communists."

Westbrook continued:

> Mr. Jacobs remarks that "Black folks are tired." I was just wondering why they wouldn't work. I was wondering why they was all on the welfare. And I was also wondering why they all went down to get their food stamps. But I guess they're tired. And I'm certainly glad to know that. They want control. They want to control the school board, the school budget. Well, I think if they would work toward accomplishing (something), as far as the school board is concerned, instead of practicing disruption of the educational system, they could certainly contribute a lot to the educational program. He says, "Yes, we want black teachers in our black schools." Well, friend, he talks my language. I want black teachers in black schools also, and I want white teachers in white schools because I think people that feel like I do can teach me more than someone that I know nothing about.

Westbrook's story was cultural: Blacks did not work hard enough, their values would drag down hard-working white children despite parental vigilance. His diatribe finally wound down, and he took his parting shot: "[Jacobs] wants to control the budget. . . . If they'll get up and go to work and get off their 'relief rolls,' I think they can have some control of the budget, but you never get something for nothing."[16]

The stories were so different: For Rosser and Jacobs black people were victims of systematic white oppression; for Westbrook black people were naturally shiftless and lazy. Both sides now spoke of disruption and the need for local control of local schools. Neither group wanted the other to be in charge of enculturating the young.

During the next month the school board revised its policy on the monthly delegation meetings to try to cope with the assertive rhetoric of people like Westbrook, Rosser, and Jacobs. As before, the board would permit delegates of school and community groups to address it at its delegation meeting, if they signed up in advance, listed the group that they represented, and specified the particular issue they would speak to. But in the future the board would refuse to hear from delegates if they had spoken on the same issue in the past three months or if the topic was inappropriate. Topics that the board expected delegates to address included the purposes, policies, laws, and grievances under which the schools operated.[17]

Meanwhile, county schools had implemented the board's new policy on student disruptions: that (1) students should not participate in disruptive activities on or near school campuses, (2) should not encourage others to do so, and (3) had to conform to all policies of the board and to local, state, and federal laws. Finally, under no circumstances would suspended pupils be readmitted to school until they and their parents committed themselves to a policy of full cooperation with the schools.

The policy and punishment were immediately controversial. Several principals suspended black students and would not readmit them because the students would not pledge to support the policy. At the May 28 delegation meeting of the school board, black community leaders accused the board of violating students' rights to free speech and assembly and protested that black students were treated more harshly (through suspensions) than white students for similar actions.[18] Superintendent Burns was steadfast. He explained the policy and its rationale carefully. Students simply had to abide by rules of good conduct. Signing the pledge of cooperation was a signal of the students' and parents' goodwill, and until they signed, they would not be readmitted.[19]

David Jacobs was back that night too. He spoke forcefully against the policy. He began by reminding the board that white students had protested at Vigor High School the year before and had not been suspended:

> Seemingly, free speech is dead here in Mobile when it comes down to black boys and black girls. There was no disruption: there was no throwing of Molotov cocktails; there was no profane language; there was no rock throwing. None of these things were done by these students. If anything has been disruptive it's been on the part of school administrators and school board officials; and it hasn't just started, it started sometime back. It goes way back to "Dick and Jane." That was disruptive when it comes down to the minds of black people. "Dick and Jane" never did appeal to black boys and girls. And the systematic exclusion of the role of black people . . . that was disruptive. It's disruptive when you have black schools in your black community with improper facilities. . . . When black boys and black girls picket the schools this upsets everybody in Mobile; the school board, the government officials—everybody becomes concerned about this, but they don't take time to look back through the years to frustrations that black people have gone through. And black boys and black girls are waking up here in Mobile. And there will be no peace and no tranquility here in this city until black folks get everything they should have—everything.[20]

Jacobs, a black Mobilian, made important rhetorical moves in this speech; he redefined *disruption* not as demonstrations and placards but as the brokenness of the system itself. He believed that black children would grow to healthy achievement only if they were freed from white power in all its manifestations: resources, textbooks, facilities. He nevertheless used the threat of the "savage" black: If you don't give us legitimate change, "he" will be unleashed.

The parade of concerned citizens continued, but they broke into two groups. One group of black citizens wanted Toulminville and Blount, the black neighborhood high schools, to be refurbished.[21] They wanted vital schools in their own neighborhoods, and these two high schools had long and glorious associations for many black people in Mobile. Some whites could attend, but the speakers wanted the schools to be prominent black community schools.

A group of white citizens, terrified by the rapidity of cultural change, chastised the board not for desegregation but other, perhaps related, matters. Marshall Covington, representing the Concerned Parents Organization, said that the schools' efforts to initiate a sex education curriculum infringed upon the God-given rights of parents to teach this aspect of life to their children. Merida P. Stearns also deplored the teaching of sex in the school system; it should be taught by parents and doctors. The story he told was commonplace: "To think that we would lower ourselves to using materials that are written by communists." William H. Cantwell also spoke as a concerned parent, but the issue he presented was different, although the underlying theme was familiar. He wanted to know what was being done to combat SDS in the schools. He had proof, he said, that when a teacher at Murphy High School had confiscated a copy of the *Great Speckled Bird,* a counterculture tabloid, from a student, another teacher had said that he had no right to take this unadulterated, pornographic material away from the student. Cantwell did not want his children exposed to this stuff, and he was sure that others felt the same way. Burns assured him that he had seen enough to know that SDS was a questionable organization, that right-thinking Americans could not approve of many of its activities, and that he had instructed school personnel to confiscate questionable material and send it to the superintendent so that he could make such material part of the board's agenda. In this way the mass media and public could know what these materials were.

Elements within the community were clearly afraid that the center would not hold, that some beast was slouching toward Bethlehem to be born. The signs, they said, were everywhere: militant blacks, socialists and communists, drugs, sex, and rock 'n' roll. They wanted traditional authority to reassert itself.

Court Action

The April 1968 order of the Fifth U.S. Circuit Court of Appeals had forbidden all school construction in Mobile without the permission of the local federal district court. In December the district court had denied the board permission to expand Toulminville High School because "it would tend to serve a school area with one dominant race, thus creating a 'lock-in' segregation area." On March 14, 1969, however, the court reversed itself; it would permit the expansion at Toulminville because the only objection to the school by the NAACP and the Justice Department was that it would be a one-race school when it was completed. The U.S. District Court explicitly rejected the appeals court's "supposition that the School Board will disregard its affirmative duty to disestablish the dual school system."[22]

A report filed with the district court in December 1968 showed that on the fourth day of classes, Mobile public schools had 74,964 pupils, 31,130 (or 42 percent) of whom were black. In 1967 692 black students had attended formerly white schools; in 1968 that number had grown to 3,484. The records showed that 253 white students were assigned to formerly black schools. All but two schools in the system had biracial faculties.[23]

In April 1969 Judge Thomas ordered the desegregation plan to be continued for the 1969–70 school year; it permitted total freedom of choice in the rural area of the county, and at the high school level in the metropolitan area, but also required pupil assignment by attendance zones in the elementary and junior high levels in the metro area. Thomas said that the board's reports on the enrollment and racial composition of each school showed that "meaningful desegregation has been accomplished and the effects of the once existent 'dual system' are being permanently disestablished."[24]

On June 3, 1969, the appellate court reversed Thomas's decision to accept the desegregation plan. The Fifth Circuit held that the district court's plan was constitutionally insufficient because it drew the new attendance zones on a *literal* nonracial basis and ignored the court's directive to make a conscious effort to locate attendance zones in a way that would eliminate past segregation. Thomas's attendance zones in the urban area were geographically compact and efficient, but he had not taken the opportunity to gerrymander the zones so that interracial contact would be maximized. The appellate court rejected the freedom-of-choice plan for the rural schools because no white children had chosen to attend traditionally black schools. The appellate judges directed the district court to request the assistance of the Office of Education at the U.S. Department of Health, Education, and Welfare to collaborate with the school board in the preparation of a new plan and "to fully and affirmatively desegregate all public schools in Mobile County, urban and rural, together with comprehensive recommendations for locating and designing new schools, and expanding and consolidating existing schools to assist in eradicating past discrimination and effecting desegregation."[25]

White Mobile was stupefied. Once again the federal courts had pushed the standard still higher. Racial mixing was clearly the most important goal of all. The school board met, decided to appeal to the Supreme Court, and issued a statement:

> One of the most crucial issues facing American citizens today is who should control education. We believe firmly that education, to be effective, must be close to the people it serves and that this can best be accomplished by citizens at the grass roots level who are able to exercise control over education through locally elected boards of education. . . . Now, the new court order in effect says that we must arrange attendance zones on a racial basis regardless . . . in effect gerrymandering attendance zones in order to create maximum integration at the expense of all other sound educational and practical considerations. We feel, as do our attorneys, that this requirement is contrary to the Constitution.[26]

Board members said the board and staff had in good faith attempted to comply with all court orders affecting the school system, that obedience to law was the foundation of the country, that they would do their best to comply again, and they thanked all the citizens of the county for their excellent cooperation in carrying out the previous court orders. However, they were deeply concerned about the overextension of the power of the federal judiciary in the operation of public schools.

The board was especially dismayed that the appellate court had continued to enjoin the board from renovating Howard Elementary School and Toulminville High School buildings. The board had been trying to rebuild these schools for more than two years, but now the court said construction would have to wait until the pattern of student needs emerged after a new plan had been implemented.

Predictably, the *Mobile Press* editorialized that "this latest ruling is typically part of an anti-South crusade, cooked up by non-Southerners to make this section a whipping boy." The paper accused the courts and federal agencies of continuing to "make Mobile and other Southern areas suffer the brunt of a hypocritical social project." Already, the courts and the federal government were withholding federal funds for alleged noncompliance with the law, and now they were threatening to require busing for racial balance but only in Dixie.[27]

At the June school board meeting a delegation of parents from Blount High School protested the suspension policy, and Jacobs took the board to task for not hiring more blacks at the central office, other than a few "showcase" examples. Westbrook, not to be outdone, stated that the board had been elected to run the schools, not to perform as puppets dancing on strings controlled by the federal government.

Massive Busing?

Immediately after the appellate court remanded the case, Judge Thomas asked HEW to send a team to Mobile. To maximize racial interaction, the HEW team had the power to draw special, one could say gerrymandered, school zones to capture residential areas populated by another race, but the team was not limited to that tactic alone. Another possibility was "pairing" a black school and a white school within one zone so that every student in the same grade would attend the same school. For instance, all first, second, and third graders would be assigned to one school and all fourth, fifth, and sixth graders to the other member of the paired schools. In order to attain racial balance in all schools, though, HEW could also create a school zone from residential areas that were not contiguous and use buses to transport students to the school building.

On July 10, 1969, the HEW team filed its desegregation plan with the court. The plan, which used contiguous and noncontiguous zoning and pairing for a few schools, would have desegregated all the schools of the county, except five inner-city elementary schools to which only token whites had been assigned.[28]

The next day the *Mobile Register* had a banner headline proclaiming "HEW SCHOOL MIX PLAN HERE TO REQUIRE MASSIVE BUSING." The plan, it said, called for "massive crosstown busing of 2,105 pupils from predominantly Negro areas" and the elimination of freedom of choice in rural schools, which would now have fixed compulsory attendance zones.[29]

In fact, the HEW plan called for busing 540 black students to Davidson High School and 305 black students to Shaw High School and for busing 1,260 other pupils from the inner city to the inner suburbs.[30] Four predominantly black schools in the inner city and four schools in the rural area would be closed.

Mobile's white elite voiced its disappointment and anger. The Exchange Club, an important downtown civic association of businesspeople, stated its opposition to busing for racial balance.[31] The Mobile City Executive Board of the Parent-Teachers Association rejected the plan as "unrealistic, absurd, and impossible" and later asked to intervene in the lawsuit in order to promote and defend neighborhood schools.[32] The Mobile City Commission called on HEW to rescind its "radical and punitive plan." U.S. Rep. Jack Edwards, a Republican, attacked the HEW plan and HEW Secretary Robert Finch. Edwards said it was an illegal "busing plan."[33] Sen. Jim Allen, a Democrat, attacked the proposed Mobile busing plan on the Senate floor; he said he was "fed up with [the] deception, double talk, and double standard" of the Nixon administration. LeFlore wrote a supportive letter to Finch and asked that the plan not be weakened.[34]

On August 1, 1969, the U.S. House of Representatives voted to curb busing for racial balance; it came as an amendment to a $17.7 billion appropri-
ations bill. The amendment favored freedom of choice.[35] That same day Judge
Thomas entered his order, saying that the task was "without doubt the most
difficult as well as important that I have ever encountered."[36] He noted that
the board had filed no plan to help the court, although the professional staff
had aided the HEW team without the approval of the school board. Thomas approved of the HEW plan for the outlying areas; this meant that area
attendance zones would be enforced for all schools west of I-65 and that the
zones were drawn to maximize desegregation. Thomas did not like the HEW
plan for schools east of I-65 and ordered the school board to prepare a new
plan by December to deal with that section of the county. Meanwhile, elementary and junior high schools east of I-65 would operate under the attendance zones used the preceding year, and high schools east of I-65 would
continue under freedom of choice. Thomas had once again proved to be
conservative. Go slow, be sure, he seemed to be saying.

Because most of Mobile's population lay in the urban center east of I-65,
the judge had essentially rejected "forced busing" for both the county and
the city. His order closed no schools. He ordered racial balance for the professional staff in each school for 1969–70 and for subsequent years "as far as
educationally feasible." He eliminated the 5 percent threshold, a school board
policy that said that a student could transfer out if he was in a 5 percent racial minority in a school. Thomas said decisions affecting hiring, firing, assignment, promotion, and pay should be made without regard for race, col-
or, or national origin except to the extent necessary to erase segregation.[37]

On August 7 the NAACP and Justice Department filed a notice of appeal
for that portion of the plan that pertained to the county east of I-65. The
NAACP wanted racial balance in the schools.[38]

Almost a hundred people came to the board's July 23 delegation meeting.
Before any of them spoke, Crane, the school board chair, announced additional procedures: (1) only one speaker for each delegation, (2) speakers
would be required to speak only on issues of public education, (3) speakers
were expected to summarize their views for and against policies and to refrain from castigating individuals or organizations, (4) speakers would have
three minutes, and no time would be allowed for debate, and (5) speakers
were expected to submit their questions in writing for answer at a later date.
The board also permitted only one observer from each delegation in the
boardroom; others would have to wait in the halls where loudspeakers had
been set up. The school board had taken these steps because of the acrimo-
ny and delay generated by other such sessions in recent months.[39]

Westbrook spoke first, about the need to resist the HEW plan. He was incensed that professors at the University of South Alabama in Mobile, especially a Professor Bjork and the Center for Intercultural Education, had helped the federal government's desegregation team. Westbrook said that "if you want an application for the SDS organization, you can get one from one of the professors at the University of South Alabama." He recommended that the board seek freedom of choice or nothing at all: "We are willing to go to jail by hundreds if necessary to back our wishes and demands for freedom-of-choice. This is what America was founded upon and we as citizens and parents will settle for nothing less. We want no pairing of schools, no closing of schools, no busing of children, no rigid boundary lines, no black history, no sex sensitivity courses, and no social welfare within our schools. . . . This is still America, we are still free, and we intend to remain free."[40] Crane interrupted him—Westbrook had exceeded his three minutes—but then the chair relented and let him wrap it up.

W. M. Shaw spoke next. He represented Citizens for Freedom-of-Choice and was accompanied by thirty-nine members who were out in the hall. He told the board that he had a petition signed by 962 people who supported freedom of choice, which they defined as "one, to put into use all of our school buildings; second, to put them in the same category as to grade and race as they were approximately five years ago; third, to give any child the right to transfer to another school of his or her choice, if this school in their neighborhood doesn't suit them."

Jacobs and Rosser attended as representatives of AFSC. They disputed the board's rules regarding speakers, particularly the refusal of the board to answer questions put to it by the delegations. Finally, Jacobs addressed the board. He said that he had noted that Westbrook had attacked individuals and groups and that the board had been wrong to let that happen. Jacobs said white protest of busing was nonsense. Busing had been used for a long time to move blacks and whites across the county. "All the cries have come from the white community and Uncle Tom[-type] colored folks who doesn't know what meaningful school desegregation is—then second, I want to attack the news media because that's where the disruption is coming from. The news media hasn't talked to people who know what's going on in the black community. They've given a one-sided view. Now I think this is primarily because . . . this is what the board wants. The board wants the white community to raise hell."

Hell was too much for one board member. He interrupted to advise Jacobs that the board did not want profanity used. He suggested that he might use "raise Cain," which Jacobs reluctantly accepted. Other people, Jacobs complained, could come in and say whatever they wanted to—why not him? "What about nigger? Is that profanity?" he asked.

> I want all the news media to get this now. I want all the news people who are here to get this. You are not treating us fair . . . you are not treating the black community fair. I'm not talking about the colored community. You have these Uncle Tom folks coming on T.V. They don't represent anybody but themselves. They might represent the views of the school board and the power structure. They don't represent us. You've never come into the black community and talked to us like we have any sense; you've talked to those people who want to keep [down] and suppress black people, and this is where the disruption is coming from, from the news media and from this school board. If blood flows in the streets come September, look here, it's gonna be your fault. It's gonna be your fault.[41]

As if to illustrate the issue of division within the black community, the last delegation heard by the board that evening was the Blount PTA. Mrs. L. B. Stewart claimed to be president, but Burns said that Blount parents had formed two groups, both of which claimed to be the Blount PTA. Undaunted, Stewart said that she and others in her group had been meeting with the central office staff but had not gotten satisfaction. They wanted the Blount students reinstated (they had been suspended for picketing the school during the previous school year) and given their report cards from the year before with no conditions attached. She set a deadline of August 22 for the board to respond. "Now today we are tired of asking, we are tired of being nice, we are tired of being treated any kind of way by the white man because of the black of our skins. We are tired of being given the runaround," she said. "We are here today demanding that our students be reinstated back to Blount."[42]

The August 27, 1969, meeting of the board was also a delegation meeting and attracted more of the same. Stewart, Jacobs, and Westbrook were there and spoke for their groups. Stewart reminded the board of her deadline and asked what had been done. Burns advised her that some things of concern to Blount people were being addressed. He hoped students and parents at Blount would work within the rules because it was the democratic way. Stewart gave the board two more weeks to get it right:

> And if those grievances don't be met in two weeks you don't need to worry about opening Blount High School because it will *not* be opened. Also, I would like to say while I am speaking, that we are not going to stand by to see that our best teachers be moved from Blount and transferred to somewhere else. Our children need a good education just like the white children do, and we want the best of teachers, too, at our school. As I overheard someone say: if you push a dog back in a corner he'll bite. We have been pushed too long, and we are ready to bite.

At the end of the speech people in the boardroom could hear loud applause from the hallway.[43] Jacobs and Westbrook also spoke; they said predictable things.

When school opened in September, Westbrook and others in the freedom-of-choice movement called for a protest-boycott of the public schools. The *Mobile Register* headlined the outcome: "25 PER CENT ENDORSE BOYCOTT OF SCHOOLS IN MOBILE COUNTY."[44] The paper's math was somewhat misleading. On an ordinary day 7 percent of the system's schoolchildren were absent, so the 25 percent figure that the paper cited that day wrongly included the normal, nonboycott absentees. Simple recalculation suggests that 18 percent stayed away from school countywide because of the boycott. The paper said absences were much higher in the rural part of the county, which for the first time had fixed attendance zones meant to maximize desegregation, so the boycott attracted much higher support in those areas, certainly more than 25 percent in many schools.

On September 23 a five-by-eight-inch ad with a black border appeared in the *Mobile Register:*

CONCERNED CITIZENS
- Do you want to protect the "freedom-of-choice" that is being denied you?
- Do you want action or talk?
- If you are tired of talk, then

PARADE
Wed. 9:30 A.M. Sept 24
- Keep your child home from school Wednesday.

Sponsored by Stand Together
and Never Divide
X-STAND Chapter
Saraland-Satsuma Citizens Group
Citizens for Freedom-of-choice
Concerned Citizens for Constitutional Rights

On the appointed day protesters paraded through the streets, then marched to the school board meeting, where Westbrook addressed the board on behalf of his group. His argument was ever the same. Jacobs was at the board meeting too. He attacked school principals who, he said, were now prohibiting students from wearing armbands and dashikis as symbols of black protest. Boos from outside the building drowned out his remarks. Bill Rosser spoke as well. He attacked the board for having a double standard, one for blacks and another for whites. He reminded the board that white students had marched downtown from Vigor High School the previous year and had not been punished, yet black students from Blount were harassed, intimidated, and suspended from school for picketing the school, something that was clearly legal.[45]

Approximately three hundred people attended a nighttime rally at Mobile Municipal Park, where they burned Robert Finch, the HEW secretary, in effigy. The rally culminated a day of symbolic activities for citizens protesting the denial of freedom of choice.[46] The whites' reawakened protest was noticeable: In seven rural schools about half the students stayed out for a day; in twelve others 40 percent appeared to have honored the boycott.[47]

Burns, the schools superintendent, attacked busing and supported freedom of choice in a major speech to the Rotary Club. He criticized the interference in the schools by the NAACP Legal Defense and Education Fund and the courts.[48] This intemperate and partisan message proved to be his swan song; he effectively ended his long tenure as the school system's chief administrator by appearing to be biased against black people.

At the October 22 delegation meeting of the board new delegations appeared, delegations that spoke to issues of fairness within each race, rather than between them. Mrs. H. J. Spikes complained that some families in her community had been allowed to send their children to the old school when they should have had to go to the new school for that area.

> They are our neighbors and in some cases relatives; and you have allowed them to exercise freedom-of-choice and denied our children the same privilege. . . . We feel that you have been unfair to the hundreds of parents who sought to obey what they thought was the law for all . . . by registering their children at the schools to which they had been assigned; and we went through proper channels of applying for transfer, only to have ours denied. We feel that you have applied a double standard in this matter and we desire an explanation of your action.

Assimilation was the issue here too. White parents worried that they and their children alone would have to bear the burden of socializing the black race.

Burns, Crane, and others sought to assure the delegation that all requests for transfer were handled according to court order and board policy. The delegation might want to appeal the denial of transfer directly to the board.[49]

Westbrook spoke at that meeting too, and his comments became even more expansive. He protested the "peace" moratoriums held all across the country, but especially at the University of South Alabama, where he found "peace-nicks, Communist-inspired, social-reforming professors and teachers who should be run out of town on a rail after being tarred and feathered, along with the school administrators who allowed such an un-American display." He commended the board for handling disruptive behavior at Toulminville but criticized the news media for suppressing all the facts about student disorder and disruptive activities. He particularly mentioned a fight after an interracial dance at Shaw High School, where about sixty weapons were confiscated.

Westbrook said he wanted all transfer requests honored and commended the board for exercising its right to grant transfer appeals. He wanted to know why the schools had such a shortage of textbooks and whether the board had taken action to move the eighth grade from Saraland to Adams.[50]

The question about the eighth grade became typical of more numerous and more frequent appeals to the board: narrow zone-specific complaints about violations of boundary lines and transfer policy by some people in the community. As long as the races were separate, parental complaints focused on issues of black versus white, but now that zone lines had changed, parents came to complain that others of their own race did not bear the full costs assessed to them, or they sought minor changes in the plan to protect themselves from costs. The costs were rarely spelled out, but they included both inconvenience and the perceived social and psychological burden of mixing with another race on that race's home turf.

Courts Respond to School Board's Continued Defiance

Although the court had ended freedom of choice for most of the county, the school board held fast to its position, which was codified in a resolution that passed unanimously at its November 12, 1969, meeting. The resolution made these points:

1. The law requires that every child, regardless of race, creed, or color, be afforded an equal opportunity to obtain an education.
2. The school board has provided equal opportunity for all children by making available to them the freedom to choose, without pressure or duress, the school that they wish to attend.
3. The Civil Rights Act of 1964 specifically states: "Desegregation shall not mean the assignment of students to public schools in order to overcome racial imbalance," and that "nothing herein shall empower any official or court of the United States to issue any order seeking to achieve a racial balance in any school by requiring the transportation of pupils."
4. In the United States, where freedom is the hallmark of the Republic, only children in the South are effectively denied the right to attend the school of their choice.

5. When children have been forced to attend schools against their will and contrary to the will of their parents, the results have been a deterioration in the
quality of education, a large increase in the number of dropouts, and defec-
tion to private schools.
6. It is the duty of the school board to provide students with high-quality education.

Therefore, the school board resolved, "The Board of School Commissioners
of Mobile County, Alabama makes it known to all concerned that it supports
a policy of freedom-of-choice in the operation of our public schools."[51] It
was an open invitation for citizens to defy the court order. The Mobile board
followed the lead of the Alabama Association of School Boards, which adopted a similar resolution at its meeting of October 28–29.

On December 1, 1969, the appellate court affirmed Thomas's August 1 order implementing his revision of the HEW desegregation plan. It noted that
the plan would fully desegregate all the Mobile County schools except the
schools in the eastern part of the city itself.[52] In December the Mobile school
board submitted its suggested plan for desegregating schools east of I-65.
HEW filed two additional alternative plans on January 15, 1970. The first alternative would have provided, as had the HEW plan revised by Thomas, for
full desegregation of all middle and high schools, but it left nine inner-city
black schools with only token numbers of whites. The second HEW plan
would have completely desegregated all the elementary and secondary
schools by a process of massive noncontiguous busing. In such a scheme
widely separated residential areas would be zoned for schools some distance
away. Buses would be used to transport the students. In this way targeted
percentages of the two races would be reached in every school. It would be
called busing for racial balance.

On January 14 the U.S. Supreme Court reversed the Fifth Circuit's decision to accept Thomas's August 1 plan and remanded the decision to the
appellate court; that court in turn told Thomas that February 1 was the new
deadline for desegregation. On January 23 Thomas asked the school board
and the government to submit revised plans to him by January 27. The government did, but the school board did not. The court then ordered the board
to submit a revised plan, but again it did not.

School officials called a press conference and claimed that the Supreme
Court did not require busing; all they had to do under the new ruling of the
appellate court was abandon freedom of choice and draw attendance zones
for the nine high schools east of I-65; the rest of the county's schools were
already using attendance zones to assign pupils to schools. The Justice Department and NAACP wanted the court not only to abandon freedom of

choice in the city high schools but also to redraw all elementary and junior high school zones east of I-65. Beyond that, they said, the NAACP, through its New York lawyers and local associate, Vernon Crawford, was urging the court to rezone west of I-65 too. The school board objected strenuously to this prospect.[53]

The January 1970 delegation meeting of the school board brought another protest from Rosser and Jacobs. They would not fill out the delegation form according to board policy. At first the board decided to suspend the rules to hear from them, but later, prodded by Crane, who was bothered by the board's violation of its own policy, board members reversed themselves. The board would not hear Rosser and Jacobs after all, "nor will anyone else [address the board], ladies and gentlemen, until they abide by the policy of this Board as long as we have this policy."[54]

The board did hear from two delegations that night; they followed procedure. Mrs. B. L. Peters spoke for a number of white neighborhoods whose residents felt that they were "sacrificed to the Williamson High School zone" in the plan that the board had submitted to the court in December. She pointed out that the Murphy and Williamson zones were extremely gerrymandered. This violated the concept of a neighborhood. Moreover, Williamson was located in the Maysville ghetto.

There is not a well informed citizen of Mobile who has not heard of the lawlessness of this little neighborhood. Every conceivable crime is a common occurrence there day and night. Militant hatred and harassment of whites by some of the residents of Maysville has made it a place to be dreaded and avoided. . . . Within the school, we are told, the principal and certain others find it necessary to carry a gun or keep one at hand for their personal protection. Furthermore, we are told body lice and venereal disease are prevalent. . . . Into this crime-ridden area we are expected to deposit our children to be further educated. Is there opportunity for advancement and learning under such circumstances?

Peters wanted the school closed and cleaned and police to be present in the school once it reopened. Crane remarked: "Mrs. Peters, we are not going to discuss your observations. We appreciate your coming, like we appreciate any delegation coming to us with proper form and appearing."[55]

Judge Thomas's Plan

The failure of the school board to cooperate with the court in producing a modified plan was provocative, and the *Press* and *Register* followed the exchanges day by day. Thomas's January 31 decree did not have the benefit of school board and staff expertise or data, because the school board never responded to his order to submit a revised plan. Thomas was plainly dismayed.[56]

The plan that he ordered that day, he said, would please no one: not the NAACP, not the Justice Department, not the school board, and not even himself. The Supreme Court had spoken and the district court was bound by its mandate. It was the law. It must be followed.

Thomas proceeded to describe the problems he had with each plan. The revised HEW plan, which the Justice Department wanted, would have required no busing but extensive pairing of several schools. HEW's alternative plan, upon which the NAACP (representing the parent-plaintiffs) insisted, would require extensive busing of children to unfamiliar areas as well as the pairing of many schools. The distance between some paired schools was fifteen miles. Both plans would have materially changed the grade structure of thirty-four schools. The government asked the court to close many of the all-black high schools. Thomas continued: "This I am unwilling to do as I think it would be unfair to the Negro population of this city. Many of them have graduated from one or more of these schools. They take pride in them. In many areas, including sports, there is much rivalry between these schools and I do not think the traditions which they have created over the years should be destroyed."

Thomas noted that under one HEW plan a child who lived in the Austin area would have to attend five different schools in six years. Under another a child would have gone to Dodge for first and second grade, Williams for third grade, and Owens for the fourth, fifth, and sixth grades. These schools were separated from each other by seven, nine, and eleven miles, distances onerous to parents and children.

The purpose of the suggested changes in grade structure, the pairing, and the busing was to achieve racial balance, Thomas said. He held that using these techniques was not mandatory for achieving desegregation, which was why his plan made minimal use of them. "I have said many times that the best thing that could happen would be for this litigation to come to an end. This is true. But I am unwilling to disregard all common sense and all thoughts to sound education, simply to achieve racial balance in all schools," Thomas wrote in his order. "I do not believe the law requires it. And this litigation will continue to be stirred as long as adequate funds are provided for those who want litigation, for the sake of litigation, without regard to the rights of the children and parents involved."[57]

In framing his plan Thomas said that he attempted as nearly as possible to comply with the mandate of the appellate court, yet to leave it humanly and educationally possible to run the schools. The objections he had to the

HEW plans were those that the school board had emphasized. In the end the plan he ordered used the attendance zones that the school board had presented in its December offering, with minor changes. Although the court ordered its plan "implemented forthwith," the school board made no immediate effort to do so.[58]

Within a month the NAACP and Justice Department had appealed Thomas's order. The school board did not seek to implement the court's order with any speed whatsoever.

On February 25, 1970, the board heard from delegations again. Cornelius Coleman spoke for the black parents of the Toulminville PTA. He reminded the board that it had committed to building a new high school at Toulminville in December 1968, and his group was there to get the project moving. He had a number of observations and suggestions. "In summary," he said, "the issues that concern us are vital to the preservation and propagation of Toulminville High *as a community school.*" Crane, as always courtly and kind, thanked the PTA for its fine letter and said that Judge Thomas was indeed "sympathetic to the board's desire to do exactly what you want, but a superior court to Judge Thomas has prevented it."

School board attorney Abe Philips spoke up to clarify the court action to that point. The board, he said, had made all the necessary arrangements: It had acquired additional property, had plans for the high school drawn up, and had everything else ready to go. But, he said, the board was powerless to build a school, abandon a school, or deal with its own property without permission from the federal court. The board had petitioned the court to have the school built, and Thomas had held a hearing. The board's proposal was opposed by "the United States Department of Justice and opposed by lawyers for the NAACP Legal Aid and Defense Fund who purported to represent the Negro community." As a result Thomas had entered an order saying the school could not be built. Philips concluded that the courts, not the school board, were delaying construction.

Crane said, "Mr. Coleman, I am sure that every board member wants exactly what you want because that's a fine, thickly populated community and that school is needed so bad." Then he summed up and advanced the narrative: "That's all we can tell you, Mr. Coleman. We thank you for coming and we will do our best to achieve what you want. If you will get down there to the court and let them know that the NAACP in this matter does not represent you and get a petition before the court, we hope it might have some weight. . . . Thank you very much."[59]

Other delegations spoke that night. Some wanted the school board to do one thing, some another. Mrs. Clyde Reasonover, representing the Westlawn group, protested the reassignment of neighborhood children when race was not even a factor. Earl Bridges was there for the Morningside community, petitioning for more delay, at least to the end of the year, based on the certain passage of a new Alabama state law that would protect freedom of choice. He closed his passionate statement with this plea against government oppression: "Now, our children are sacred to us. They are inviolable. Believe it. But if they can come in here and tell us, and tell you, that our child must go to this school, to this particular school. . . . The next step they are going to tell us, 'All right, you've got to go to a particular church.' Then they are going to eliminate our church. Gentlemen, we've fought too long and too hard in other wars, and our children are fighting now, some of them, to prevent this type of government. What I say is: 'Don't let this type of government start here.'"[60]

Community Control

In early March 1970 Roy Innes, the national director of the Congress of Racial Equality (CORE), unveiled CORE's plan for the creation of *segregated* school districts. There was considerable irony in this move. CORE was an interracial spin-off of the Fellowship for Reconciliation, the Quaker-led international pacifist organization, and CORE had worked for decades to blunt Jim Crow separation wherever it could. CORE had taken the lead in the Freedom Rides across the South in 1947 and 1961, when its people had been beaten as they entered "whites only" bus terminals. In 1970, though, CORE had set up STEP, Step Toward Educational Excellence, a program for local communities that advanced the idea of separate school districts for blacks and whites. Three Mobile residents were in Washington, D.C., for the announcement of STEP's formation: Loycelyn Finley, a teacher at Central High School; George Langham, a guidance counselor at Toulminville High School; and Vincent Washington, a seventeen-year-old prime minister of the United Students Action Movement, a black students' group.

Finley said that a number of teachers had been telling their students about the CORE plan, and "the response has been really enthusiastic." Langham said, "What we're trying to get away from is the idea that the only way a black kid can get a quality education is to sit beside a white kid in school." Innes said that he felt that the plan had a better chance in the South than in the North because white southerners, unlike their northern counterparts, "are willing to admit they don't want integration—in their schools or anywhere else." The plan formulated for Mobile would create two unitary school districts, one predominantly white, the other predominantly black. Each district would be funded according to the existing state and county laws, but each would have its own school board. Innes did acknowledge, though, that local NAACP leaders and other civil rights groups backing integration had strongly opposed the CORE proposal to split the seventy-three-thousand-student Mobile County school system, Alabama's largest, into two districts, one white and the other black.[61]

The notion of black community schools struck a particularly resonant chord with blacks who wanted to strengthen Toulminville and Blount. And a national organization was taking their feelings seriously. The people in these communities did not want to be assimilated into the white culture. Instead, they wanted the resources to develop on their own. The CORE initiative hardened a split within the black community, reinvigorated the white radicals, and called into question the liberals' whole program. However, the courts took no notice.

Continued Resistance

On March 4, in an act of clear defiance, the Alabama state legislature passed the Freedom-of-Choice Act, and shortly thereafter the Mobile school board passed a resolution saying that it would *not* follow the federal court's January 31 desegregation decree but would instead operate as it had before, under freedom of choice, as most recently mandated by state law.

On March 16, 1970, Thomas ordered the school board to comply with the January 31 decree within three days—"to desegregate now" or he would fine each member of the board $1,000 per day. The board moved quickly, albeit reluctantly, to comply.[62] Burns announced that students should report to their assigned school on March 20.

Significantly, the board also announced a "nonconformers" policy. Under it, if parents signed a form stating that the board had not encouraged them to defy the court order, families could send their child to the school of their choice. The child would not be denied access to regular classrooms, school activities, resources, and bus transportation. Under the policy nonconformers would *not* have the privilege of officially enrolling in the school and receiving report cards or diplomas.[63]

Thomas's plan affected six to eight thousand students; it closed two schools, altered many school zones, and enforced school attendance zones for Mobile's nine high schools east of I-65. More than one hundred teachers were transferred.

At Davidson High School about one hundred white students protested outside the school because they were now compelled to go to another school.[64] By the end of the first week, however, fewer than 250 of the thousands of students involved in the recent court-ordered changeover had failed to report to their assigned schools. Most were white students who failed to report at Williamson. The actual number of "official" nonconformers was only twenty-four, including fifteen at Davidson and six at Murphy.[65] But the white threats of disruption proved hollow. It was not clear whether whites were exhausted, resigned, accepting, or simply clever enough to take evasive action.

Summer brought more court-ordered change. On June 8, 1970, the Fifth Circuit reversed Thomas's January 31 order. Judge Griffin Bell, writing for the majority, noted that the traditionally black schools east of I-65 were still not desegregated. The court ordered that the school district implement the plan that HEW had submitted to the district court on January 27. This plan reduced from twelve to nine the number of schools with all-black or virtually all-black student bodies. The percentage of the urban area's black youngsters who would be assigned to all-black schools fell from 60 percent under Thomas's plan to 28 percent under the HEW plan. One school affected by this change was Toulminville High School, which the appeals court ordered desegregated even though the HEW plan did not call for it. The court also directed Judge Thomas to establish a majority-to-minority transfer policy and to create a biracial committee to advise the school board and court on the operation of the school system, including transfers, site selection, and zone lines.[66]

Thomas began to issue a series of orders on June 12 that complied with the higher court's directions. The plan called for only five all-white schools and two all-black elementary schools; Thomas's plan had allowed for six all-white and nine all-black schools.[67]

In late July more than fifteen hundred people attended a mass meeting at Murphy High School. Robert Dawson, who led the meeting, told parents that they had three choices: a total boycott of the schools, total defiance by taking children to the school of their choice, or mass legal action by all parents. The highlight for many was the speech by W. O. Powell, a black man and president of STEP. He said that the mass shifting of children by the court's order would do nothing but "heap hardships on families of this county, particularly the poor families, mostly black. . . . Integration has not worked and has contributed nothing but unrest." He argued in favor of Roy Innes's plan for separate school districts in Mobile.[68]

The July 22 meeting of the board was Burns's last; he retired from the school system and public life. In the delegation portion of the meeting Westbrook sang his praises: "Public education in Mobile County will have lost one of its greats; and with your courageous leadership and high standards of honesty, sincerity, and integrity you have brought public education to the forefront in the minds of all our citizens in Mobile County." Westbrook went on, of course, to blame the "vindictive Federal bureaucratic bungling in our Mobile Public Schools" as the reason for Burns's retirement.

Westbrook, the white radical, spoke in favor of the STEP plan, so long as the zone lines were drawn according to his map. Westbrook told a story of the NAACP's betrayal of black interests: "And as for the NAACP, I have very few words for them and certainly no sympathy. They have fought [against] their own people. They have fought [against] their progress in the courts and in the streets, and the colored citizens of Mobile have suffered. They would now have a new high school, second to none, in the Toulminville area if [the] NAACP had not fought against them. This racist organization, the National Association for the Advancement of Colored People, should have been called the National Association *Against* Colored People." Of course, Westbrook went on to denounce communist-inspired court decisions, the United Nations, and biracial "brotherly love" committees. Then he repeated his theme: "The people of Mobile County and the City of Mobile are best qualified to handle the problems of local education in Mobile and certainly from not a faraway place. We will not submit our children to the vultures of mongrelization, be they white or black."[69]

The *Register* had not lost its voice or its passion, nor had it lost its theme. Its editorial screamed: "This is an outrage, a stench in the nostrils of justice, a brazen offense to the American tradition of fair play. . . . The South is treated as a region apart, a region singled out for persecution with the blackjack of forced integration as all other regions pursue their segregated ways without coercion or penalty. In its outcry against 'discrimination,' the federal government makes itself a clamorous, conspicuous practitioner of discrimination against a whole region. . . . The South's case for protest is beyond tenable question or challenge. A stronger case has not existed in American history."

The deep feeling of legitimate grievance and the necessity of righteous protest was now tempered, as it always was, by the publisher's fundamental law-and-order conservatism. Nevertheless, the paper still saw outsiders as the root of the problem, but it encouraged people to bear the pain as a sign of the South's moral superiority:

> If law and order must be abused, if basic American principles must suffer and if lawlessness and disorder must occur, let these things happen outside the South and let others bear the blame and the guilt. Let none happen in the South and none stain the traditional character of the South as a region and a people moved by the highest motives in the pursuit of the goals that give the best promise for all America. . . . In the school year 1970–71, the people of the South, including the people of Alabama and Mobile, should not be surprised to find agitators in their midst, bent on provoking them and causing trouble. Whether of out-

side or local origin, these agitators may be counted on to operate under the common influence of hostility for the South. Their design at this time and in this circumstance will be, as always, to harm the South, to smear its good name and bring about more severe persecution of it, using—if possible—Southerners themselves to help gain these malicious ends. The choice for the people in Mobile, elsewhere in Alabama and over the South generally, is to conduct themselves in a steadfastly creditable manner in the face of discreditable attitudes and actions by many others toward the South. This way, and only this way, can the people of the South be sure of continuing to stand high above the low level of their traducers and persecutors.[70]

Discussion

Black citizens rose up in protest against blatant discrimination in public accommodations and schooling, but the federal government compelled the greatest changes in southern cultural practices. Separation and discrimination would no longer be tolerated, whether by popular culture or by law. In Mobile, as all across the South, school desegregation meant more than simply opening schools to children of another race. It meant the assimilation of two cultures into one. The terms of this assimilation were not known at that time, perhaps, but everyone sensed opportunities and threats.

The more aggressive spokesmen for the black movement, Jacobs and Rosser, feared continuing white oppression within desegregated schools. After all, they believed that southern whites had always conspired to remain on top. School desegregation could simply reify racial inequality in a new setting. To establish a strong position they insistently told a public narrative of grievous injury and necessary rehabilitation; they were not grateful and respectful supplicants. To them, rehabilitation meant the power to change established narratives and resources. Oppressive stories and inadequate facilities injured black children, so Mobile would have to set aside the white man's narrative: no more Rebel flags or Dixie pep bands, no more biased textbooks, and no more second-rate schoolrooms. "Black" jobs in the schools' central administration and representation on the board would ensure that problems would be remedied and no new injury permitted.

Westbrook and many others, the white radicals' heirs, still preached black inferiority, sometimes biological and sometimes cultural: Look at the violence and depravity in the black community, they asserted. More than that, the worldview of radicals was so rigid that even the countercultural symbols of sex, drugs, and rock 'n' roll were anathema because they were given impetus by black culture.

Ironically, Westbrook, the spokesman for the white radicals, related a public narrative that seemingly belonged to disaffected members of the African American community. Westbrook said that desegregation, particularly the end of freedom of choice, would destroy the black community and that the supposed liberators of black people, the NAACP and federal government, were really its oppressors. This move was a political innovation. He sought to make common cause with those in the black community who wanted neighborhood schools because they would be responsive to local communities. In this way Westbrook's lamentation on behalf of some black people served to undercut the leadership of the NAACP within the black community and before elected officials.

The *Press* and *Register* represented the old conservative position: The South would be fine, if only northern politicians and agitators would not stir things up. Always be careful: Things could fall apart. Even the local federal judge could not restrain his conservative soul. Judge Thomas, too, repeatedly counseled prudence in the face of aggressive federal mandates. He favored community-based schools and found the HEW plans both onerous and unfair.

White liberals did not voice their public narrative at the local level. Either they did not have courage or, more likely, they felt it unnecessary because the federal courts and the president had the power to move things in their direction without help. And the liberals' goal was not clear: Was it modest desegregation or assimilative integration? Would the policies favor absorption, fusion, or some new form of cultural pluralism? Because Mobile's white liberals were so unorganized and unassertive, their stories did not permeate the public or private spaces, and without controlling the narrative, they could not hope to shape the direction of the community once federal power was withdrawn.

Outside the South, during these years whites easily believed that racial discrimination in schooling was a southern problem. That was the story they heard and told. Only much later, when the courts finally compelled busing for racial balance in Louisville and Boston, would they face the full force of the black movement and its implications.

4. Busing

THREATS OF BOYCOTT and the mass exercise of de facto freedom of choice hung over the opening of schools in September 1970, but some voices urged stability and reason. The new schools superintendent, Dr. Harold R. Collins, announced that schools would operate normally and within the orders of the court. The League of Women Voters urged parents to send their children to their assigned schools and reminded everyone that the schools would lose $1.37 in state money for each day that a pupil did not attend her assigned school. The Justice Department sent John LeFlore a letter that said that the department would take whatever steps were necessary to ensure compliance with the orders of the federal district court.[1]

The school board did not surrender; its lawyers appealed to the Supreme Court, seeking to overturn the June decree from the Fifth Circuit. The U.S. District Court ordered the board to implement the HEW plan pending appeal.

George C. Wallace came to Mobile on September 7 to speak at a Labor Day celebration at Prichard Park. He was no longer governor, but he remained hugely popular. Wallace had served as Alabama's governor from 1963 to 1967, then had caused his wife Lurleen to serve in his stead. Upon her death from cancer in 1968, Albert Brewer, Lurleen's lieutenant governor, served until George Wallace could reclaim the governorship in 1971. A crowd estimated at six thousand gathered in the park that day to hear what he had to say. He urged the people to use the Alabama Pupil Placement Act: "If I were you, I'd exercise my freedom of choice." Wallace said that the exercise of freedom of choice should be carried out peacefully; the problem was political, and the solution to the problem was political. Wallace reminded the crowd that Richard Nixon had been elected because the white South had believed him when he said he would help preserve neighborhood scho[illegible]. Wallace asserted, had won Nixon the election. Wallace warned [illegible] Nixon administration responded to demands from the S[illegible] the court orders, Nixon was going to be a one-term president. [illegible] lace that day was a coterie of other politicians, including [illegible], the lieutenant governor; Pierre Pelham, a state legislator and local leader of the white Citizens Council; and John Tyson, a Democrat who was running for the House of Representatives.[2]

At this and other rallies and meetings a group called Concerned Citizens passed out detailed instructions for how parents should behave at the opening of school. One flyer showed a picture of a parent and child approaching a principal and saying, "This is the school of my choice. I will not leave until my demands are met!" Listed below the slogan were specific instructions:

> (1) Go with your child to the school of your choice; (2) demand your child be given a seat and [illegible] schedule, books, and teachers; (3) stay with your child at school if necessary, and do not be herded into a cafeteria, gymnasium or auditorium to be lectured to; (4) continue to escort your child if necessary for one full week, even if this means taking off from your job. Freedom Comes First! (5) *Do Not Sign Non-Conformist Papers!* You are legally within your rights to choose the school in which to have your child educated; (6) the school board alone is under court orders. We, the people, who are God fearing citizens and hard working tax-payers are not under the court orders. Do not be brainwashed. This is a peaceful movement. Keep it cool. (7) Discipline = respect. Respect = maturity. Maturity = citizenship.[3]

This notice made clear that a new theme had emerged: The movement of massive resistance by southern whites had been transformed from assertive superiority over a lesser race into a claim of individual liberty against an oppressive government.

Registration at the [illegible] county's eighty-three schools totaled 62,094: 26,001 black and 36,093 white students. The number of students was sharply below expectations; the district had expected seventy-one thousand students to enroll. Awaiting action were twenty-six hundred new transfer requests that had been submitted to the office of pupil personnel. School officials announced that 1,102 had registered as nonconformists. Vigor had the largest number—284—most of whom had come from the Blount High School zone, where only thirty-five whites reported for classes. At Vigor and at other schools members of Concerned Citizens staffed desks set up at the entrance to the school and provided information to "nonconformers." Williamson High School was expected to have 323 black and 786 white students, but attendance on the first day had been 50 blacks and 219 whites. Both sides had stayed away. At Murphy High School, long considered the crown jewel of the public schools, things were somewhat better: The HEW plan anticipated 1,456 black and 1,114 white students; 1,283 blacks and 844 whites showed up.[4]

On the second day of the new school term a pushing, shoving, shirt-pulling brawl erupted between groups of black and white youths at Murphy High School. Before the scuffle ended, seven or eight cars of police arrived to quickly break up the melee. A teacher at Murphy reported that it was "a brawl, and it looked bad," but Police Chief James J. Robinson said it was "just a scuffle" and the whole thing was best forgotten.[5] Enrollment the second day was 66,094 systemwide, or 4,200 students more than the first day.

On the third day five black youths were arrested as Mobile police and school authorities "got tough." Bernard Little was charged with assault after one of several dozen law enforcement officers said he saw Little roughing up a white student in an attempt to extort petty change. The principal said white students were afraid to go into the restrooms because of widespread extortion attempts by black students. Another school official said the practice of extorting dimes from intimidated students was common at predominantly black schools, "and they just figure they can get away with it here at Murphy." Other black students had been arrested the day before after failing to disperse from off-campus aggregations.

The fears of the black "savage" and the base culture out of which he emerged seemed to be confirmed by news accounts of the recent happenings, but just as quickly peace between the newly desegregated groups was established by firm authority. About sixty members of the police department's specially trained riot squad patrolled the streets surrounding Murphy High School, while state troopers and FBI agents observed from unmarked cars parked outside the main entrance. The massive show of force was the school system's main response to the disruption of the day before. Superintendent Collins said, "We are going to maintain order here at Murphy and at all other schools in the system. We'll do whatever is required to accomplish this." Chief Robinson was also perturbed: "I'm not going to tolerate any more foolishness of this type in the public schools. I am tired of it."[6] Only 331 of the 883 white students previously registered at Murphy High School showed up for classes on the third day of the new school year.[7] Police stood by at Vigor High School, but nothing happened.

Part of the problem at Murphy was the difficulty of determining who was and who was not a student. The newspaper reported that during the first two days of school, large numbers of blacks milled around in the school's hallways and on campus. The second day was much more controlled than the first. The principal, R. B. Taylor, announced over the public address system that anyone found in the halls after the bell rang would be arrested as a trespasser.[8]

A determined group of white parents set up a "private" school inside the Chickasaw-area public school. They put their children in two vacant classrooms at Hamilton Elementary School and waited outside while substitute teachers taught their children. The parents had hired retired teachers with state certification to begin teaching the next week. The principal, C. J. Wallace, said the parents were orderly and very nice, and he said he had no authority to arrest them or send them from campus. The children were fifth and sixth graders assigned to Robbins Elementary School in Prichard as part of the pairing arranged by the court order. Robbins, a traditionally black school, had fewer than ten white students enrolled at that time, but when reporters asked why the parents preferred Hamilton to Robbins, they offered nonracial reasons. Abe Philips, the school board's lawyer, said he was not sure whether the Hamilton situation was unique, but he said it was up to police to eject the students.[9]

On Monday, September 14, the schools had their first full day of classes, and at Murphy two black youths were arrested when they could not justify their presence in the main building. A room-to-room search was conducted at about the same time for two other blacks who were said to have grabbed a white student and taken 60 cents from his pockets before school opened. Principal Taylor announced over the public address system that "any student who is threatened, assaulted, accosted, intimidated or abused in any way, verbally or physically, please note the description of the person and report the incident immediately to a faculty member." Riot-trained police ringed the campus to back up his warnings. Taylor told the police, "We'll either keep it quiet or close it down."[10] School officials reported that thirty-five hundred students had requested transfers by the end of the transfer request period that Friday.

Protesting the End of Neighborhood Schools

The court-ordered fixed attendance zone plan had permitted six all-black or nearly all-black elementary schools. Enrollment reports in September showed that there were in fact nine, not six, elementary schools in that category. The all-black elementary schools had enrolled 7,651 students, or 64 percent of the total black student population in the metropolitan area of the county. None of the junior high and senior high schools in the metropolitan area of the county were to be all black under the plan, but in September, 6,747 students attended all-black or nearly all-black junior and senior highs—about 50 percent of all black students east of I-65.

White students found ways to avoid going to the "black" area schools. Some registered as nonconformers; some sought and won transfers from the central office or the school board; still others changed the address of the family to another area of the county in order to get into the attendance zone they wanted. The number of formal nonconformers was 1,185 on September 10; they had signed the papers. Their number had declined to 471 by September 21. Most were children from families who refused to send their elementary children to formerly all-black schools.

The largest number of nonconformers were not formally identified. They were largely high school students who misrepresented their addresses in order to register at high schools they wanted to attend. More than one thousand white students who were assigned to schools east of I-65 actually showed up at schools west of I-65. Davidson High, for example, had been designed for eighteen hundred students, but twenty-nine hundred had enrolled.[11]

The board had not bought buses to serve most of the students who were assigned to more distant schools. The board had 225 buses and said it would transport only those who had had transportation the year before. Black parents at Trinity Gardens thought this unfair and complained to the school board because their children had to travel much farther to their newly zoned school this year. NAACP lawyers filed a motion for the court to require the board to provide transportation. This proved to be a key issue in determining the sincerity of the board when the Fifth U.S. Circuit Court of Appeals later reviewed the Mobile case.[12]

Street theater has always been key to getting one's story across because these symbolic displays are dramatic, metaphorical, and therefore newsworthy. The message of white radicals had increasingly become a woeful lamentation more than a rebel yell; they seemed determined now to resist government oppression more than to oppose "savage" blacks. On Thursday, October 1, four thousand people rallied at Municipal Auditorium and then marched to the Federal Building, home of the U.S. District Court. The editorial board for the *Press* and *Register* gave its interpretation: "Participation in the protest march manifestly exceeded expectations. Similarly significant was the minimum of fanfare in organizing it. This was not a show-off promoted in the Madison Avenue tradition. . . . Their petition for redress of these grievances cannot go unanswered without perpetuating a glaring injustice against a region nowhere excelled in its devotion to the principles upon which the nation was founded and endures."[13]

Another demonstration, the Fathers' March, occurred later in the month. In pallbearer fashion protesters bore caskets labeled "freedom of choice" and "neighborhood schools." A fourteen-year-old boy played *Taps* as the caskets were placed on the steps of the Federal Building.

Judge Thomas later met with parents from Chickasaw in his chambers; it was not the first time that Judge Thomas had met parents—he had also done so in August. Mainly, he listened.[14] Meanwhile, the number of official non-conformers had decreased: Chickasaw now had ninety, down from 143, and Vigor had only thirty, down from three hundred.[15]

Barton Academy, as the administrative and school board headquarters was known, announced that it had approved 1,284 applications for transfer and denied 2,020 others—279 of those denied had been appealed to the board and each had been granted.[16] Public records do not specify the race of these students, but the board seemed sympathetic to anyone who had reason to thwart the court's desegregation plan.

The U.S. Supreme Court Takes the Mobile Case

The U.S. Supreme Court agreed to hear Mobile's *Birdie Mae Davis* case as a companion case to *Swann v. Charlotte-Mecklenburg* and heard oral arguments in mid-October 1970. Speaking for the U.S. government, Solicitor General Erwin Griswold said that the desegregation plan that was in force would work, that the school board had practiced dilatory tactics, and that a return to neighborhood schools would return the district to segregation. Abe Philips represented the school board, which had appealed the case, and argued that Mobile had indeed had a dual school system in 1963 but that it had been disestablished. The present plan was onerous, he claimed. Because of it, four thousand students simply had not enrolled in school; none of the one thousand white students assigned to Blount had enrolled there. The school system had had six different plans thrust on it since January, and this had created an almost "comic game of fruit-basket turnover" for teachers and students. He wanted the Court to send the present plan back to the district court so that Thomas could eliminate some of the worst cases of school zone gerrymandering.

Samuel L. Stockman, a Mobile lawyer, spoke for the Countywide Parent-Teacher Association, which had intervened when the case went to the Supreme Court. He said the PTA wanted neighborhood schools. Under the present plan a family could have three children in three different, widely scattered schools. The bus rides were too long, in many cases twelve to fifteen miles.

Both lawyers claimed that under the present plan, "the race of the child has been the sole basis for assignment." Jack Greenberg represented the NAACP Legal Defense Fund before the Court. He said his organization did not necessarily accept the plan then used in Mobile, but it did reflect the type of plan that Mobile needed. He complained about the confusion in Mobile, especially the difficulty the NAACP had had in getting a hearing before

Thomas, and the large number of nonconformers. In order to eliminate racially identifiable schools, the Court could compel school districts to use the same methods to integrate that they used in the past to segregate: portable classrooms, gerrymandered zones, and busing.[17] The Supreme Court withdrew to its chambers; its decision would come in the spring.

In January 1971 Judge Thomas announced plans to retire. Wendy Grosskoff took notice and alone wrote a letter to the editor of the paper to give witness to her long-time friend: "His highly developed sense of right and wrong served this community very well indeed at a time when such a man was most needed."[18] This was faint praise for the long-embattled judge.

When twelfth-grade students at Blount High School were assigned their fifth teacher of the year, right in the middle of exams, parents complained to the school board. They brought other issues too. They charged that the district had sent *elementary* school teachers to Blount as well as teachers who were qualified in one subject but were being asked to teach others. A parent, Mrs. Mary L. Heningburg, told the board that Blount needed five qualified teachers, adding, "These students and parents will not take any more of this." J. R. Martin, the assistant superintendent for personnel, replied that Mobile was coping with a severe teacher shortage and that there were some schools where "teachers just won't go." He said Blount had lost nine teachers at once. School board member Norman Berger added, "We've lost a lot of teachers to private schools." School board members did not have to explain that a large part of the problem was that the court order required that 60 percent of each school's faculty be white. It was difficult to get white faculty to go to or stay at Blount.[19]

Others spoke at that January delegation meeting too; in all, twelve delegations made statements and appeals. The Reverend J. McIntyre asked for science and other equipment for Toulminville High School, and he requested protective devices to stop the extensive vandalism at the school. Mrs. Lynn Hobbs asked that the board allow "sit-in" pupils (nonconformers) to receive grades and credit at the Griggs school, which now had only thirty such students. It was one of the largest delegation meetings in months, and the new boardroom at Barton Academy could not hold them all.[20]

In February HEW turned down Mobile's request for $1.14 million in emergency school assistance funds. HEW cited three reasons for not granting the money—faculty ratios in seven schools were not 60-40 white to black; attendance zones were not drawn to maximize desegregation; and Davidson had transfer students that the department regarded as illegitimate. Representatives of the American Friends Service Committee had asked HEW to refuse the grant request. Thirty-two other southern school districts were also reported to have been denied aid.[21] The *Mobile Press* and *Register* editorialized once again about the hypocrisy of the federal government. It accused Washington of deception: It forced desegregation, said it would provide money to help the process along, then denied the money to those that needed it most.[22]

Calls for mass boycotts of the Mobile schools continued throughout the winter. The interracial Greater Mobile Ministerial Association urged black and white citizens to work together peaceably. The group issued a statement that said in part: "We believe that most of the citizens of our communities are lovers of peace and progress, are deeply concerned with educational advancement, are dedicated to the principles of law and order with justice and are, therefore, opposed to riot and ruin—fire and frustration. . . . We must energetically exert every effort to prevent combustible and inflammatory incidents in our schools. If we do not, then God save America."[23]

The *Press* and *Register* reported that the growth of private school enrollments was a consequence of the problems in the public schools. Their stories brought an immediate reply from the Roman Catholic Diocese of Mobile. The monsignor, the Reverend Oscar Lipscomb, wrote that "immediately following the local court desegregation orders last year, registration at all Catholic schools was closely restricted to those who had valid reasons for enrollment (change of address, promotion, etc) and effectively closed to those who sought transfer for racial reasons." He said there were 7,170 students in Catholic primary and secondary schools, only fifty-five more than the previous year. They did have ninety-two more teachers, though, which the monsignor said simply reflected the effort the diocese had made to enhance its program.[24]

The *Swann* Decision

The axe fell on April 20, 1971. The *Press*'s headline told the tale: "MOBILE SCHOOL PLAN OVERTURNED—BUSING APPROVED BY SUPREME COURT."[25] The Supreme Court had ruled unanimously in the cases from Charlotte, North Carolina; Clarke County, Georgia; and Mobile. The Charlotte case was primary. In *Swann v. Charlotte-Mecklenburg County,* the Court said federal courts could order busing as a means of achieving racial integration. It rebuffed the preference of the Nixon administration and the South for neighborhood schools. The Court said that there was no absolute requirement that the racial makeup of each school be the same as the district as a whole and that some one-race schools could be permitted; nonetheless, the courts would pay close attention to ensure that the schools achieved "the greatest possible degree of actual desegregation."

Chief Justice Warren Burger read the opinions quietly before the tourist-filled courtroom as a cluster of law clerks listened just outside. What he said was sweeping: "Having once found a violation, the district judge or school authorities should make every effort to achieve the greatest possible degree of desegregation, taking into account the practicalities of the situation. A district court may and should consider the use of all available techniques including restructuring of attendance zones and both contiguous and noncontiguous attendance zones. The measure of any desegregation plan is its effectiveness."[26]

In its opinion on Mobile's *Birdie Mae Davis* case, the High Court cited the crucial facts showing the ineffectiveness of the desegregation efforts there. First, it concurred with the Fifth Circuit in its conclusion that the school board had "almost totally failed to comply" with earlier orders directing faculty and staff desegregation. With regard to pupil assignment the Court disapproved of the Justice Department's plan, which the Fifth Circuit had accepted and which treated the eastern and western sections of the county as distinct areas. The desegregation plan had used a major north-south highway (I-65) to divide the Mobile County school system. West of the highway, schools were 12 percent black, and they had been easily desegregated. East of the highway schools were 65 percent black. The desegregation plan that Thomas had originally approved for the area east of I-65 had left twelve all-black schools serving 90 percent of the black elementary students in the metropolitan area. The appellate court had rejected this, adopting instead a modified HEW plan that left only six all-black schools serving 50 percent of the black children in the metropolitan area. This plan, which took effect at the beginning of the 1970–71 school year, had not achieved the intended result. By September 21, 1970, the eastern section of the county had nine, not six, identifiably black elementary schools serving 64 percent of the area's black children.

Given this record, the Supreme Court said, the plan had given "inadequate consideration . . . to the possible use of bus transportation and split zoning." The Court remanded the case to the district court "for the development of a decree that promises realistically to work and promises realistically to work now."[27]

The reaction in Mobile was mixed. U.S. Rep. Jack Edwards said he was unhappy because the decision had upheld busing and would mean another year of disruption. A. J. Cooper, a local attorney for the NAACP Legal Defense and Education Fund, called the decision a victory for the parent-plaintiffs and the community. John LeFlore was pleased; for him, busing was a normal educational practice, not a terrible burden: "We have consistently felt that the busing issue is being overplayed because busing has been a mode of transportation throughout the years. One of the primary causes of our filing the school desegregation petition in 1962 was that black high school children living at Hillsdale Heights were being transported 52 miles to St. Elmo when Shaw and Davidson were within three and four miles."[28]

The school board and its attorneys had no immediate response. Others did, and their theme was the moral implications for "the South." One citizen, Geraldine Koffler, wrote to the paper that "the Supreme Court, in its decision on school desegregation, has given us who live in the South a rare opportunity. We are now in a position to change our image in the nation and the world from a section of racial bigots to a people with a deep love of humanity." But the Reverend Reese Farnell Jr. had another, older idea. He wrote, "The Supreme Court's ruling on Tuesday is once again a direct hit against the South. When it comes to the full justice and human benefits which should come to all people of this nation, the same kind of handing down of high court decisions should apply to all the land."[29]

At the delegation meeting of the school board on April 28, 1971, white people argued about the terms of assimilation. Westbrook attacked racial sensitivity training, now required of teachers by the Supreme Court decision, and threatened a taxpayers' revolt. Edna V. Wade, representing the Unified Concerned Citizens of Alabama, spoke about the public health problems in some of the schools, suggested preventive measures, and cautioned the board about the health implications of busing and pairing. Mrs. Clyde Reich represented the Murphy High School PTA. She said PTAs could not function as they had in the past because of the disruptive elements in society, communistic in nature and scope, which invaded the schools both locally and nationally. She called for people to unite to drive them out of the city. She also attributed the breakdown of the PTA to the destruction of the neighborhood school by the federal government.[30]

LeFlore did not often appear at these board meetings, but he was there that night to plead for harmony and justice. He directed his plea to black separatists as well as whites:

> Today the Nation finds itself at the crossroads in its society. It is imperative that men of different races learn to live together as brothers, lest all of us perish. To the minds on one side that have attempted to brand me as a troublemaker, permit me to say that I owe no man an apology for my belief in respect for the dignity of the individual and shall continue to work for principles acceptable to that concept. To those on the other side who have attempted to label me as an Uncle Tom because of my belief in moderation, permit me to say that I cannot be a racist, for we have already suffered long from that evil. It has brought only disgrace and turmoil in our country wherever its ugly head has been reared. Those who would keep us divided into first and second class strata of citizenship, one

white, the other black, whether they be [white] segregationists or [black] separatists, are rendering our country a serious disservice as they seek to perpetuate
the unworkable social experiment of the past 352 years. That system of racial
proscription has spawned a quagmire of prejudice, hatred and confusion. It
cannot be expected to provide the answers to the problems in race relations that
an accommodating political power structure has helped to create.

LeFlore closed with a pointed observation: The significant deterioration in
race relations over the past ten years had been occasioned by the resistance
to school desegregation.[31]

Separatists were still at work in the black community, despite the integrationist thrust of the *Swann* and *Birdie Mae Davis* decisions by the High Court
in April. The traditionally black high schools were the focus of attention,
especially Toulminville. The black community was sharply divided about
whether it wanted a new Toulminville high school that was sure to remain
all-black or nearly all-black or whether it should favor integration with whites
at another new or rebuilt suburban high school. The issue became so divi-
sive that the local chapter of the NAACP addressed it directly that summer.
Dr. Robert W. Gilliard made the following statement:

> A small combination of black and white opportunists is seeking to undermine
> the confidence and distort the minds of our young people and their parents by
> attempting to make them believe that they must have an all-black school to have
> identity and pride. . . . We reject the idea that there is any pride or dignifying
> identity for either black or white young people in a segregated school system or
> a segregated school. At the present time, this false doctrine of pride and identi-
> ty is being preached to the Toulminville School community. We condemn those
> who seek to promote their selfish interests by sacrificing the minds of our black
> and white youths. It is the same bigotry proposed by Governor Wallace in 1967
> in his Freedom of Choice teacher plan. It is the same bigotry proposed by the
> Innes or STEP Plan. The acceptance of this sham will give our black youths the
> feeling that they are inferior and cannot compete in an integrated society.[32]

The NAACP clearly favored assimilation—social integration—not just
token desegregation. The organization wanted busing for racial balance, so
that each school would be a microcosm of the whole community and so that
two racial cultures would become one. The terms of assimilation, however,
had not been settled.

In mid-May 1971 the school board had announced that the nine-year fight
about desegregation had cost Mobile taxpayers almost $250,000.[33]

The school board had changed considerably during the school year. The
archconservative Sidney Phillips had withdrawn rather than seek reelection

in November 1970. Other members of the board lost their races. Charles McNeil, one of the moderates on the old board, became the most influential member of the new board, and as president he had practically handpicked Harold Collins to be the new superintendent.

A New Story: Let Our Children Learn

After the Supreme Court decision Collins and McNeil went to the Fifth Circuit to consult with Judge Griffin Bell, who was the most active jurist on the court in the area of school desegregation. Bell indicated that the appeals court would not remand the case, because he was convinced that this would delay the process still further. Bell urged Collins and McNeil to go to the NAACP and negotiate a plan for the 1971–72 school year.[34] That is what happened.

Collins attempted to develop a new plan with citizen participation. He called in representatives of thirty interested groups and organizations to show them "dot-spot" maps of black and white children scattered across the county at elementary schools, junior highs, and high schools. He tried different zone lines to show the effects on school enrollments. The school board's plans were initially not acceptable to the parent-plaintiffs, but negotiations continued. Lawyers from the NAACP's office in New York came to take a look. They used HEW's "total desegregation" plan as a basis of comparison and agreed that the school board lacked the resources to put that plan into effect by fall. They made some specific changes in the board's proposed plan, including which schools might be closed. Black community groups were also brought into agreement. After round-the-clock negotiations both sides agreed on the new plan. It was less integrated than the NAACP had sought but more than the school board had wanted. Significantly, the NAACP agreed not to challenge the plan in court for three years; the school board would have that time to achieve desegregation.[35]

On July 8, 1971, Judge Thomas received a historic letter:

> Dear Judge Thomas:
> Please find the attached plan for the operation of the Mobile County School System which has been agreed upon by the defendants and the plaintiffs. The defendants believe the plan comports with the constitutional obligation to create a unitary school system and plaintiffs believe, if successfully implemented, it will meet the defendants' constitutional obligations. Our signatures below indicate that we agree to this plan as to form and content.

The letter was signed by A. J. Cooper for the parent-plaintiffs and Dr. Harold Collins, superintendent of the school system, for the defendants.

The next day Thomas issued a historic order: "The Board of School Commissioners on July 8, 1971, filed in this Court 'a Comprehensive Plan for a Unitary School System' which said Plan has been agreed to in form and content by the plaintiffs. This plan has been considered and approved by the Court and is hereby adopted by the Court and ordered into effect immediately." The order said that the court would retain jurisdiction to determine whether the plan resulted in a unitary system. The plaintiffs had agreed not to challenge the plan for three years to give the school board time to achieve unitary status and the pupil enrollments projected by the plan.

Cooper said that the plan "reflects many needs and desires of plaintiffs and the black community." Both sides had made concessions, he said, and "because of the willingness to compromise, the community has been spared another unpleasant trial, another appeal and the attendant confusion and uncertainty." He called for all segments of the community to support the plan. Charles McNeil, president of the school board, said that the plan "represents concessions never received before in this school system through the federal courts and most likely never agreed upon before in this school system on an informal basis with the plaintiff."[36]

Significantly, the plan called for busing blacks across I-65 from east to west and whites from west to east into the city. This was the major concession by the board. For example, approximately eight hundred to one thousand white students would be bused to noncontiguous inner-city elementary schools, generally across I-65. The number of white students riding buses would increase over two years to bring about a fair distribution of the two races. Overall, nineteen elementary schools would have noncontiguous zones.[37] Five elementary schools were to remain all black.[38] Two formerly all-black schools would close.[39] Five middle schools were to have noncontiguous zones, as would four high schools. Toulminville High School, which many thought would be closed, was to remain open. However, the plan pointed to the need for a new high school in the Shaw-Toulminville area—Toulminville itself was to remain open only until the court approved another school and the school board selected a site. White enrollment at Blount and Toulminville high schools (9 and 2 percent, respectively) was to be increased and stabilized. The plan called for the appointment of a black assistant superintendent and further desegregation of the central office staff at Barton Academy. Finally, the school board would notify the NAACP of any new construction before it awarded any contracts.[40]

The plan also contained detailed guidelines for various aspects of school life, including special orientation programs for students and teachers, the responsibilities of principals to implement the plan, the establishment of interracial human relations committees, and so on.

The structure of assimilation was in place but not its full dynamic. Whose values would prevail? The plan had a few real problem areas, as well, which were known to McNeil and others close to the negotiations: Although A. J. Cooper, the local attorney for the NAACP, had agreed to the plan, it was not clear that he spoke for the parent-plaintiffs as a class, and deep suspicions soon arose about his position among black citizens of both separatist and integrationist leanings because Cooper had been so heavily wooed by the school board's negotiators and allegedly had compromised so much. Also, some projected racial ratios in the schools would probably not hold up, making the schools once again racially identifiable, and the intensely felt issue of what to do with Toulminville High School had not been settled.

The League of Women Voters of Mobile commended the board, staff, and Cooper for their cooperative effort and challenged the community to follow their example to make it work.[41] The Roman Catholic bishop said, "May the Catholics in Mobile do their full part with all men of goodwill to build a community of peace here in our beloved city."[42] Gilliard, who spoke for the local NAACP at a question-and-answer session at Mount Zion Baptist Church, lauded the school plan: "In its endeavors to convey its dedication to a unitary school system, the school board has worked untiringly to gain input from all segments of the community, and to include in its planning that which is relevant and applicable to development of a total and racially *unidentifiable* education system."[43] Kathryn Reid wrote to the editor of the *Press* to acknowledge the paper's recent editorial in support of compliance: "Your editorial proves to me that even the most recalcitrant position can be changed when necessary, and gracefully."[44]

The participants at the next delegation meeting of the school board were not new; their positions were known. Westbrook castigated the board; he snidely complained that the plan nowhere mentioned the word *busing* but that was plainly what it was. He complained about the cost of the busing ($500,000 for new buses); about the discipline problems sure to plague the schools in the fall; about the violation of people's rights. He told board members that they had betrayed the people who had elected them and called for their resignations. He got applause from the crowd.[45]

Millie Hobbs came next, representing the Concerned Citizens of Tillman's Corner. She complained about the "reckless" purchase of new buses "for the sole purpose of attaining a social goal desired only for the benefit of a minority people." She said it would cost an extra $5 million to implement the desegregation plan and that that was a waste of money. She talked about white resentment of government policies that used whites to socialize the poor and the black: "So much effort has gone into making things easier for both the disadvantaged children and their parents: Headstart Programs, Free Lunch Programs, Free Breakfast Programs, day care centers, and many others. What about the children and parents of other groups? Do they have no consideration left for them at all? Doesn't anyone care for them anymore? Has it become a Misfortune to be Fortunate? Are they to be forgotten? Will they be bused, cussed, beaten, shook-down, and utterly deprived of a quality education just because some in our society have had the misfortune to be 'disadvantaged'?"[46]

Mrs. Edna Wade spoke for the Unified Concerned Citizens of Alabama. She complained that the white citizen groups that had participated in desegregation planning had not been invited to talk with the black community groups that also were called in. She said not a single recommendation of the white group had been included in the plan. She accused the board of betraying the people. Mrs. Murrell R. Wheeler spoke for the Women for Constitutional Government. She wanted every parent and child to receive a copy of the schools' discipline code, which she insisted be the same in all schools, and that police officers be assigned to each school to enforce it.[47] The parade of white people had a common theme: The interests of hard-working whites had not been taken into account; white people were being forced to associate with uncivilized blacks and to pay for it through the suffering of vulnerable white children.

The *Press* and *Register* conducted an informal survey of teachers about their effectiveness the previous year. The consensus was that desegregation itself was the top problem. Reporters gathered these comments from teachers at Murphy High School: "No child or teacher did their best work. It was a very bad year, and children were hampered in getting an education"; "I was afraid for the children, not so much for myself"; "I wouldn't say education was above average"; "We had some good days and some bad days. I feared campus disruptions more than those in the classroom."

From Dunbar: "You can't police and teach at the same time. . . . I babysat for 9 months."From Phillips Middle School: "It was almost a wasted year. I spent a large part of my time trying to keep order in the classroom. It might partially be my fault. Until three years ago I had taught only whites except for a sprinkling of Negroes. And perhaps it could be a generation gap." From Davidson High School: "The teachers did an excellent job in trying to teach in the overcrowded situation, but it just isn't possible to teach under those circumstances." (Davidson was built for nineteen hundred students, but three thousand had enrolled in 1970–71.)[48]

Discipline, distraction, overcrowding—the teachers seemed to be saying that educational processes were disrupted by efforts to desegregate the schools. The newspaper presented no countervailing story.

* * *

In August 1971 the *Press* published the results of recent achievement test scores under the headline "PUBLIC SCHOOL STUDENTS GRADES LOWEST IN SIX YEARS."[49] That year saw a sharp decline in the average scores on the California Achievement and Mental Maturity Test. The test was designed to produce a grade-level score: Mobile's eighth graders should have had a score of 8 to be at the national average. In the past year they had fallen from 7.1 to 6.9, or more than a year behind the national norm. In the eleventh grade the difference was more marked—a decline from 9.7 to 9.1 in one year—and almost two years below the national standard (see table 1).

In June 1970 Floyd Replogle, the Mobile school psychologist, presented a report to the board that showed a gradual but consistent decline in test scores based on his six-year study. Replogle said the decline was most noticeable in the elementary grades and that many other systems had seen similar results. The testing of eighth- and eleventh-grade pupils was state mandated, but Mobile had also tested grades four and six until 1969. The school board had made comparisons of white and black schools. The results showed that white schools were at or above the national norm in grade four, while black schools were four months behind the national average. At grade six the results were more disparate. Using the same testing program, white sixth-grade students fell five months behind, while black sixth-grade students fell eighteen months behind the national norm.[50]

Disruption, whatever its origin, seemed to be hurting the students. This rising sentiment suggested a new and important story among many people of both races.

Schools opened in September 1971 with no significant disruption. Thirty people picketed the area where the school buses were parked, and one black student was suspended indefinitely at Vigor, but that was all. Two national television networks sent camera crews into Mobile to cover the action, but they were disappointed.[51] McNeil, the school board president, attributed the orderly opening to Mobile residents' familiarity with the plan before it was implemented.[52] But both black and white leaders went out of their way to

Table 1. Grade-Level Scores for Mobile Public School Students on the California Achievement and Mental Maturity Test

	1965–66	1966–67	1967–68	1968–69	1969–70	1970–71
8th grade	7.2	7.2	7.1	7.0	7.1	6.9
11th grade	9.9	9.9	9.9	9.8	9.7	9.1

Source: Mobile Press and *Register,* Aug. 19, 1971.

enjoin disruption. John L. LeFlore, for instance, issued a statement which said in part, "No misguided youths or adults, irrespective of race, have a prerogative to abridge by vulgar or unlawful means the rights of others to enjoy a peaceful atmosphere in their quest for learning."[53]

A New Story

From riots to reason, from antagonism to amelioration, from tumult to relative tranquility: How had Mobile done it? Answer: A new story emerged from the historical mess, and it was told by the NAACP's LeFlore, by superintendent Collins, and others. This story said that pragmatic cooperation could make good things happen. The subtext was that the school board had finally surrendered to the authority of the Supreme Court.

Liberals locally were energized by the possibility of meaningful change. During 1970–71 the Human Relations Center at Spring Hill College held intensive race relations workshops for a variety of community people, including school and law enforcement personnel.[54] Geraldine Koffler, president of the League of Women Voters, had been especially active in support of full, peaceful desegregation. During the spring and summer she and the league had worked hard to establish a "Make It Work" campaign in cooperation with other community groups like the American Friends Service Committee. This campaign included writing to civic and business organizations to urge peaceful compliance and support, holding workshops and meetings, and passing out lapel buttons.[55] The Mobile Committee for the Support of Public Education was formed and mounted an intensive public relations campaign aimed at reducing the level of school conflict. A public relations firm was hired and produced a sixty-second television spot; the spot showed scenes of desegregated groups in classrooms, halls, labs, and school grounds. These scenes were overlaid with guitar music and a message: "School years should be good years, a time to learn, a time to enjoy; not a time of conflict. Mobile County has good schools with highly qualified teachers. They are handicapped by racial strife. They need help from all of us . . . students and parents, and citizens who know how conflict cripples a community. We can help by encouraging racial harmony in our schools. Only a few people of both races are causing the turmoil. It's time we said to them: 'Please stop. Let our children learn.'"

The message aired on both local television stations for nearly two months during the early and late evening news shows. It was featured on programs popular with teenagers. Similar spots were broadcast on radio stations, and more than one hundred billboards carried the message. Handbills were circulated. No disturbances occurred during the period of intense campaigning.[56]

Others gave credit to Collins, the superintendent, for the change and the peace. First, he reshuffled (transferred or fired) key staff members. Then he initiated outreach and openness. Collins enthusiastically enlisted black and white citizens and parents in the planning process between April and July. Most significantly, he included the NAACP, the very people he had been fighting in court. The Mobile Exchange Club stated that it supported the school officials who "have shown initiative and determination in working to bring together all segments of our society in unified effort to solve the problems facing our schools and to provide a quality education to all children of this county."[57] The Chamber of Commerce had issued a similar statement back in July.[58]

Last Days of the Old Story

The *Mobile Press* reported in August 1971, just before busing began in earnest, that a new church, "the Assembly of Christian Soldiers Church," had been incorporated.[59] Among its founders were well-known Klan members, and the church was part of a statewide effort by Asa Carter and Jesse Mayberry, both acknowledged leaders of the Original Knights of the Ku Klux Klan of the Confederacy, to found a system of private schools. The scheme included founding churches and having the churches create private schools and "commissaries" that would sell supplies to members; the "profit" would be used to pay the private school's tuition for those unable to pay. In Mobile the Christian Soldiers managed to get a good start toward their goal when a local medical doctor loaned them $35,000 to stock their commissary. Within a few months, though, the operation fell apart when they could not get financing from the banks, and the original membership of several hundred began to fall off. Their school limped along for many months, then disappeared. Other private schools were founded and did somewhat better.[60] Most of these "segregation academies" were small and met in Sunday school classrooms of mostly fundamentalist churches.[61] Race and religion became still more closely fused.

White protesters also tried once more to undermine the desegregation of Mobile's schools by more direct means. In early October the Unified Concerned Citizens (UCC) of Alabama called for a one-day boycott of the schools to protest crosstown busing. This was to be the opening action in a campaign of disruption. Absenteeism increased by 28 percent at the seven metropolitan high schools; overall, the schools' central office estimated, attendance was 9 percent less than usual.[62] Wade, president of UCC of Alabama, also planned a mothers' march to Washington, D.C., to take petitions to U.S. senators calling for a constitutional amendment to ban busing.[63] Nothing practical came from the effort.

Gov. George Wallace got the legislature to pass a law that directed school boards to transfer a student to a school of his choice whenever his parents determined that time or distance of travel to a school was a risk to the health or safety of their child or significantly impinged on the educational process. In a state court lawsuit based on this act, the Mobile school board was ordered to permit the transfer of twelve students who had made a request under the new state law. The school board agreed to comply with the order. Abe Philips, the board's lawyer, said the board had done so while waiting for the courts to decide the issue. The federal courts took little time in striking down the state law.[64]

On May 28, 1972, at the end of the first full year of busing for racial balance, black students made up 42 percent of the county's school population. Twenty-two of the county's eighty-one schools were more than 90 percent segregated. The 1971 desegregation plan negotiated with Cooper and approved by the district court was actually less effective in desegregating the black inner-city schools than were the plans rejected by the Fifth Circuit and the Supreme Court. Even if all the projections had been met, the negotiated plan contained two high schools, three middle schools, and six elementary schools with student populations that were more than 90 percent black.[65]

There was an attempt to change the composition of the school board in 1972. Geraldine Koffler, who had led the League of Women Voters' "Make It Work" campaign, sought the Democratic nomination for the school board seat held by Homer Sessions, a conservative Democrat. Westbrook sought the same seat in a highly contested primary. Koffler got more votes but not enough to avoid a runoff. Westbrook was eliminated in the first round and threw his support to Sessions. Albert S. Foley, a Catholic priest and professor at Spring Hill College, asserts that Westbrook launched a smear campaign that included the accusation that Koffler had attended a human relations program at Spring Hill (Sessions had also attended), that she had signed an agreement with the NAACP to achieve total desegregation through busing, that she had been active in NOW and the Non-Partisan Voters League, that she had entertained blacks in her home and had been photographed in the company of black males, and that she had gotten 92 percent of the black vote in the first primary. Sessions handily won reelection.[66]

That fall Nixon carried Mobile County by a huge margin over George McGovern, arguably the most liberal candidate the Democrats had ever put forward. Republicans had first won Mobile's House seat in 1964, and they won it again, by a wide margin. The radicals were making good on their threat: The Democrats were being paid back emphatically at the polls.

Discussion

Public narratives are ultimately judged by attentive citizens. If stories are to have popular appeal, they must be cohesive and seem truthful. White radicals told a story of racial antipathy, that blacks were biologically and culturally inferior; blacks were either "beasts" or "savages" who would tear down white people and their achievements at the first opportunity. Whites should resist government-imposed school desegregation because white children were threatened. They could win the struggle if only the school board would maintain its defiance of federal courts.

The white radicals' story failed to win the allegiance of most whites. Most white parents did not see the threat of black children as immediate or horrible. Integration was worrisome but not catastrophic. Radicals described the world in black and white, both literally and figuratively, and many whites did not think that way. Whites were not all the same, and neither were blacks. The predicate of the white radicals' claim was also suspect. This time the school board could not defy the Supreme Court. The radicals' threat also proved hollow in the end: Whites did not massively, persistently, and violently protest full desegregation. Instead, a new story began to emerge from the white radical camp when the white "rising" did not come. It was a lamentation. The new story portrayed the once threatening and defiant whites as persecuted victims of unremitting federal power.

Other stories were also told, but these were still being tested. Some blacks and whites supported extensive integration; they told stories of pragmatic cooperation or morally compelling harmony in the service of a new southern culture. Other blacks and whites favored the racial separatism inherent in formally desegregated but nonetheless plainly community schools. Implicit in the contest of these stories were separate worldviews and different policies of cultural assimilation; the stories evoked metaphors of fusion, absorption, or cultural pluralism. But no clear winner emerged in Mobile, where subcultural separation and hierarchy had been culturally supported for many, many decades.

PART 2

Accommodation

5. Power Transitions

DEBATES ABOUT DESEGREGATION fell off sharply after implementation of the 1971 plan, as students, parents, teachers, and staff were caught up in the process of adjustment. The school board rarely spoke about desegregation, and on all topics many fewer delegations requested time to address the board than in previous years. In May 1972 the board loosened its delegation policy so that representatives of groups no longer had to prepare written texts of their statements; later, delegations were no longer required to request speaking rights a week ahead of time.

This pattern of civic quiescence persisted. In 1973 and 1974 the board heard from no racially charged delegations, nor did the board itself have any public comments about school desegregation. The radical whites who had predicted disaster and resistance no longer told their stories in public places. Whatever concerns the board had about the *Birdie Mae Davis* case, not surprisingly, it kept them to itself. Throughout this time the board consisted of McNeil, Sessions, Williams, Berger, and Crane, all veterans and representatives of the old business leadership.

Some prominent participants took time to reflect. For eleven years Judge Griffin Bell of the Fifth U.S. Circuit Court of Appeals had rendered decisions on school desegregation in cases from Florida to Mississippi. In July 1972 he gave a rare interview to the Associated Press, and he said he favored neighborhood schools: "I've had the personal view that public education would be preserved and enhanced without anyone's rights being damaged if we would just agree to send every child to the school nearest his home."

To many whites Bell's assertions offered reassurance and reasonable limits; others read him with disbelief. In the interview Bell expressed concern about the exercise of power by the courts, especially in the wake of the *Swann* decision. "The American people are accustomed to obeying the laws," he said. "Damage is being done to public education because there is no certain standard that the public can understand as the end requirement. The lack of a permanent rule is one of the main reasons for the flight from the public schools. Parents do not know just what the future holds." Bell wondered about liberty when children were assigned to schools solely by race: "It's doubtful that adults would allow this sort of infringement on liberty." He spoke about the right to know the law by telling a story: "There was a Roman emperor named Caligula who took spite on his people by posting his laws in high places in small print. We must be careful not to give the same treatment to the school law." He blamed Congress for not passing legislation on pupil assignment, but he drew back from criticizing the Supreme Court for having gone too far in *Swann*. As a parting shot, he said, "The real issue is and ought to be a quality education for every child, regardless of race."[1]

The real issue ought to be "quality of education for every child"—the esteemed federal judge who had forced school desegregation on so much of the South was offering a new and strangely ironic twist. Quality of education, not integration, should be the focus of public efforts.

In Mobile itself ordinary people coped with busing in different ways. In one case reported in the press Edna Wade, president of Unified Concerned Citizens of Alabama, a group opposed to busing, had sued in federal court in 1971 to prevent her twin boys from being bused to St. Elmo Middle School for the seventh and eighth grades. She had put the twins in Theodore Middle School as nonconformers, which meant that they were schooled but not registered and received no grades. After two years they finally registered at Theodore High School, because that was their official assignment for the ninth through twelfth grades.

The two were placed in academic classes appropriate to their grade without any penalty whatsoever. When asked about this in April 1973, Bobby R. Clardy, assistant superintendent for pupil personnel, said, "We have done no more for them than we would do for a kid who has quit school and wants to come back. Although he quit in the seventh grade, when he comes back, we would place him where we thought he could succeed on the basis of test scores, age, and maturity."[2]

The upshot: The system encouraged nonconformers, but no one kept records to find out how many there were. Nevertheless, white flight from the school system was estimated to have reduced the student population by 20 percent between 1970 and 1975. The principal beneficiaries were forty-six private schools with about ten thousand pupils; these schools were mainly one-race church-based institutions. About six thousand students attended Roman Catholic parochial schools, which had been desegregated in the 1960s. Despite a stern admonition by the local bishop against allowing the Catholic schools to be havens for white flight, they enrolled a large percentage of non-Catholic students, and some were all or nearly all-white institutions.[3]

The three-year moratorium on the NAACP's challenges to the 1971 school desegregation plan ended in 1974, and the NAACP brought in a special consultant, Dr. William Feild, from the South Florida Desegregation Center at the University of Miami. He examined the semiannual enrollment reports submitted to the court in order to address two questions: Had the plan been substantially implemented? And had the plan achieved maximum desegregation and a unitary school system? He answered no to both questions.[4]

Feild said that the school system was actually run as two distinct systems by the board, one rural, where blacks accounted for 19 percent of the student body, and the other metropolitan, where black students were 59 percent of the school population. By 1974 only twenty-three of fifty-three schools (43 percent) came within five points of the racial composition specified in the 1971 plan. In order to be unitary, according to the Supreme Court, no schools should be identifiably black or white, Feild said. He said that Mobile had failed this test because 41 percent of the metropolitan area's black high school students were in historically and presently all-black schools (Blount and Toulminville); 32 percent were in black or nearly all-black middle schools (Dunbar, Mobile County Training School, and Booker T. Washington); and 56 percent of the area's black elementary students were in nine all-black elementary schools, six of them historically black.[5]

Feild found that the teaching staff was distributed proportionally in the schools, but he said the data showed racial bias in the placement of principals in the integrated schools. Of the twenty-three black principals who were able to retain their positions as principals after desegregation began, nineteen were at all-black schools, three at white schools, and one at an integrated school. Forty-nine of the fifty-eight white principals were at white or integrated schools. No white was assigned to head an all-black school.[6]

The Feild report supported the NAACP's motion for additional relief, which it submitted to the district court in March 1975. The organization alleged that the plan had failed to achieve unitary status for Mobile County. The complaint summarized the situation: Eleven historically black schools had never been desegregated, and 44 percent of black students were still attending substantially all-black schools.

* * *

The *Birdie Mae Davis* case was now before a new district judge, Brevard Hand, who had replaced Thomas. The NAACP asked him to order the school board to use a wide variety of methods to further desegregate the schools, including realignment of attendance zones and pairing of contiguous and noncontiguous school zones (i.e., busing). The NAACP also asked the court to order the reassignment of principals on a more random basis, rather than having white principals at historically white schools and black principals at historically black schools.[7] In short, the NAACP attorneys wanted more integration. The black community itself was not directly involved in these legal maneuvers.

Hand did not act for two years. He offered no explanation, and observers speculated that he had no love for the NAACP, which had asked him to disqualify himself in a related case because of personal bias. Upon appeal the U.S. Supreme Court had rejected the complaint that Hand had erred in not disqualifying himself.[8] The whole issue had left a bad taste in Hand's mouth, it seemed. In any case, hearings on the issues remaining in *Birdie Mae Davis* did not begin until March 1977.

When federal courts compelled busing for desegregation in the North, they relieved the South of some of the onus, much to the delight of many southerners and especially of the *Mobile Press* and *Register,* which had long complained of northern hypocrisy. The eruptions of violent protest in Boston seemed particularly revealing. Many people, including news media there, sought to portray it as manifestations of community insularity, not racial antipathy, as was always the interpretation offered about the South. Although most schools desegregated peacefully, violent protest at South Boston and Hyde Park high schools captured national headlines, and the governor called out two specially trained units of the national guard. The persistence of an organized boycott kept the issue in front of the American people the whole year. Only 40,000 to 60,000 students showed up out of a potential enrollment of 80,000.[9]

Power Shift on the Mobile Board

The election of November 1974 significantly changed the makeup of the school board. Dan Alexander and Ruth Drago replaced Charles McNeil and William Crane. This was more than a change in personality; it represented the rise to power of people who were not of and selected by the established business leadership of Mobile. The new representatives emerged from and represented the interests of white lower-middle and working-class people, and this represented a substantial departure from the past. And when Hiram Bosarge joined these two in November 1976, the populists' power seemed secure.

The traditional leadership selection process had failed to produce viable candidates. In part this was because none among them wanted a job on the board of school commissioners—commissioners were more likely to be vilified than honored in this new age—and partly the change was due to the distrust that many plain people felt for the old regime. The conservative elite had failed to hold the color line and had let the schools sink under the weight of pupil overcrowding and financial neglect.

In the new regime gracious manners gave way to pointed elbows and waspish tongues. Dan Alexander became the dominant force on the board for the next decade. Alexander was a young storefront lawyer. He represented change. He liked public conflict and was irrepressible in front of the media. Alexander could argue like a lawyer, but he could also tell a story like a bayou pirate. Some people later likened him to George Wallace for his combative spirit and his racial politics. Alexander himself said he admired Huey Long and modeled himself on that example: populist not racist, colorful yet tough. Whatever the model, Dan Alexander was intelligent, and he could be charming, but most of all he was ambitious, very ambitious, and he soon showed he knew how to get and hold power.

Although the two had no previous connection, Ruth Drago became Alexander's loyal supporter. Drago was a retired schoolteacher and former president of both the Mobile County Education Association (MCEA) and the Alabama Education Association (AEA), each of which was a professional organization with real clout in politics. She had run unsuccessfully for the Board of School Commissioners in 1970. She had strong views based on her years as an elementary school teacher in Mobile's schools, including (1) the need for a preschool testing program to put children in special education programs if they needed to be there; (2) the elimination of the large number of portable classrooms across the county; and (3) the return to freedom of choice in place of busing.[10]

The "old" members still on the board—Williams, Sessions, and Berger—maintained their conservative, close-to-the-vest styles. They served with poise and civility. They wanted to continue to meet and to discuss in secret and to project a united front to the public on issues before them. This was not Dan Alexander's approach.

By February 1975 he was causing trouble on the board. He visited schools and talked to the press, although it was against board policy for individual members of the board to speak with journalists. Alexander wanted the policy changed so that members could speak to the press as long as it was clear that they spoke only for themselves and not for the board.

Williams, Sessions, and Berger were opposed to this notion; they wanted the board to continue to speak with one voice. But in March, Alexander forced a new public information policy on the still-reluctant board.[11] In this instance he had the support of the media. The board agreed to establish a public relations office at Barton Academy. Moreover, the new policy stated that reporters could come onto school grounds and interview students, teachers, and staff, provided the principal granted permission (something forbidden by earlier board policy); the board would have press conferences if three of the five members agreed to one (and indeed it became increasingly common for the board to take questions from reporters in the boardroom immediately after policy debates); and individual board members could talk to the press so long as they made it clear that they were expressing their personal opinions. The voice of the board would still be expressed as a written statement approved by a majority of the board before it was released.[12]

The shift in policy served Alexander's political and personal agendas. He sought to use the media to frame the problems of the schools in new ways, and he needed publicity in order to tell a new and better story of what was wrong with the schools and what might be done to correct those ills. If the board had kept its "one voice" policy, the storyteller would have had no forum by which to reach his audience.

Alexander did not make his full agenda clear at any point, but right from the start it was clear that he wanted power and "accountability." He wanted the board, and particularly him, to have direct power over the schools and what was done in them. This put him in conflict with the established patterns. Over time he challenged the independent authority of superintendents, senior staff, and principals, and he threatened the security of teachers.

One of Alexander's early proposals stimulated African Americans to respond. Alexander wanted the board to appoint an "ombudsman" for the system. According to Alexander, the ombudsman would listen to parents and investigate complaints about teachers and principals. In this way the board could circumvent the nominal oversight by principals and assistant superintendents. Dr. Robert W. Gilliard, the articulate black dentist who headed the Mobile NAACP chapter and was one of LeFlore's lieutenants, objected strongly to Alexander's idea at the next delegation meeting. He said the plan was racist and compared Alexander's ombudsman to Hitler's, who he said ruled over conquered territories in World War II; the ombudsman, Gilliard asserted, would be a superspy within the administration designed to undermine black personnel. "In summary," Gilliard said, "we denounce the Ombudsman idea as subversive, dictatorial, racist, expensive, and unnecessary."[13]

Black leaders were suspicious of almost every move Alexander made. Black citizens had been deceived and manipulated so often by white authorities that their distrust was almost automatic. Gilliard feared that the ombudsman would collect information that white school officials would use to undermine the standing of black teachers and principals.

Alexander lost on the ombudsman and other issues by a 3-2 vote. The old guard (Williams, Sessions, and Berger) slowed the political takeover that Alexander so badly wanted to achieve. But sometimes he won. He got a new policy through the board regarding legal matters. Henceforth, individual board members or the superintendent could request legal opinions; copies of requests and responses were to go to all members.[14] This allowed Dan Alexander to use the board's lawyer directly in order to shape the issues he wanted to bring to the board and to monitor the actions of others, especially the superintendent.

Alexander sought to control the superintendent or to replace him. He wanted the board to *really* appoint key administrators, particularly central office staff, and this violated the professional norms of career educators as well as the practices of the old board, which thought that the superintendent, as the principal professional, should direct and execute board policy. Alexander wanted more direct control, and that was viewed as threatening. Alexander managed to keep the professional staff and board opponents off balance because he spoke for changes that opened up the system, a breath of fresh air, so to speak, after a generation of elite secrecy.

Alexander visited schools, gave talks, and listened to what people had to say. Then he told stories to others, and embedded in the retelling were certain themes: unresponsive school staff, inefficient and unfair educational practices, and always the need for change.

One early confrontation occurred in September 1975. In June, Alexander had been frustrated by the control over new appointments exercised by the superintendent, Dr. Harold Collins.[15] Collins and previous superintendents were used to having the board defer to them on almost all administrative appointments. Alexander complained and later brought to the board a series of revisions in its policies aimed at letting the board, not the superintendent, control the selection process. Heretofore, Alexander argued, all the board got was the name and educational background of people nominated for administrative appointments. He wanted to see the whole profile for each candidate, and more than one candidate for each administrative post, and thus be able to judge for himself whether each person was able to do the job.

The implications of Alexander's maneuver percolated throughout the system. At the September 10 meeting of the board Burt Silverstein, president of the Mobile County Council of the PTA, approached the board as a delegate to say that "the Mobile County PTA believes that the school Board should hire the superintendent and establish policies by which the schools were administered; but, the actual administration of the programs and the conduct of school business should be left to the superintendent and the professional and non-professional staff *he selects to work for him*" (emphasis added). Silverstein proceeded to grill Alexander and Drago extensively about the meaning of their collaboration: Was Alexander trying to take authority away from Collins and the staff? Was Drago her own person or simply Alexander's tool? The two denied any sinister collaboration and stated that they were making sure the board, which had ultimate responsibility, also had adequate control.

Later that night, when the issue of control came up for formal discussion and vote, Alexander lost. He and Drago voted aye, but Berger and Sessions voted no. Williams did not vote, thus killing the measure. Berger clarified his position. He said it was the job of the superintendent to find and promote people who could do the job; he did not want people getting jobs through their contacts with school board members.[16] Implicitly, he, like Silverstein for the PTA, worried about the politicization of the school system.

In November 1975, a year after being seated on the board, Alexander brought back, in more limited form, his proposal to give the board more information, earlier, about new hires and promotions. He said he had not intended to include all jobs in the system, especially bus drivers, custodians, and so on; he meant professional personnel only. Clearly, he had assessed the politics of the situation: This was a bid for the votes of Sessions and Williams. Dr. Richard LoDestro, deputy superintendent, then told the board that the staff had objected because the policy permitted no exceptions, when there might be good reasons for one; he wanted Alexander's proposal made into a procedure that the board and superintendent would agree to follow, not a hard-and-fast policy. Williams moved to create an amendment to exclude supervisors, coordinators, and assistant principals from the positions affected. It passed. Alexander qualified his affirmative vote by saying that the limitation was the only way to get the proposal passed, and he wanted to walk away "with a little piece of the pie." Then the board passed the amended proposal 4-1, with only Berger holding out. The new policy would affect candidates for principal, director, and assistant superintendent. It said that the board would receive staff and superintendent recommendations for vacant positions with profiles before the position was placed on the action agenda of the board and that the board would have three days to notify the superintendent of any disagreement, in which case the board would have to hold a special meeting.[17]

Alexander had gotten more than a little piece of the pie; it was a substantial victory over the professional educators and the closed system. In January 1976 Collins resigned as superintendent.[18] He had lost control of the situation. In time LoDestro replaced him.

Meanwhile, the NAACP Legal Defense and Education Fund also turned its attention from school desegregation to a frontal attack on the distribution of political power in Mobile County. While white populists like Dan Alexander sought to yank power from the professional educators and old business elite, the NAACP filed lawsuits that sought to break the white monopoly of positions on local governing bodies. The election laws favored whites in this way: Each commissioner was elected countywide. Because whites were a majority in the county, and most whites voted only for other whites, whites alone were elected to every important office in the county.

The NAACP's 1975 lawsuits, *Bolden v. City of Mobile* and *Brown v. Board of School Commissioners*, charged that the county's at-large electoral system for school board, the city commission, and the county commission abridged black citizens' constitutional right to fair representation. *Bolden* asked that elections be based on small districts, not the whole county, so that black people could be elected to some posts.[19]

In the *Bolden* case the federal courts forced Mobile to change its election laws so that representatives were not elected countywide but by geographically distinct districts. This change allowed blacks to be elected to top posts for the first time since Reconstruction. The *Bolden* precedent stimulated a wave of lawsuits across Alabama and the whole South that changed racial politics forever.[20]

While the blacks pressed ahead with their lawsuits, the power struggle among the white activists continued. In 1976 Robert Williams, one of the old guard who had served as school board president for several years, was replaced by Hiram Bosarge.

Hiram Bosarge was a retired army man. He chose to represent the white working class, men and women employed in paper and petrochemical plants or who labored at docks and fishing fleets in southern Mobile County. Bosarge became the swing vote; he was crucial to Alexander's grab for power. With Bosarge in place Alexander claimed the board's presidency.

Competency Testing

In April 1977 Alexander opened a new campaign, one that was to dominate public discussion for a long time and aroused black leaders' steadfast antipathy. At the April 27 meeting of the school board he announced that he wanted the board to develop a policy of testing students to ensure their competence for promotion from grade to grade. He said poorly educated children were passing through the school system, and this blighted their employment prospects.

Alexander had come up with the idea of frequent competency tests for Mobile's schoolchildren on his own; he had not attended national or state meetings where competency testing had been touted. Conservative activists had not put him up to the move. His effort had been stimulated, he said, by stories he had heard directly from parents and employers about young people who had received diplomas but could not read.

In addition, Alexander told the board and assembled reporters that he had contacted Nat Sonnier, a state legislator from Mobile, and Sonnier had introduced a bill in the legislature that mandated testing of students at certain grade levels and, if they tested below standard, would provide them with remedial courses; under the current system students were not tested until the twelfth grade, which often meant that students who tested below average could not graduate with their class. If the legislature enacted the measure, Mobile might get some money from the state to pay for the tests and the remediation, but the Mobile school system ought to go ahead anyway, Alexander said.

Superintendent Richard LoDestro said the staff had already been working on plans for testing and remediation, but he seemed defensive and reluctant. LoDestro was more a bureaucrat than a storyteller, and he was a poor match for Alexander. Alexander cited student papers with poor grammar and spelling; LoDestro cited the need for additional study and proper procedures. Alexander said impatiently that he wanted the new policy to be implemented by the next school year.[21]

Alexander's move was not altogether new; other people had demanded testing in other venues. The move was not so much the consequence of a mass reform movement as the simultaneous invention of fertile minds. During the preceding three years thirty states and many school districts had mandated some form of competency testing to measure whether students had skills and knowledge regarded as minimums for high school graduation. For instance, Florida took a tough line on testing. Tests were designed to measure minimum math and communication skills, and 42 percent of Miami's high school juniors failed the math portion. Forty-five percent of Jacksonville's flunked.[22]

Black parents in many communities where the federal government forced desegregation saw a racial motive behind competency testing, because disproportionate percentages of blacks and Hispanics failed competency tests. Minority parents said testing had not been an issue until desegregation, and then it was introduced ostensibly to protect standards. The effect of competency testing, they feared, would be resegregation within schools, by means of academic "tracking."[23] Once again, minority children would be stigmatized and held back. Tremendous tension arose in place after place as advocates sought to both define the problem of public education and to offer a solution.

At a school board meeting in January 1978 Alexander demanded that the board receive copies of all written staff communications—letters, memos, reports, and the like—whether confidential or otherwise, that the superintendent or his deputy had sent to the assistant superintendents during the previous three years. He would not say why he wanted these materials, only that the board had a right to see anything.

Alexander publicly accused the superintendent of failing to move forward fast enough on student testing. He said that the board had made its views known but that the staff had dragged its feet. The two men disputed whether this had been the case, and ill winds blew across the table.

Alexander said that he was trying to make a general point. He did not question LoDestro's professional competence but was calling into question once again the attitude of the professional staff toward the lay board.[24] This was what had to be corrected. The board had priority.

Board members moved away from the tension between the two men into the specifics of how they could test the "survival skills" of students. The board worried, again, that some young people graduating from high school could not read or write. Employers in particular complained of this. The staff said that many parents felt that in giving competency tests, the system was going to do something bad to their children.

Alexander jumped on that assertion; on the contrary, he said, the system was trying to do something good for their children. He said the system was not doing students any favors when it allowed them to be promoted year after year and then handed a diploma to students who could not read, write, or add and subtract. Such students could not get jobs anywhere, and the system was at fault for fooling them into thinking that they had learned what they needed to know during their twelve years in the public schools. At the end of the extended discussion LoDestro promised to provide for the board information about testing, remediation, and different types of diplomas at the next meeting.

Then, at the end of the meeting, the staff came forward with boxes of materials from their files. It was both compliance with Alexander's demand for information and a defiant, in-your-face gesture. Alexander, Bosarge, Drago, and the staff discussed the volume and security of the information, and after some discussion Alexander decided it would be best if he took the boxes to his law office. The information would be easily available to him and secure.[25]

When the press found out about this maneuver, it had a field day. Why had

Alexander taken the records? Would he try to alter them? Wasn't taking records like that illegal?

Alexander called a special meeting of the board for January 16, but Sessions was in the hospital and Berger would not attend. More than one hundred observers and reporters packed the room. Alexander had directly challenged the norms of professional educational administrators and implicitly snubbed members of the politically powerful Alabama Education Association.

At the meeting Alexander tried to blunt criticism directed at him. He pointed out the irony: that he had always favored openness with the press and now the media were skewering him. He had taken the records only to make it easy for him to study them; they were secure. He had called the board into formal session to clarify his right to keep the records for his study.

Drago was obviously primed. She noted that she had had many calls about the situation. She pointed out that Alexander did not have any of the superintendent's original files nor any of the deputy superintendent's, either. She said the source records were therefore preserved; if someone attempted to alter files, it could be shown quickly and easily. She moved that the board approve Alexander's having the records under the circumstances, and her motion passed easily by a vote of 3-0.

LoDestro, Drago, and Bosarge discussed issues and postured; LoDestro had a lawyer at his elbow, and Alexander himself was schooled in the law. During questioning from reporters LoDestro acknowledged that Alexander had asked him to resign. Alexander talked around the substance of the issues, namely, an intense struggle about who exactly controlled the schools' policies and personnel. The media pressed for details. Everyone asked questions or had something to say, but LoDestro and Alexander made little clear about the substance of their disagreement.[26]

In executive session at a special meeting on January 25, the board and LoDestro came to an agreement: The charges against LoDestro, which were not disclosed, would be sealed until he could respond at a special executive session of the board on February 20. Meantime, he could have contact with the senior staff only through the deputy superintendent.[27]

The populists on the board had taken political power from the old, conservative business elite, and when they found themselves stymied by professional educators' stubborn insistence on their own power and prestige, Alexander, Bosarge, and Drago had walked over them too.

Not coincidentally, LoDestro announced at the January 25 meeting that he and the staff were now recommending competency-based testing. The staff members explained that they had checked with the state department of education and found out that nothing precluded their setting graduation requirements higher than the state's. The staff now recommended annual testing of all students in the eleventh grade on basic competency skills and a test of survival skills that checked more than reading and arithmetic ability.[28] The staff also recommended that passing the competency test at a minimal level be a prerequisite for graduation; students who did not pass would be remediated and given other opportunities to pass the examination.

The staff recommended also that the district offer different types of diplomas: The regular diploma would require twenty credits, as was now the case, and a passing grade on the competency exam; those who could not pass the exam but who did have seventeen credits would receive a certificate; and the district would award an honors diploma to students who passed the exam and met many other requirements, including a high grade-point average and special coursework.[29] Finally, the staff recommended testing procedures and four methods of remediation, one of which was free summer school in place of term-time remediation.

Drago asked whether the staff had plans for testing in earlier grades. She was told that the system would test this year in eleventh grade only, so that graduation requirements could go into effect the following year. The staff recommended full systemwide competency testing in grades three, five, and eight beginning the next year. A rough estimate of the cost was $460,000.

Berger moved that the board approve the recommendation for competency testing, remediation, and diplomas, and it was passed unanimously. Mobile became the first major school system in Alabama to move so fully and comprehensively in this direction. Alexander had won.[30]

Alexander called a special meeting of the board for February 15 as a "prehearing" for LoDestro. They resolved their dispute in executive session. When the board reconvened in open session, it dismissed all charges, reinstated LoDestro to full powers as superintendent, and sealed permanently the specific charges that it had dropped. Alexander said the conflict had been about the proper relationship between the superintendent and the board. In general, he said, the charges alleged that the superintendent had not always effectively followed through on recommendations by some assistant superintendents, nor on some instructions by board members.[31]

A week later the truce was tested. During a meeting of the board Alexander began his attack on student achievement from another front. It began with a simple question directed to the superintendent: What was the system's policy on social promotions?

LoDestro immediately stated that he understood that grade-to-grade promotions were earned. Alexander replied that this policy was *not* being carried out in the system. He knew of specific instances in which supervisors and central office staff had gone into schools and told teachers that they should take into consideration other factors in promotion decisions, including age, size, and whether the child had already been retained twice. LoDestro countered. He would need to investigate these instances; would Alexander give him details? Alexander said no, all the superintendent had to do was send out a memo to all teachers stating that they were not to make social promotions, that academic factors alone should determine promotions. Would the policy affect special education children too? No, of course not, they had their own program. Other board members joined the debate; they questioned and commented but on the whole supported Alexander's thrust. They decided to take up the issue at the next meeting.[32]

At that meeting on March 1 LoDestro read the pertinent part of the system's promotion and retention policy: "Decisions concerning promotion and retention shall be based on the student's total background of growth and achievement in the conditions under which his learning needs can best be accommodated." LoDestro passed out material that showed how teachers used this policy in various subjects and grades. Each child was assessed, he said; the decision was made cooperatively by the teacher and the principal. He pointed out that the number of students retained in grade had increased from fifteen hundred in 1974 to thirty-eight hundred in 1977. Although the policy could be revised and strengthened, LoDestro emphasized that the system needed a viable alternative program for students who had trouble with the regular program but could not qualify for special education.

Alexander responded that he earned his living as a lawyer interpreting laws and rules, and nineteen Philadelphia lawyers and one hundred educators could not figure out what this policy meant. Policy, he said, needed to be narrow enough to accomplish what was necessary. He said he had been at the Old Shell Road school the night before, and teachers there had said that they had been told that promotions were to be given on grounds other than academic achievement.

Larry Newton, the deputy superintendent, responded that a degree of interpretation did exist in the policy as to whether a child has to pass certain academic requirements or whether educators could consider the social, emotional, and physical development of the child. This, Alexander asserted, meant that children who continued to fail a subject would be passed to the next grade anyway; that is what people meant by social promotions. He wanted the system to adopt a new policy, promotion on academic grounds alone, and implement it before the March 10 report cards were sent out. If they waited until the May report card or for the next academic year, they would be seen as condoning social promotions.

The discussion continued, point by point. Bosarge wondered what would happen to children with dyslexia under the new policy. Berger wondered about equity issues embedded in alternative programs—he wanted more pressure put on teachers and students to do well now. Sessions wanted promotion to be based solely on academic achievement; the children who did their homework would pass, and those who did not deserved to fail.

Staff members were alarmed by that proposal. They pointed out that in five schools more than half the fifth grade would be retained this year if the board adopted its new policy: What would happen to these students? No one said, but everyone knew, that these were mainly poor black students in predominantly black schools. The question was about program and logistics, but the issue of race hung in the air. Berger and Bosarge wanted to wait, to look more closely at the implementation, but Alexander, Drago, and Sessions voted to change the policy immediately and to base promotion only on academics.[33]

The consequences of what they had done became clear during the next two weeks. At the March 15 meeting of the board the staff said that the school principals strongly favored maintaining the the policy of limiting promotion to students' academic achievement *based on their level of ability.* The staff estimated that under the board's new policy, which required students to be at or above grade level in all academic subjects in order to be promoted, thirty to forty thousand of the system's sixty-six thousand pupils would be retained in grade. How honest would teachers be when faced by a problem of this magnitude? the staff asked. What standards would teachers set for grades? If a student in the eighth grade passes a sixth-grade math class, is the appropriate grade a C or an F? The discussion finally ended as board members faced the morass of mind-boggling potential problems.[34]

At the delegation meeting of the board on March 22, board members heard some of what they must have anticipated—objections from professional educators and blacks.

Shirley Banks appeared on behalf of the Mobile County Education Association. She said the confusion and unanswered questions recommended that the board postpone implementation of its retention policy until the next year, after more study had been given the issues. Anything done in haste that spring, with 80 percent of the school year over, could affect a child's outlook on her entire education. The school system could use the summer to develop programs and procedures everyone could understand.

Alexander interrupted: The problem was clear, he said; we have an educational system that puts children in a grade when they are not up to that grade level in academic achievement. Anything the board did was going to be traumatic, but the problem would not be cured by running away from it.

Banks retorted that some of her students had achieved two grade levels this year but were still behind; it would traumatize these students if she now had to tell them that they had not really worked hard enough this year. It was too much.

Alexander asked Banks if she would like to see a letter that he had received from a female high school senior. He asked whether Banks thought that the board ought to let the young woman pass through the system when not one sentence in the letter was grammatically correct. If the board postponed the matter, he said, many others like her would be graduated into the community. The real trauma, Alexander went on, was caused by allowing low standards to prevail for so long. The time for planning had passed; the time for some action was now, Alexander closed.[35]

Gilliard came forward to speak for black interests. He wanted to see the results of the competency tests, to see whether there were racial differences in the pass rate. He said he had always opposed social promotions, but he had reservations about the board's rush. Graduation of some students without proper academic training had been going on since 1940, and he did not think the board could correct that mistake between March and May this year.

Alexander replied that he did not think that time was a factor. He did not see withholding graduation as punishment of the child but as an opportunity to try to give the student something. "If the system retains more blacks than whites under the new policy, would that be racist?" Alexander asked. On the contrary, he answered himself: Discrimination exists in the "diploma mill," a social promotion policy whereby children are run through the system just to be rid of them and are not taught anything. If this is done to blacks more than whites, that is where the discrimination lay. Gilliard agreed and added that if more blacks than whites were retained in grade, it would mean the educational system had not been doing for blacks what it was supposed to do.[36]

Alexander had made his points, told his stories, and overall his agenda guided the board, but on this night the other board members agreed with the critics—they were moving too fast. After taking time to say how much they deplored social promotions, the board backed down. They postponed implementation until the staff developed alternative academic programs.

Teacher Competency

Talk about student competency tests had raised fears among students and parents. Many told Alexander that it was unfair to hold students accountable for their failure if teachers were actually to blame; the students could not learn language arts, science, or math if the teachers did not teach them correctly.

Parents sent him examples of teacher incompetence, and Alexander called a press conference on Friday, March 24, 1978, to highlight the issue. One letter in particular aroused his fury. He told how a parent had received a note from her son's teacher that was grossly wrong in grammar, spelling, and punctuation. Moreover, the teacher who did this was a tenured Mobile schoolteacher with both an undergraduate and graduate degree from an Alabama state university. He passed out copies of the offending letter for all to see: "Scott is dropping in his studies he acts as if he don't care. Scott want pass in his assignment at all, he a had a poem to learn and he fell to do it. Mrs. [Name] I feel that you should know this." Alexander had blotted out the name of the parent and teacher, so that the teacher would not be publicly identified. The parent, however, did not mind being known and stood at his side as Alexander attacked: "It is inconceivable to me that a language teacher in our school system could write such a letter." The problem, he said, was widespread, and he urged other parents with such complaints to call the school board. Alexander said he intended to ask the board to change the policy so that teachers judged to be incompetent by principals could be immediately removed from the classroom.[37]

At a special meeting on March 29, 1978, the board signaled its direction when it decided to cancel the contract of a nontenured teacher because the board found the teacher to be incompetent. Under Alexander's prodding the board confirmed its interest in revising procedures to deal with teachers it regarded as incompetent. They would be suspended without pay pending a termination hearing, because parents would not put up with inferior teachers even for a short time. Bosarge seconded Alexander's motion and asked to put into the record a letter dated March 23, 1978, that he had received from one concerned citizen.

Dear Mr. Bosarge,

The student achievement program advocated by certain members of the school board is certainly commendable. In addition to this, to be totally fair with all students, a system of Teacher Achievement likewise needs to be established. . . . Teachers who cannot or are not teaching should be warned through the personnel system and should be immediately required to take refresher teacher training with highly qualified instructors and be subject to review. Sufficient appeals should be available to protect the teachers, but their responsibility is teaching and they should be like pilots, doctors, and others who must constantly maintain their sharpness.

[signed] Frankie M. D'Olive Wheeler

Alexander stated that this letter summarized what a lot of people had been saying. He agreed with Drago that the system had a lot of good teachers, but he felt that the time had come to let everybody know that the board was interested in and wanted to know about problems. Some had criticized him for releasing the infamous ungrammatical note from the teacher, but it clearly showed the kind of problem he had in mind.

At this meeting, as at every board meeting now, the board took questions from the press. The questions were directed to Alexander, and he was an eager and articulate politician. Bill Capo of WALA-TV asked how many complaints Alexander had received about teachers. Alexander could not, or would not, say. WKRG-TV reporter Pat Riddle said people would accuse Alexander of a witch-hunt, with parents coming in and giving information or anonymously phoning in and alleging teacher incompetence. Would not teacher competency tests diminish this aspect of the problem? she asked. Alexander replied he did not think that teacher competency tests could be instituted soon enough to help children. He objected to Riddle's use of the term *witch-hunt*. He said it was a teacher-hunt, an inadequate-teacher-hunt.[38]

By April 1978 delegations addressing the board were beginning to register polite protests.[39] Teachers' representatives warned of the presumption of incompetence involved in the new procedures, and they worried that disgruntled parents would complain in order to harass teachers they did not like. Dr. William Hanebuth, the head of the Mobile County teachers' union, offered a proposal that the board, the administration, and representatives of the Mobile County Education Association work out a revised teacher evaluation procedure. They could discuss the feasibility of a competency test for teachers; at the end of those meetings, after the board and the association had reached agreement on evaluation procedures, the proposals should be placed before the board and the MCEA membership for a final vote. Alexander cut him off. The board, he said, was not interested in a collective bargaining agreement with anybody.[40]

Black people had mixed feelings about all this talk about student and teacher competency tests. Norman G. Cox, a retired air force lieutenant colonel, spoke to the board directly about the issue. It would begin a long relationship. Cox said citizens were shocked at the results of the recent so-called student competency tests; however, he was sure that no board member was. The California Achievement Test results from the previous year showed the same pattern. Mobile County was more than two years below the national average, and most of the black schools were one to two years below that. Recently, he said, a board member (Alexander) had told reporters that he was trying to help black students. Cox wanted to know when that aid was coming. He noted that nothing had been done in the past, even though the students' level of achievement was known to be low. Cox said students had to pay to go to summer school, thereby making summer school education open only to those who could most afford it. Schools that served the black community had few summer school teachers, he said. Of the fifteen high schools, traditionally black Blount had the worst scores on the Stanford Achievement Test last year. Yet Blount had had only three summer school teachers. Traditionally black Toulminville ranked next-to-last, and it had only five teachers in its summer school. But Murphy High, Cox continued, which had scored well above the national average, had had fifteen summer school teachers. Cox implied that blatant racism had a hand in the assignment of teachers. His statement assumed an old story: Whites would discriminate against blacks at every turn unless they were watched closely.

Cox was immediately told that the number of teachers assigned to the summer school depended upon the number of students who enrolled for the summer program. For his part, Alexander stated that what had gone on in the past was not adequate; he guaranteed that remediation would go where it was most needed. Drago said Cox's statements were misleading, that Mobile had participated in a number of federal programs designed expressly to help poor people. She named the Elementary and Secondary Education Act of 1965, Head Start, and Title I.

Board member Berger then implied another story: that black culture itself was deficient. Berger said that based on what he had learned at a recent National School Board meeting he thought one key was increased parental and community involvement. If parents would become interested and expect more of children, children would do better in school.[41] This was a portentous statement. Berger was Jewish. His father had run retail businesses in Mobile's black community for decades. Now, publicly, one minority was telling another minority that its cultural values and practices were flawed.

Berger was not through for the night. Later in the meeting, he said he wanted to go to the core of the problem of teacher competence, which he said was the lenience of colleges. He wanted the board to use its influence to change the admissions and graduation standards of colleges that trained teachers. Sensitive black listeners heard in this rhetoric an attack on historically black teacher-training programs. Again, Berger was implying that black institutions were at fault for the lower educational achievement. Because Mobile had the largest school system in the state, Berger said that it could effectively take the lead, and if joined by other school boards and teacher organizations, something important could be done. Bosarge immediately agreed with the idea.

Alexander agreed that the problem of incompetent teachers clearly started back in college. He referred to the ungrammatical, "famous letter" he had made public earlier and pointed out that the teacher had undergraduate and master's degrees from an Alabama university. (He pointedly did not identify the university. Nevertheless, the media and informed citizens knew that it was historically black Alabama State University in Montgomery.) Alexander noted that the teacher had worked in a parochial school for one year, in another public school system for another year, and had taught for the Mobile public schools for three years. She had received satisfactory evaluations from supervisors and principals during this entire period. All of a sudden this letter was printed, and the teacher said she never knew she was doing anything wrong, he continued. It was sad, Alexander concluded, that this teacher was given the benefit of the doubt, that nobody ever told her she was doing anything wrong.

Berger regained the floor. According to one study, he said, the school from which this person was graduated had been rated the lowest in the state in turning out "quality teachers." If the board moved ahead on his proposal, this school and others would have to come up to standard and stop turning out ineffective teachers.

Berger argued that the board could model teacher testing on that done by other professions; he noted that he and Alexander had to pass the law and dental exams. Alexander agreed. Bosarge said that he did not think any member of the board thought that many teachers were incompetent; he thought 18 percent at the outside, and that was not bad. The superintendent agreed to set up a meeting of the board and the staff of the personnel office to discuss these issues further.[42]

The Mobile board, at Alexander's urging, became one of the first in the country to press for teacher competency testing. It garnered Alexander and Mobile considerable national attention, including a photo in *Time* magazine.

During May the board continued to fuss with the ways it could improve the teaching staff. Alexander wanted to begin testing teachers for competence but realized that legally the school board could not do that until the following year; testing would have to be written into the teachers' contract. Another formidable problem was which test to administer.

Still, Alexander pushed; he wanted to do something now. To illustrate his frustration he pointed to the file of another nontenured teacher. The file contained evaluations that said that the teacher had poor language and speech patterns and trouble with discipline. One intern had reported in November that the teacher had broken down in front of the children. Alexander asked how this teacher could still be in front of a class. Who had hired this teacher? he asked. What sort of evaluative system would hire a person deficient in basic language skills and then, when deficiencies were discovered by principals and other evaluators, permit her to continue?

Alexander wanted the board to require all principals to certify that every teacher under their supervision had a good basic grasp of the English language and use of proper grammar. He suggested that principals then notify those who had deficiencies, thereby laying a foundation for subsequent dismissal. He referred to a teacher whom the board members had found to be deficient but whom they could not fire because they had not given sufficient notice; instead, they had had to give her a year's leave of absence in which to make up her deficiencies. In that particular case the teacher had been teaching for more than two years before she was cited for poor use of the language; clearly, said Alexander, the system of evaluation was flawed. Alexander wanted each principal to certify the language competency of each teacher by name this year; it was the only way to move forward immediately.

The board stumbled into technical aspects and rhetorical gibes. In the end, right at the board table, Alexander drew up a new certification form for principals, supervisors, and interns to use, and the board unanimously approved the requirement that all teachers in the system be evaluated by the end of the next week.[43]

The board members met in special session on May 19 in order to get the results of this exercise. They found that the central office staff had given them the names of about fifty-nine deficient teachers; some were tenured and some not. The board directed that the staff prepare separate lists of tenured and nontenured teachers, because each category required separate action. The board approved a resolution that all teacher contracts be revised to include the possibility of a teacher proficiency test, despite the reluctance of the staff to take this step. And under the tutelage of its attorney, the board began to use the term *job-related deficiency* in place of *teacher incompetence* in some communications.

Bosarge and Alexander, questioned by reporters, seemed disappointed that so few teachers had been identified as job deficient. Alexander said some principals seemed to have certified everyone, and because he had parents' complaints about many teachers who had been deemed competent, he was going to investigate further. It was not clear whether he meant to investigate the incompetence of some teachers or the recalcitrance of some principals. Bosarge emphasized that principals from the schools where students scored the lowest on the tests had not identified a single deficient teacher. Everyone knew he meant the black community's schools.

Questions from the media revealed the interpretive "frames" that they used. Riddle, one of the television reporters, asked whether "job-related deficiency" included the English language requirement the board had been so exercised about the week before. Gleefully, Alexander informed her that the board's attorney had said that a court would not necessarily recognize the inability to read or write as a deficiency so far as teaching was concerned. The board would have to prove, through the use of expert witnesses, that competence in English was a job-related skill. The board felt it could do this. The board, Alexander said, still looked on gross deficiencies in the English language as a job-related deficiency.

Bill Capo, of WALA radio, asked if all this talk about teacher incompetence was not just a tempest in a teapot, because the principals had identified only fifty-nine as deficient and the supervisors only eighty-seven, whereas the board had thought it might have as many as five hundred incompetent teachers. Alexander said the problem was enormous to the parent of a child stuck in a classroom with an incompetent teacher. He did not think all the incompetence had been identified; the system had twenty-seven hundred teachers. If the board could get rid of 150 incompetent teachers, that would be significant.[44]

At the May 24 board meeting Riddle asked the telling question: Given that the court order in *Birdie Mae Davis* required racial balance in the employment of teachers, what would happen if a disproportionate number of blacks were fired as the result of the board's policies? Alexander said that he was aware that many people had tried to insinuate that these policies were racially motivated, but they had nothing to do with race. He said he was talking about competence. If more whites than blacks were judged to be incompetent, then more whites than blacks would be released and vice versa. He said he was perfectly willing to replace any teacher found to be incompetent with another teacher of the same race. He wanted the board to employ the twenty-seven hundred best people it could find, no matter what color they were. Berger stated that in hiring and firing he hoped the board would stay with the ratio the district had at that time: 60 percent white and 40 percent black.[45]

Student Competency

Toward the end of the meeting of May 24, 1978, Berger brought the board back to student competency. He had heard from a lot of parents who were confused. He asked Dr. Henry H. Pope, the director of the curriculum development, to inform the board about the standards by which students would be judged the next year. Pope said that there were problems in regard to what the board had meant by "grade level." He said the norm could be national, regional, or local. Moreover, what were the minimum skills the board wanted to define as passing? Alexander pointed Pope to the recent standardized test results and said that he had been told that Mobile's eighth graders had scored at the sixth-grade seventh-month level. Pope replied that those were average scores in different subjects compared to the national norm. By definition 50 percent were below the average. This did not define the minimum. Alexander showed irritation. He had been told long ago that the system had the information it needed to specify at what level each student was performing. Pope launched into a description of norm-referenced and criterion-referenced tests.

Bosarge headed off the conflict by suggesting a working conference between the board and the staff on the issue in a few days. Alexander said that he was beginning to think that the problem was never going to be solved because the board could not get its own staff to understand what it wanted. LoDestro said that defining minimum skills for promotion was a nationwide problem, and specifying grade level was terribly difficult. Alexander reminded everyone that the board had instructed the staff to send a letter to every student this year who would not have passed had the promotion policy been made effective immediately. Now, he said, the school year was ending and the staff had not figured out to whom the letters would be sent. Pope quickly said the letters would be sent out on the basis of staff perceptions of grade levels. The board was not pleased and requested detailed information for its next meeting.

At the end of the meeting the press had questions. Pat Riddle wanted to know how the staff could make plans for the summer remediation program if no one knew how many students would have failed this year. The board could not respond directly; members said they would have to wait for more information from Pope. Anne Reeks of the *Press/Register* asked whether letters requested by the board had gone out to parents of children identified as deficient; the letters offered access to the summer remediation problem. Pope said that some letters had gone out based on general criteria of success, and others would.[46]

As May 1978 wound down, the board met yet again to consider teacher contracts. The board had twenty-five nontenured teachers whom the supervisory staff had identified as deficient. The staff recommended that eleven teachers not be given new contracts and that fourteen others be given contracts that required that they attend the newly formed Staff Development Center in order to work toward the elimination of their deficiency. The eleven teachers whose contracts were not renewed could put themselves through a remedial program and reapply for a job in the fall. The board had no program to deal with teachers who were both tenured and deficient but agreed that some sort of remediation might be put forward later.

In the middle of the meeting the board moved into a private executive session and cleared the room. When they returned to the public meeting forty-five minutes later, Dan Alexander said that Superintendent LoDestro had tendered his resignation. The board unanimously accepted his offer. He would get $4,000 per month for six months to act as a consultant. LoDestro made a statement. In it he said all the nice, polite things—how much he loved Mobile and its people—how much he had enjoyed his five years at the top of one of the best systems in the country—how much they had achieved together. And then he said some things in code: "While the board and I have had some certain differences in the past, I leave with the perception that they were philosophical in nature and not personal. I trust that we both have learned something valuable from our experiences. I would ask that the community take ever more interest in the affairs of this school system as the board and staff cannot make a success of this system [alone]. If you agree with the directions the board is taking, let them know that you support them. If you disagree, let them also know, but do it in a positive manner. This board and system need your help and your support to overcome the difficult times still ahead."[47]

Dr. Larry Newton, LoDestro's deputy, became acting superintendent and proceeded to implement the board's policies. In June the staff told the board that 13,082 more students would have failed that year had the new policy been in effect. Alexander disputed these figures because, he said, the staff seemed unable to define any grade-level standards. Pope could not say how the staff had come up with the number, but he guessed they extrapolated it from the national norms of the standardized achievement tests that spring. The staff and board grappled with the meaning of averages and national norms and then abandoned the discussion. At another point the staff recommended that the board hire consultants to develop a teacher competency test. The staff had gathered expert opinion to this end. The staff asserted that the development of valid instruments for measuring proficiency was beyond its capability. Alexander seemed perturbed but voted with the whole board to contract with Dr. Raoul Arreola for this purpose.[48] Throughout the summer the staff brought to the board plans for the implementation of the board's student and teacher competency programs, particularly ideas for identification and remediation.

The board hired a new superintendent, Pete Landrum, in July and that proved a fateful step. Alexander had personally found Landrum and brought him to the board's attention. Berger and Alexander had a falling out about the hiring that signaled a permanent realignment on the board. It came to light at the July 26 meeting of the board. Alexander announced to the board that Pat Webb, president of the Mobile Council of the Parent-Teacher Association, was suing the board, claiming that it had hired Landrum improperly. She apparently alleged that there were "under the table and behind the scenes" dealings, but the suit focused on technical aspects of Landrum's employment, including his failure to obtain a doctoral degree. Alexander blasted Berger: Webb was the treasurer of Berger's reelection committee, and language in her complaint was similar to that which Berger had used to describe Landrum's hiring. Webb, Alexander asserted, had done a number of things during the past few years to frustrate actions of the board, and that was a shame. Berger tried to defend himself and Webb, but Alexander would not hear it.[49]

Instead, his response came at the August 2 meeting. Landrum had sent out a letter to staff and board stating that Webb was not to have access to the staff and facilities at Barton Academy. Alexander said the woman had sued the board and that meant no one in the central office should have contact with her. She had had, he explained, free access to Barton Academy in the past, but that was no longer the case and rightly so. Again, Alexander and Berger sparred, to no real effect except to separate them still further.[50]

Discussion

When Griffin Bell, one of the federal appellate judges who had compelled racial integration across the Deep South, made a public statement about his own views in 1972, he worried about the use of federal power to diminish individual freedom. He said, "The real issue is and ought to be a quality education for every child, regardless of race." Education, not forced mixing, was a legitimate goal. While he did not say anything about the first attempt by the federal government to reconstruct the South after the Civil War, he surely knew that Reconstruction had stimulated an intense and retrograde Redemption.

This belief was echoed by Mobile's nonconformers, those parents who chose to put their children in schools without formally registering them rather than send them to the schools to which they were assigned by the court-ordered plan. Surely, those who moved their children to private schools cited individual freedom as their reason for doing so, even if they did not cite Judge Bell directly. The story they told each other, and anyone who would listen, was that they were protecting their children against the excesses of federal power.

John LeFlore and the parent-plaintiffs in *Birdie Mae Davis* brought in Dr. William Feild to show that the school board had not yet ended the old dual school system. Feild said that there was discrimination in the assignment of principals and that the rural and urban areas of the county were treated as separate systems, thus allowing whites in the rural areas to escape full integration. The story of Mobile's schools, according to black leaders and white liberals, was that white school officials were not trustworthy—they continued to resist equity and to discriminate whenever they could.

When Boston became violently opposed to busing, Mobilians and almost all southerners metaphorically wagged their fingers and said, See, y'all aren't any better than we are. Boston parents had complained that busing destroyed their communities, a familiar refrain in the South.

Dan Alexander heard all this and responded. He became the axis about which individuals and groups arrayed themselves. Alexander saw himself as a populist politician. He ran for the school board because the post would help his law practice and his long-term political ambition. Once elected, he wanted to accomplish things for ordinary people and was hampered in that effort by two established groups: the old business elite and professional educators. When he sought to wrest power from these people, he demonized them and was demonized in turn.

Alexander repeatedly told stories based on a metanarrative new to those embedded in the hierarchical culture of Mobile: that people ought to be judged on their individual merit, not on the basis of race or class. And, more important, they needed to measure up to a reasonable standard. The story—that achievement in school led to good jobs for individuals and economic progress for the community—was simple and compelling because it was the American culture's most fundamental story.

When Alexander brought out the ungrammatical letter from a tenured black teacher, his dramatic interpretation trumped others. Professional educators could hardly defend manifest incompetence, so they were silenced. Black leaders were frustrated and enraged, but they were rhetorically impotent. Blacks distrusted Alexander because they believed that the competency tests for children and teachers would show that blacks were disproportionately deficient and that whites would use these temporary failings to deny to blacks resources, access, and power. In that sense, they feared the tests would become a self-fulfilling prophecy. They could not counter the notion of present incompetence by claiming that historical abuse excused it without at the same time encouraging the deep prejudice of white people.

Alexander was chided by prominent citizens, challenged by black leaders, provoked by reporters, and ignored by the old elite, but they could not, with any force, impeach the values that he espoused or counter the stories that he told. After all, individual accomplishment in a competitive world was the very foundation of the American dream.

6. Community Schools

MOBILE'S SCHOOLS had been chronically overcrowded and underfunded since the tremendous population influx during World War II. Black people felt especially aggrieved because the 1971 desegregation plan had closed many traditionally black schools. As the school board contemplated new school construction programs under the constraint of court-ordered school desegregation, blacks became increasingly alarmed. If whites would not attend schools in black areas, the district might close even more traditionally black schools; black children would then be bused out of their communities into white areas to desegregate schools there, and that was unfair. The Toulminville community was center stage in the first round of rising black protest, and Blount would be the focus of a later confrontation.

Behind the hard feelings expressed at PTA meetings and debated among lawyers was the priority given to the assimilationists' construction of the problem of racial inequality. Racial balance in the schools, the hallmark of assimilationist thinking, followed from the conceptual narrative of how black children needed to be in schools with whites in order to fully claim equal social status and where they might be challenged to achieve higher academic standards.

Toulminville

Well into the 1950s Toulminville had been an essentially all-white community. What became the all-black Toulminville High School was in those days an elementary and junior high serving the white families in the area. Urban renewal and demographic movement slowly changed the city, but the dismantling of the dual school system in the 1960s rapidly created virtually all-black schools in the area. At one point, before the 1971 court order, two hundred whites had been assigned to Toulminville High School in order to desegregate it, but few attended. The 1971 order itself had required 107 whites to attend, but they disappeared over time.

The middle-class blacks who had replaced the whites in Toulminville were proud of their community, and they had come to feel that the old, inadequate school building would have to be replaced with a big new one. It was owed to them, they argued.

The school board had tried to build a new high school at Toulminville for several years, but the courts had thwarted that effort. On December 20, 1968, following one early proposal to build a school in the area, the federal district court had expressly forbidden the construction of a new Toulminville high school because it would "tend to serve a school area with one dominant race, thus creating a 'locked-in' segregation area." Both the NAACP Education and Legal Defense Fund and the Justice Department had strongly argued this position.[1] The parent-plaintiffs and the federal government wanted a new school to be built between the black and white communities so that the new school's attendance zone would naturally include meaningful percentages of both races.

Nevertheless, in March 1969, acting on the school board's motion to reconsider, U.S. District Judge Daniel Thomas approved its Toulminville project. He wrote: "The only objection of the plaintiffs and the plaintiff-intervenor is that the new school may be totally or at least predominantly Negro when completed. Such objection has as a premise, the supposition that the School Board will disregard its affirmative duty to disestablish the dual school system." The court found that supposition faulty; it wanted to give the board room to both desegregate and be sensitive to community preferences.[2]

The NAACP and the government immediately appealed to higher courts and vigorously pursued the action.[3] The Fifth U.S. Circuit Court of Appeals consolidated thirteen desegregation cases, including *Birdie Mae Davis,* and heard them en banc. The 1970 decision in the consolidated cases, known as *Singleton v. Jackson,* gave instructions to Judge Thomas and set the standard for the whole region: "All school construction, school consolidation, and site selection (including the location of any temporary classrooms) in the system shall be done in a manner which will *prevent the recurrence of the dual school structure* once this desegregation plan is implemented."[4] That statement had legal power in Mobile, even though local activists did not fully understand its implications.

The NAACP and school board agreed to the "Comprehensive Plan for a Unitary School System" in July 1971. Mobile's plan stated that "the system is in need of an additional high school facility in the area of Toulminville and Shaw communities" but that Toulminville High School would remain open only as a transitional facility until a new school could be built to serve the two areas. Additionally, the Board of School Commissioners agreed to involve the respective communities in the selection of a site.[5]

A. J. Cooper, the young black Mobile attorney who represented the NAACP, participated in the negotiations leading up to the Comprehensive Plan, and his approval of this approach, guided as he was by the NAACP in New York, seemed to many to signal the end of Toulminville High School. The NAACP and the Justice Department generally wanted new schools to be built somewhere between the centers of black and white populations so that both races would bear the burden of desegregation, but that policy was not sensitive to community sentiments on either side.

The school board appointed a biracial site selection committee, and it became a scene of immediate frustration. Representatives of the preponderantly white Shaw community wanted to preserve and enhance their own high school, and those of the Toulminville community insisted that a new school be built in their community. At first the community representatives were dimly aware of the constraints set upon the situation by the courts, and as they learned more about the requirements of the courts, they became indignant. Construction of a new facility *between* the two communities seemed the only solution, and that course was unacceptable to each community's partisans. Strangely, activist blacks and whites—nominal opponents—used the same arguments and similar stories to justify community-based schools.

Many in the Toulminville community were outraged by the position taken by the NAACP. By pressing for racial balance in court, the NAACP had denied the community a new high school, or so it seemed. On March 8, 1972, community fervor reached a high point. More than two hundred students from the Toulminville area spent the day at Barton Academy protesting the contemplated construction of a new high school between the Shaw and Toulminville communities. School officials met with them twice that day to explain the situation; on three occasions, they told the students, the board had wanted to build a new high school in their community, and three times the court had denied them permission because of the NAACP's objections on behalf of the parent-plaintiffs. It was not the board's fault. Toward evening the young black demonstrators marched to the home of Dr. Robert W. Gilliard, president of the NAACP's local branch. They wanted a new and predominantly black Toulminville high school in their own community, not somewhere else, and they blamed the NAACP for creating the problem.

Gilliard was not intimidated. As the crowd approached his house, he came

out and fired a shot into the lawn to stop their advance.[6] He would not negotiate with the crowd, but he offered to discuss the issues with a few of its
delegates. That did not work; the evening ended in a standoff. So Gilliard
wrote a piece for a local black newspaper to convey his views: "I am sure
Governor George Wallace appreciates the help he is getting from Mobile to
convince the voters that the neighborhood schools are best for all. As to the
position of our organization, as expressed many times before, segregated
schools have been and always will be inferior both for black children and
white children. In the case of black schools, they have been and always shall
be inferior. The federal court has decreed that the new high school shall be
constructed between the Toulminville and Shaw areas."[7]

The confrontation represented a deep divide within the black community. Some, like Gilliard, saw assimilation into the mainstream culture as the
only way to secure black opportunity, while others told stories about black
achievement that raised community identity, solidarity, and tradition above
the value of social integration.

The board was caught between federal law and community desire. Its lawyer advised that the U.S. Supreme Court had taken a more demanding line
than the Fifth Circuit had in *Singleton*. Abe Philips said that the Supreme
Court "has sometimes taken the view that school construction must be located in such a manner not only as to prevent the recurrence of the dual
school structure, but that it must be located in such manner as to actively
assist in dismantling a dual system."[8]

Strong feelings in the Toulminville and Shaw communities, ambivalence
on the school board, and the press of other issues delayed a decision on the
Toulminville-Shaw project. Eventually, the renewed site selection committee, which was initially divided by race, found a compromise, made its recommendation, and the board agreed in 1975, three years after the committee began work. The Mobile school board petitioned the court to permit the
renovation of both high schools and the construction of a new high school
between the two, at Wolf Ridge. Shaw would have a student body of fourteen hundred students and be 30 percent black; Toulminville would school
one thousand students and be 100 percent black; and the new high school
would house one thousand students and be 50 percent black.[9]

It was a grand compromise. People in each community got some of what
they wanted, but the NAACP objected to the plan because the upgraded
Toulminville High School was projected to be all black. The organization said
that this was unacceptable because Mobile's Williamson High School, which
had been all black before 1971, had 30 to 35 percent white students in 1974.[10]

If it could be done at Williamson, the NAACP argued, the board could make it happen at Toulminville.

On March 28, 1975, Judge Brevard Hand, who had replaced Judge Thomas in the *Birdie Mae Davis* case, reluctantly rejected most of the board's plan, but he gave his personal opinion in a footnote: "The Court feels compelled to parenthetically note that the solution to the problem suggested by the School Board and submitted by the Bi-Racial Site Selection Committee is in the opinion of the Court a viable solution for the problem at hand. . . . Were it not for the prior decisions of the Courts which preclude the establishment of an all-black school . . . even though common sense, reasonable practicality, history, child safety, educational stability, disciplinary considerations, community pride, lack of government creation of the problem, un-needed consumption of fuels, etc., all mitigate in favor of such decision, this Court would approve the proposal submitted to it."[11]

Hand approved the renovation of Shaw "inasmuch as the evidence convinces this Court it would in no way affect segregation or desegregation within the Mobile School system and inasmuch as any further delay would only serve the office of increasing the costs of those buildings due to inflation." But he rejected everything else in the board's plan.[12] Subsequently, Hand ordered that a new plan be submitted by July 1, 1975.

The activist parents at Shaw seemed not to understand what the judge had said. John L. Devery, president of the Shaw PTA, wrote a letter to Superintendent Harold Collins with observations and suggestions about what could be done. Devery's primary recommendation was that Shaw be renovated and a new Toulminville high school be built on the present site, with "open enrollment" in either school for students from the two areas. He was not equivocal about the outcome: "Since we are in fact experimenting anyway, what possible harm is there in using John Shaw High School as an all white school and Toulminville High School as an all black school. This will be, in my opinion, the result of an 'Open Enrollment' policy in these two schools, especially if the New Toulminville High School is constructed as near to the exact plan of John Shaw High School as possible, no better no less."[13]

Devery submitted a three-page analysis to support his microlevel freedom-of-choice plan. Special circumstances warranted this solution, he argued. After listing several attributes, he concluded, "The Toulminville Community can therefore be considered unique in that the happy coincidence of the desire of the people and enabling Federal programs have created a healthy, stable, near perfect, self sufficient, black community." The unasked but implied question was why destroy that community? The same was true of Shaw:

It was equally good, and it had already been successfully desegregated, he argued. Again, why destroy it?

He listed the proponents of this solution: residents of the Toulminville and Shaw communities, the school board, and the federal district court. He listed the opponents too: the NAACP's New York office, Justice Department, HEW, and the Fifth U.S. Circuit Court of Appeals. It was the locals versus the feds.

Embedded in Devery's figures lay the decisive issue. Shaw then had eighteen hundred students, 31 percent of whom were black. Toulminville High had fourteen hundred black students and no whites.[14] If the students of the two areas were pooled, blacks would be 62 percent and whites only 38 percent; if racial balance came to the high schools in the Shaw-Toulminville area, *whites would be in the minority,* and the implicit assumption was that that would not work. He did not have to say why because everyone there knew the subtext, that white people would not willingly submit to a black majority. In the popular imagination of many whites the old stories still held sway—stories of blacks' innate and cultural inferiority and antiwhite hostility.

The Board Responds

On June 6, 1975, seven years after the federal courts first thwarted the school board's plans to build a new Toulminville high school, the school board, senior staff, and lawyer met to discuss the Toulminville situation yet again. Procedurally, they decided to ask the court to delay the deadline for the new facilities plan until late fall. Beyond that, they agreed that another biracial committee should be part of the planning process, as should some experts from the colleges and universities in Alabama. Substantively, the board recognized that the problem was twofold: The need to satisfy the community groups, particularly the Toulminville militants who wanted a school in their community, and the need to ensure that the schools were sufficiently desegregated to pass court scrutiny.

The board dealt with a perplexing ecology. As the board's lawyer summarized a week later, "It was further recognized that any solution which may involve pacifying the Toulminville community by keeping the school open as some sort of special school, if this could receive Court approval, must take into account the fact that the 1400 black regular high school students attending Toulminville must be assigned somewhere and that assigning them all to a new school (unless the new school is very large) will run the risk of creating simply another all black school, while assignment of them to nearby schools such as Vigor, Murphy, etc. runs the inevitable risk of tipping those schools over and causing them to become all black."[15]

The board and senior staff began to think more and more about a special magnet school program at Toulminville to get enough whites on campus to desegregate the school. More significantly, the staff began to work with the newly restructured biracial committee to move these ideas along.[16]

The committee began its study anew in October 1975. It wanted all sorts of information, but it signaled its mounting frustration when it told the superintendent that "the unanimous feeling of the committee is that its recommendations were not presented to the Court in a positive manner [in June]."[17] The committee's implicit belief was that the court had erred and that a more reasoned argument would persuade the judge.

On November 4, 1975, the committee made its report to the superintendent. Its recommendations were similar in many respects to those of the earlier committee, but in important ways they were different. The committee recommended *unanimously* that the district should build two new high schools, not just one, each with the capacity not to exceed fifteen hundred students. One was to be at the Wolf Ridge site, located about halfway between Shaw and Toulminville, and the other on the present Toulminville campus. Thus the committee challenged directly the logic of the NAACP and Justice Department; its solution would honor sentiments within the black community, and this in turn would minimize desegregation in the other schools in the area. The Wolf Ridge high school was to be "first class in every respect," and the new Toulminville high school "would be complete with all of the necessary mechanical and architectural features to insure educational excellence and an atmosphere acceptable to students of all races." Most important, the committee recommended (but not unanimously) "that this new facility be integrated to the best degree possible by student assignment." The committee felt that if a first-class facility were built, integration of the new Toulminville school was possible. The white population to be assigned was not specified, however.[18]

The committee, the board, the staff, and the NAACP's new local attorney, James U. Blacksher, a white civil rights lawyer, met at various times to try to iron out pupil assignment. Discussions dragged on through the winter, with some effort made to sell the ideas to the communities involved.[19] The committee briefed and sought feedback from various community delegations, including the American Federation of Teachers, Mobile County Education Association, Mobile County PTA Council, John LeFlore for the Nonpartisan Voters League, Robert Gilliard for the local branch of the NAACP, and the Chamber of Commerce. Each group expressed general support for the concepts involved, including the hope that the new Toulminville high school could be integrated through special curriculum offerings.[20]

The legendary civil rights leader John LeFlore died while the biracial committee was working on its recommendations. He was buried on February 2, 1976, from the Big Zion A.M.E. Church. LeFlore was described as "a loving and peaceful man but a LION in his fight for human rights and unbending in his belief that each and every man deserved a world in which justice prevailed." He worked tirelessly for racial equality, and his successes were almost too many to mention. Among them, he served as the executive director of the Mobile branch of the NAACP for thirty-eight years. His protests led to the desegregation of dining and Pullman car services on eight railroads. He had retired in 1966 after forty-five years with the postal service.[21]

The senior staff of the school system prepared a plan that fleshed out the biracial committee's ideas, and the school board accepted it. The plan called for three schools: The enhanced Shaw and two new schools, Wolf Ridge and Toulminville on its long-time campus. When renovation was finished, Shaw would serve thirteen hundred students from the western end of the present Shaw-Toulminville area. Wolf Ridge would have a student population of fifteen hundred students from the eastern part of the present Shaw zone and the western part of the present Toulminville zone. The new Toulminville school would have nine hundred to one thousand students drawn from the area right around the school, as well as five hundred to nine hundred students attracted to the school because of new, specialized alternative (magnet) programs. All three schools would have the curriculum of a comprehensive high school, but Toulminville would "provide a specialized instructional program of a highly advanced and/or technical nature for academically talented students in the metropolitan area." White students would have priority in assignment to the alternative magnet program. Moreover, the school system would provide transportation to and from any area, and students could opt to take the alternative program for one-half day and the traditional curriculum at their home school for a half-day, or they could do the whole day at Toulminville.[22]

The board submitted this plan to the court on February 28, 1976. In fact, the plan was remarkably similar to the one that the court had rejected a year earlier. The only real difference was the provision that the Toulminville school would be desegregated by adding an alternative program that, it was said, would draw enough whites to meet the minimum standards required by the court; otherwise, the new school would continue to serve the black population from the neighborhoods around it.

The Justice Department concluded that this provision for desegregation had little real chance of working, and it filed its objections with the court.[23] Moreover, the board's proposal to offer white students priority enrollment would constitute a denial of equal educational opportunities to black students. Thus, in the eyes of the Justice Department, if the plan worked, it would be racially discriminatory because it denied black students access; if it failed, it was racially discriminatory as well, because all-black schools were inherently unequal.

Throughout the summer and fall the attorneys for the Justice Department, school board, and NAACP met in conference and exchanged drafts of proposed consent decrees.[24] The board tried to maintain the position that it had staked out in the plan, although it had readily conceded that black students from the Toulminville area might apply for the alternative program; in the original plan only students from outside Toulminville could apply for admission to the alternative program at Toulminville. Still, the board continued to press for a selection process for the alternative program that would favor white students (and thus advance desegregation of the building). The Justice Department wanted the specialized programs offered at Toulminville to include both advanced academic and technical-vocational courses of study and a proviso that no other high schools in the county could duplicate these programs. The government also wanted only those students who were enrolled in the special program to be able to attend the regular academic program of the new Toulminville high school; that is, it would have no traditional students. Jim Blacksher, the NAACP attorney for the parent-plaintiffs, wanted to set aside one hundred to two hundred places in the alternative/specialized programs at the new Toulminville high school in a way that would give priority to black students outside the zone.

The clear irony here was that the magnet school was supposed to attract whites so that the whole campus would qualify as desegregated, but if the magnet program was so good, black children should be able to attend as well. But—and that was a big but—if the magnet and the campus as a whole were preponderantly black, would any white students show up?

The board and NAACP reached a compromise and joined in a consent decree that Judge Hand accepted on February 7, 1977; the Justice Department was not a party to the compromise agreement. The consent decree specified that eight to nine hundred places at the new school would be for students from the Toulminville area and that they could enroll in either the regular or alternative/specialized programs. White students from outside the zone would have priority for four to five hundred places in the alternative/specialized program, and black students from outside the zone would have priority for one hundred to two hundred places. At most, whites would make up about one-third of the population of the school, provided that the white population met the target envisioned. In its decree the court approved the con-

Over time, disputes and conversation continued, and both sides sought more and more data. The ecology of school construction and desegregation meant that one significant change affected others, not always in known ways. In July 1978 the court approved a negotiated consent decree that blessed the construction of Baker High School and reaffirmed the construction of the Toulminville high school but rescinded all other construction pending more extensive plans and the agreement of all parties to them. Construction of the Wolf Ridge high school was therefore on hold.

The school board directed Campbell to write to Judge Hand in September 1978 to complain: "The Bi-Racial Site Selection Committee and the outside experts recommended that the Wolf Ridge school be built simultaneously with the Toulminville school in order to insure maximum desegregation. If the Defendants are not allowed to move forward with the construction of Wolf Ridge Road school in conjunction with the building of the Toulminville school, the alternative magnet concept . . . stands little chance for success. In other words, *Defendants* [the school board] will be responsible for building an all new, all black school in the Toulminville area."[32]

The board sought permission to begin construction immediately on the Wolf Ridge school, but it was denied, stalling both school construction and zone assignment plans.

Controversy at Blount

More and more attention centered on Blount High School. Blount was a traditional black high school with a statewide reputation for athletic superiority. It had not been effectively desegregated; whites assigned there by the 1971 consent decree had not stayed. The building itself was in poor shape, and the campus was too small to house new construction. Nonetheless, the community strongly supported refurbishing the old facility or building a new school at the same site. The Justice Department wanted to close Blount and build a new Eight Mile school north of the Blount zone that could also accommodate whites from suburban Citronelle. The central office staff and school board were ambivalent, but they worked to put together a school construction program that was palatable to the other parties and the court.

As time passed, the Blount community grew increasingly restive. Blount residents saw that Toulminville's citizens had succeeded in getting a new school in their neighborhood and that they had succeeded through unremitting pressure. Now, the Blount residents felt, the same technique could work for them, and this time they had an advantage: African Americans had been elected to the school board for the first time in the twentieth century.

In November 1978 two black members of the board were elected from areas designed by court order to be majority-black electoral districts. Norman Cox, the retired air force officer, and Gilliard took their places at the board table. Their addition altered the interpersonal dynamics and staff planning. In particular, the staff now took pains to show that the Justice Department, not the school system, was pressing for Blount's closing. Cox wanted to leave Blount where it was and enhance it, and Gilliard wanted either to integrate it or, failing that, to close it outright.

By June 1979 a proposed settlement of the construction issues was circulating for board discussion. It was the product of staff projections and negotiations among the three parties, but the black members of the board were not pleased. The board formally considered the plan at a meeting in early August. The plan provided for a portion of the Shaw zone (Hillsdale and Mobile Terrace) to be assigned to the Baker High attendance zone; construction of a new Toulminville high, to be desegregated by a magnet program; reduction of the Blount High School zone commensurate with the size of its campus and buildings; construction of an addition to Shaw to accommodate three hundred Toulminville-area students; construction of a new high school at Eight Mile; and construction of a new Satsuma high school at a new location.

The board's vote on this plan split along racial lines, with Cox voting no and Gilliard abstaining. The reasons were clear. Cox wanted to support the black community at Blount. Under the proposal Blount parents would not get a new school in their community, but they would be saddled with the old facility and lose some students to the Eight Mile school. Gilliard, on the other hand, was caught between the assimilationist thrust of the NAACP and the intensely held views of many people in the black community. Whites would suffer some dislocation under the plan, but each of the white neighborhoods got something good—its schools were to be enhanced as well as desegregated.

The board's plan might indeed be the basis for a consent decree among the three parties. The effects of the plan were communicated through the NAACP attorney and board staff to Blount partisans, and they came in number to the August 22 meeting of the board.[33]

John Langham, the Reverend R. L. Dawson, and James Taldon spoke out. They argued that Blount's problems were of the board's making. Renovation of Blount was only fair, they argued forcefully. Paul Smith spoke for the Save Blount High School Committee. He petitioned that Blount be kept open permanently by not building Eight Mile and using that money to upgrade Blount instead.

A. J. Cooper spoke too. He was now the mayor of Prichard, which Blount served, and he was the local black lawyer who had represented the NAACP for tendance was Howard Feinstein, the Justice Department's negotiator. A discussion of the board's construction plans and the proposed consent decree was on the agenda. Alexander summarized the situation: attorneys Campbell, Feinstein, and Blacksher, each representing his own party to the dispute, had negotiated a compromise school construction agreement, which the board had approved in early August. Afterward, when the Blount partisans had protested the implicit closing of Blount, Blacksher had backpedaled, saying he could not sign the proposed consent decree at that time. A week earlier the board had asked the court to identify the plaintiff class because it needed to know which party it was negotiating with. If Blacksher had gone back on the handshake agreement this time, what was to prevent him from doing so on other occasions, after he consulted with local communities? The board had also decided to petition the court to dismiss the case. This action was sure to cause legal conflict that would impede the school construction program.[36]

Therefore, the purpose of this special meeting with the Justice Department was to redirect the board's lawyer if the board deemed that necessary. It might be advisable to suspend the motion to dismiss *Birdie Mae* until later, after the new schools had been built and had proved to foster desegregation, and to try to find a way to settle the construction issues now.

The latest draft of the proposed plan/consent decree did not specify that Blount would be reduced in size. Instead, it said: "No provisions of this Order shall be construed in any manner to negate the continued existence and viability of Blount High School as a grade 9 through 12 facility. Defendants shall take all necessary measures to ensure that the physical plant and facilities and the educational and extracurricular programs offered at Blount are on a par with other high schools in the school system."[37]

Feinstein said the Justice Department was satisfied with the proposed consent order and was ready to sign it. He agreed that if the NAACP challenged the agreement, the Justice Department would side with the school board. But the Justice Department would oppose the motion to dismiss the case if it were brought forward now. Once the schools were built and housed multiracial populations, the board could move for dismissal.

After discussion and disagreement Bosarge moved that the board withdraw its petition for dismissal and accept the consent decree. The motion passed over Drago's objection. Alexander thanked Feinstein, and for the record he reminded everyone that in the past the NAACP and school board had negotiated some agreements, only to have the Justice Department object at the last moment. Today, he said, it was clear to the Justice Department that the board wanted to faithfully comply with the 1971 decree.[38]

Discussion

In 1968 the federal court had been unwilling to let the school board build a new school in the predominantly black Toulminville area because it would "lock in" racial segregation, yet a decade later the court approved a new school at Toulminville and an enhanced building at Blount. What had happened?

The NAACP Legal Defense Fund and Justice Department lawyers all believed that the desegregation of the South could proceed most effectively if new schools were built on sites that were not identified with communities that had long histories of being home to one race. Their thrust was entirely assimilative; blacks and whites would have to go to school together if the second reconstruction of the South was to take hold. Old values and patterns of conduct were manifestly racist, and new schools were the best way to fashion a new nonracial culture.

Many leaders and ordinary citizens in the black communities rejected that logic. Their life stories often included those old schools, and they did not want those memories trashed. They did not want to sacrifice something important just so whites could be accommodated once again. Instead, they wanted more resources to be put into the traditional black schools and just enough whites made or encouraged to attend so that the schools could be called desegregated.

Whites were loath to attend "black" schools. Those assigned to Toulminville and Blount in the past had not stayed, which meant a new approach was necessary if desegregation was to work. That something was to build a new school to satisfy the black community and to develop a special school within a school to attract whites.

In the event, the creation of a magnet program at Toulminville worked to a degree. Enough whites from across the county attended the special program so that the overall school building could claim to be desegregated, although at nowhere near racial balance. And that solution meant much less racial interaction than would have been occasioned if the Wolf River school had been built and Toulminville closed. And Blount? It just limped along with almost no white students.

Black leaders, and especially the new black members of the school board, were caught in cross-pressures. Where once the federal government, both the courts and Justice Department, had been active in securing black civil rights, increasingly they were seen by black citizens as advocating the destruction of black community institutions. By the end of the 1970s many blacks, like many whites, waved the banner of community in the face of federal power.

What is crucial to note is the failure of the new members of the school board to find and agree on one story that explained why blacks were where they were. White radicals had claimed all along that busing hurt the black community. Now, when black parents rose up and attacked plans to close Blount and Toulminville, they were using the same story. Cox and Gilliard chafed at agreeing with hostile whites. The two black school board members could not seem to find a way to strengthen community schools without giving up on assimilation itself. This lapse gave Alexander time and space to play out his own interpretation: Blacks had been treated unfairly in the past, that was clear, but the only way for them to become competitive was to submit, as everyone must, to higher performance standards. This could happen in predominantly one-race schools; it did not require busing.

7. Blacks on the Board

SOMETIMES POLITICAL LEADERS act out underlying narratives rather than simply speak them. Nevertheless, a discerning observer can find beneath their actions a narrative that gives meaning and context to their otherwise bizarre behavior. The interactions of Mobile's school board members were revealing in just this way. Dan Alexander persistently offered a new story about inequality, one that on its face left out any racial animus. Alexander said he wanted quality education for every child, certified by high and consistent standards for teachers as well as for students. That move frustrated and scared many black leaders. Attempts to rebut Alexander's construct animated Mobile's politics for a long time. First, though, some background.

Vote Concentration

The movement for black equality was not only about quality schooling. It was also about getting and holding political power. To that end, in 1976 Lila G. Brown and others, representing the black voters of Mobile County, filed a lawsuit against election officials and the school board, *Brown v. Moore,* that alleged that the county's at-large method of electing board members impermissibly diluted their voting strength in violation of both the Fourteenth and Fifteenth Amendments to the U.S. Constitution and the Voting Rights Act of 1965.[1] In a bench trial U.S. District Judge Virgil Pittman agreed with Brown and the other plaintiffs and ordered that the county be divided into five single-member districts, two of which had to contain a majority-black population. The school board appealed *Brown v. Moore* to the Fifth U.S. Circuit Court of Appeals, but that court affirmed the lower court's ruling.

The U.S. Supreme Court decided not to hear *Brown v. Moore* on appeal by the school board; it was too similar to the *Bolden v. City of Mobile* case, which the Supreme Court did take up.[2] The board did not give up easily, though; it wanted its attorney to petition the Supreme Court to suspend the September 1978 primary and November general elections until it could appeal on other grounds. The board did not prevail. That November two black members of the board—Norman Cox and Robert Gilliard—were elected from areas designed to be majority-minority districts, and they took their places at the board table. Blacks had finally achieved positions of power, and the two men used their power fully.

In *Brown v. Moore* Pittman formed a temporary six-member school board made up of two newly elected black members and the four sitting board members. But Pittman feared that the board could be made ineffective if it split 3-3, so he ordered that either Alexander or Drago should become its *nonvoting* president until 1980 when their terms expired. This scheme was compromised early on when the newly constituted board divided 2-1-1-1 when it voted on committee chairmanships. The panel voted in scattershot. No member of the board could get the majority necessary to chair a board committee. In response to a letter from the school board, the judge ordered that "for this two-year period of time only, 1978–80, the chairman will have the right to vote only in the event of a tie vote, which would be the occasion of abstention, absence or any other reason." Pittman defined a tie: "A tie vote means a 2-2 or 2-2-1 vote. If three constitutes a quorum, it could be a 1-1 with an abstention or a 1-1-1 vote."[3] The federal district court was now micromanaging the school board.

Alexander became the nonvoting president of the board. He could control the agenda and rule on procedures, but he found that the two new members began to question even simple procedures for managing board affairs. Cox and Gilliard wanted everything done by the book. Norman Berger had frustrated Alexander from time to time, but Cox and Gilliard began nearly every encounter with Alexander from a position of deep suspicion. If Alexander wanted to move something up on the agenda, they said no. They voiced concern that they were not privy to some key discussions among other members and the senior staff and that certain papers were not sent to them on time.

More important, the two black members challenged Alexander's substantive policies. Gilliard placed a discussion of high school diplomas on the agenda in December 1978, right after he was elected to the board. He said he was especially concerned about the certificate of attendance in lieu of a diploma.[4] Gilliard wanted a new study and report done of that type of "diploma." Dr. Henry Pope, director of curriculum development, wondered what bothered Gilliard: The certificate-of-attendance was to be given to students who had been enrolled for twelve years, completed two semesters of twelfth grade, and had earned at least seventeen high school units but had not passed the high school competency test.

Gilliard retorted forcefully. He alleged that a racial motivation lay behind the test and its consequences; it was intended to discriminate against and discourage black children. The effect of this certificate was, he said, far reaching. Students who received the certificate rather than a regular diploma would not get into a trade school or a junior college without passing the general equivalency examination. Such a student could not get a good job unless industry was willing to do something special to remediate, which was too big a burden for business to take on. Some students could fail this competency test because indifferent teachers had failed to teach them the material. Or students may not have been able to learn under the circumstances in which they were educated. Some teachers, Gilliard said, could make A's on the teacher competency tests but were nonetheless unable to get a point across to students. For that reason the certificate of attendance was not a valid reflection of anything. It was unfair and implicitly racist. It was something that the school system had done to students and not something the students had done to themselves.

Gilliard's hypotheticals were based on the old metanarratives of white discrimination against blacks and the heavy burden that black children carried because of white neglect. The dentist made it plain that he had heard from many black parents, and many told stories of white teachers who did not teach black children all they needed to know. They said the certificate of attendance was institutionalizing second-class standing for black children. Jim Crow simply had a newer face.

Pope responded for the staff. He argued individual responsibility. Pope said that students did not have to accept the certificate. They could decide to stay in school to complete their requirements for graduation. The failure to complete graduation requirements, not the certificate, was what made students ineligible for trade schools and junior colleges. The certificate was simply a recognition that the student had spent twelve years in school. Gilliard responded that Pope was splitting hairs. It amounted to the same thing. Students were leaving school with nothing of value.

Dr. Abe Hammons, the new superintendent, tried to focus attention on the underlying issue: How does the system identify and then specify the level of proficiency of each student? Gilliard jumped on that. He stated that whether a student received a diploma or not, the system was based on a test devised

Alexander came in for strong criticism too. At the school board's next delegation meeting Shirley Banks appeared on behalf of the Mobile County Education Association to complain that no test could measure teacher competence and that Alexander was insulting teachers when he said that 20 percent could not pass the eleventh-grade student competency test. She said the board should find another way to evaluate teachers.[10]

Hammons, the superintendent, then directed the board's attention to the three high school diplomas that the system offered: honors, regular, and special education. The board had rescinded the certificate of attendance for those who had completed twelve years of school but did not qualify for one of the three remaining diplomas. The staff outlined a new proposal for these students: a conditional diploma for those who achieved below grade level. The conditional diploma could go to two types of student: those who stayed in school and earned twenty credits but failed the competency test, and those who earned fewer than twenty credits but passed the competency test. The latter could stay in school until the age of twenty-one to pursue a regular diploma, which meant twenty units and passing the competency test at grade level.

The proposal immediately focused board attention on the meaning of *grade level.* Norman Berger found that the staff had no single definition of *grade level.* Cox observed that students who were in the "alternate program," that is, those who were not taking courses at grade level, would not get a regular diploma even if they passed the minimum competency examination. He said that was unfair. If you could pass the test, you should get the regular diploma. Pope then explained that the minimum competency test was evaluated at the seventh- or eighth-grade level in math and reading.

Alexander was incredulous: The eleventh-grade competency test was evaluated at the eighth-grade level? Yes. The real difference in diplomas, then, was whether the student took regular or alternative courses. The staff tried to show that twenty units of regular work were somehow more advanced than twenty units of alternative work, but they had lost the board. Gilliard said that the people he talked to felt that requiring students to pass any competency test in the eighth or eleventh grade was unfair. He moved that the action on diplomas be postponed.

The discussion persisted around the theme of fairness. Alexander said diplomas should reflect the level of individual achievement; that was fair. But Bosarge broke ranks. He worried about the *honors* diploma. Some high schools did not have foreign-language teachers, so their students could not qualify for the honors designation. When the vote came, Bosarge and Berger joined Cox and Gilliard in voting to postpone action on diplomas.[11]

The board immediately took up teacher competency testing at Gilliard's request. Alexander reminded them that the board had unanimously approved the policy of teacher testing a year earlier. Gilliard said he was concerned about the whole idea of teacher testing. He wanted teachers to be evaluated in the usual way and left to teach children.

Drago disagreed strongly and at length. She had worked for forty years to upgrade teachers' certificates. She blamed colleges and universities for failing to educate and train teachers; they declared too many ready to teach when they were not. The supervisors' and principals' evaluations of the previous year had been ineffective at identifying deficient teachers, so testing was certainly appropriate.

Berger wanted to know about the specific testing instrument. He would vote for it only if teachers were tested in their areas of certification. Alexander pointed out that Berger had already voted to test teachers. Berger said the terminology he voted for said only that teachers "may" be tested, and at issue was which test. Alexander said the board had never suggested that it would give a poorly designed test. But the bad blood between Alexander and Berger was evident to all present.

Cox said no written test could determine whether a teacher was competent. It might flag an illiterate teacher, but it could not measure competence—the only measure that mattered was the classroom growth of children. Bosarge retorted that a test was essential; if teachers did not know their subjects, they could not teach.

Gilliard wanted to know what Alexander meant by "a simple competency test." Alexander said he did not know, but what he did know was that senior administrators had told him that 20 to 30 percent of the teachers in the system could not pass an eleventh-grade competency test.

Alexander cited the national pattern of testing teachers. For example, he said, 585 Dallas school system teachers took a standardized test and failed. Teachers in Mobile had failed to clean up their own ranks, but they screamed when the board tried. Alexander asserted that he had been misunderstood; he had not said that the board should give the eleventh-grade competency test to teachers. The National Teachers Exam would do. The school board had a duty to see that children had proper instructors.

Alexander continued. If Mobile's teachers would take the national test and 70 percent received a passing grade, he would resign. Berger interrupted and said that he resented Alexander's political grandstanding. Alexander retorted that his actions were not political; he was trying to do what most people wanted done. After all, he said, that was how the system worked; in order to get reelected a person had to do what the people wanted. He, Dan Alexander, crimination. Discrimination occurred when the system did not care enough to educate black children. Incompetent teachers hurt black children more than white because in the past white parents were better prepared education-ally and could help their children more when they had an incompetent teach-er. Black children with incompetent teachers could not get the same help from their parents.

Whiteurs said he was aware of the conditions, but he felt that hiring more teachers was more important than trying to weed out a few incompetent ones. Alexander replied by pointing out that if tests revealed only ten poor teach-ers, they still were affecting the lives of three hundred children.

Whiteurs said one did not need to test all teachers in order to weed out a few; the board could find other, more appropriate methods. Alexander re-minded Whiteurs that he did not want teacher testing to be a racial matter; he had proposed months earlier that any teacher eliminated by a test be re-placed by a teacher of the same race. He said he failed to see that this was racial discrimination.[17]

All this discussion took place during the delegation portion of the board's meeting, but it was not wasted because teacher competency was on the for-mal agenda. At the appointed time Hammons, the new superintendent, rec-ommended that he form a community-based committee to look at the whole issue of teacher evaluation. He wanted to develop a system of evaluation that included direct observation as well as any testing.

Hammons's recommendation precipitated more debate. Bosarge said all the talk about testing as racism was ill founded. What the board needed was a way to test teachers in their areas of responsibility. He supported Ham-mons's recommendation that a committee should use every avenue available to develop a system of teacher evaluation.

Gilliard said that he needed to set the record straight. He said he had a few bitter remarks to make, but he wanted people to know that he was not vin-dictive. He read from a prepared statement, but his statement was a story about incompetence and malice:

> A few days more than a year ago, this board, as then constituted, embarked upon a sea called competency testing. It first directed the staff to design a test for elev-enth and twelfth grade pupils of the 1978–79 school term. Reports coming from the schools indicate that those tests are riddled with errors and are a source of confusion to teacher and pupil alike. The then-board proceeded to authorize the staff to expend good taxpayers' money to pay someone, once found, to design a test to determine the competence of teachers. The question lay dor-mant during the spring and summer while attention was given to preventing the two new board members from gaining their positions through the elective

process. Immediately after the new members took their seats, there was a revitalization of the interest in the competence of teachers. Some members of the board proceeded to whip themselves into a fever over the issue and, in so doing, mesmerized some segments of the community into some sort of teacher competency cultism. The philosophy of the cult vacillated between a staff-designed test, a consultant-designed test, and the NTE. Now as it turns out, the consultant who has been paid good taxpayer money does not recommend his own work. The NTE testing service refuses to participate and the staff wisely did not attempt to perform the task. Now we are hearing the same designers of the comedy of errors come forward like great godfathers saying they have found a solution to their own errors by spending some more money. The fact of the matter is that the board is now in an untenable position as a result of those errors, and the only sensible solution is to abandon the whole idea of teacher testing and implement a concentrated system of evaluation.[18]

Alexander immediately said that he resented Gilliard's remarks about Alexander's trying to keep him off the board. He reminded Gilliard that the board had supported single-member districts, and he, Dan Alexander, had honestly said in court papers that blacks could not be elected in countywide elections even though that hurt the school board's case. In Alexander's opinion everyone had been treated fairly since he had been on the board.

When the motion to permit the superintendent to form a community-wide committee to investigate teacher evaluation was put to a vote, it carried. Cox alone chose to abstain rather than vote for the measure. The board, voting along racial lines, approved a subsequent motion by Bosarge to have the superintendent identify tests that could be used to measure teachers' competence.[19]

At the school board's meeting on February 21, a parent spoke about why he had pulled his children from the public schools. The Reverend John Hamilton said that sixteen families from his church had withdrawn their children from the schools in recent months because they were not being properly educated. He said Dan Alexander had suggested that the minister come to the board meeting to testify about his congregants' situation. Hamilton had gotten no satisfaction from the principal or staff when he had taken his complaints to them. Board discussion quickly moved beyond this one statement to the general issue of teacher competence as well as the competence of principals. Several board members, particularly Berger, were incensed when they found out that Hammons had appointed thirty-two people to the committee to develop a teacher evaluation system and all but four were professional educators within the system. Parents especially needed to be consulted, Berger said. They were the ones complaining.[20]

During the days and weeks that followed, Alexander kept up a steady stream of public comments. He spoke to the Sertoma Club, where he excitedly told the group that after he had received "a hundred examples" of teacher inadequacy, he had approached the staff at Barton Academy. "They weren't even surprised; I think that's what shocked me the most," Alexander said.[21] For her part, Drago prepared a long persuasive essay that she sent to all teachers. Drago, the veteran teacher and association leader, strongly supported both student and teacher testing. She argued that testing was one part of an effort to restore public confidence in the schools. "A written test is at the present time the most efficient and reliable means available to us for measuring and documenting knowledge and understanding," she wrote.[22]

The End of Teacher Testing

Hammons presented several recommendations about a teacher evaluation system to the board at a special meeting on March 7. When he finished, Gilliard moved that competency, literacy, or any similar type of tests be abandoned as part of the evaluation system. Alexander immediately asked Gilliard to take the chair so that he, Alexander, could offer an amendment. Gilliard refused to do so; he believed that this was a clever ploy by Alexander to get him, Gilliard, into a nonvoting position at a crucial time. Bosarge said he would offer Alexander's amendment for him.

Alexander said he wanted to offer a substitute motion, that the school system give a test to every professional, including teachers, principals, and other administrators. He said he would not identify the test for security reasons; the board did not want copies of the test circulated. The test was published by the Psychological Corporation and was designed to measure the level of educational achievement among adults. He said that the test did not produce a final grade. It would simply permit a comparison of professional people against national norms. Bosarge said he would make the motion to accept Alexander's statement.

Alexander gave his pitch once more. He did not know why competency tests for teachers caused so much controversy when competency tests for students had not. A competent teacher has a number of abilities. Knowledge—a reasonable mental ability—is one component, he argued. If a teacher were incompetent or inadequate, a test could show that the teacher was deficient in one of those components, say, mental ability.

The board's lawyer, Bob Campbell, took the members through the legal issues involved. Alabama law permitted the board to require proficiency tests of teachers. The issue had been litigated, and the Alabama Supreme Court had made it clear that school systems could administer such tests to their teachers. What was not clear was what use the school system could make of the results. Teachers could challenge the validity of the test. Under federal guidelines, if the results of a test disproportionately excluded one race from some benefit, and the test was not related to job performance, excluded teachers could sue.

Gilliard interrupted: What if the test showed blacks had lower scores than white teachers, and the district used the results to remove some teachers? Campbell explained that if the test was shown to exclude African Americans, its use would be questionable.

Alexander regained the initiative: The issue before the board was whether to give the test, not what was to be done with it. Alabama law was clear; the district could give the test, and employees who refused to take it could be fired for insubordination. Two weeks earlier, Alexander continued, the board had directed the superintendent to look into the issue of tests for teachers, and he wanted to know what Hammons had done.

Hammons said he and his deputy had researched the issue and now had their conclusion: "In assessing the overall effort of this endeavor, information received indicates it would be unwise to attempt to administer a test to in-service staff members. The general opinion indicates that comprehensive evaluation and an enrichment program which is presently in effect is the most appropriate way to address the teacher competency issue."[23]

Berger said he would not vote for a test he had not seen. Drago did not attend at the board meeting, but she had sent a letter expressing her point of view: Postpone action on teacher testing to see whether the newly developed evaluation system could identify weak teachers. Gilliard said that blaming teachers for the failure of some students to achieve was wrong. Societal factors were to blame. Bosarge said he had heard all the debate and had done his own research, now it was time to end the uproar and resolve the matter.

Alexander called for a vote on his substitute motion, to test all professionals; it failed—only Bosarge voted aye. When the board voted on Gilliard's main motion, to eliminate testing of teachers and other professionals, only Bosarge voted no. Gilliard, Cox, and Berger were in the majority. Berger had switched sides. By court order Alexander could not vote.[24]

Bosarge then said that he could not see how the board and the community could hold students accountable and require them to take a competency test developed by the same educators who now were saying they could not develop a competency test for teachers. The board could not then hold students accountable because they could be taught by incompetent teachers.

This provoked much posturing. Berger said he had worked for years to keep competent teachers and get rid of incompetent ones, but it was more complicated than Bosarge imagined. Gilliard said he did not favor incompetence, but the notion of teacher and student competency tests originated as a punitive measure, and that was why he opposed them. He opposed pupil testing in the eleventh and twelfth grades but favored it in the early grades. Bosarge then moved that the board eliminate competency testing in the eleventh and twelfth grades until the board could find out more definitively whether the test evaluated students effectively.

At Hammons's request Pope said that the issue of student testing had gained the attention of students and parents the first time. The results of the eleventh-grade competency test that year had been gratifying; fully 77 percent of this year's seniors had passed the eleventh-grade test. If students were to be held accountable, the board had to establish some objective checkpoint. It was unfortunate that in some cases teachers had not taught what they should have taught, but allowing a child to leave the system without the necessary skills to survive as an adult was almost criminal. Pope opposed the motion strongly.

Alexander would not let the moment pass. He asked Pope how the test results could be valid for students but not teachers.

Cox wanted to limit the motion to eliminating testing in the eleventh and twelfth grades, and Bosarge accepted the amendment. Alexander pointed out that if the motion passed, students who had failed the test that spring would then get a regular diploma. The vote was 2-2: Cox and Bosarge for and Berger and Gilliard against eliminating the test for eleventh- and twelfth-grade students. Alexander could have voted to break the tie, but he chose instead to abstain. He said he wanted the debate to continue at the next meeting.[25]

Student Testing Revisited

Student testing was on the agenda for the March 14 meeting. Alexander reprised the issue: Could students fairly be given competency tests when the competency testing of teachers was still in question?

Cox said he expected the test to be on the material taught. The test and the material taught did not mesh in Mobile, he pointed out—Mobile teachers taught modern math and Robert's English series, but students were tested for basics. Hammons reminded the board that when the test was first given the year before, 50 percent had failed; this year the failure rate was only 13 percent. He wanted the board and the community to recognize the effort and achievement that had taken place during the past year.

Gilliard said the question was, "Should students be tested when teachers were not?" He answered his own query, saying the two were not the same. Alexander explained that literacy is literacy regardless of whether a student, a teacher, a principal, or a lawyer was being tested. This prompted a now-familiar round of comments and digs about teacher competency.

Finally, Gilliard moved to accept the staff's recommendation that competency testing of students continue. Alexander offered a substitute motion that called for testing everyone, including students, teachers, and principals, or no one. No one voted to consider Alexander's substitute. On the main issue the board voted 4-0 to retain student competency testing. Berger and Bosarge had voted with Cox and Gilliard.[26]

They had cut Alexander down. Although he had spearheaded the competency issue, and it had carried the day, he was angry. Pittman's order had made him impotent. He decided to force the issue.

Power Play

An opportunity to compel action occurred at the April 11 meeting. Two members of the board claimed that they could not attend, Berger because he was ill and Gilliard because his wife had had some sort of accident. Cox was unaccountably absent, although some close observers said that he had come and gone because he did not want to create a quorum only to be outvoted. That left Alexander, Drago, and Bosarge alone at the board table. Alexander said that they had a long agenda and should not keep postponing various items. He ruled that the three of them constituted a quorum and said they would proceed, but he knew that he was testing the limits of Judge Pittman's order.

With ease Alexander, Drago, and Bosarge unanimously approved changing the prices charged for providing photocopies of personal records and printing briefs for the *Brown v. Moore* court case. Then they moved into deeper water. They turned to teacher evaluation, which was indeed on the agenda. They permitted the superintendent to present his report, but then the three unanimously modified his recommendations. They adopted a policy that called for using scores on the National Teachers Exam to establish norms that could be used to screen prospective teachers. They said that based on the teacher evaluation program for 1978–79, the superintendent should start remediation proceedings for the 160 teachers identified as needing enrichment and termination proceedings for seventeen teachers regarded as beyond remediation. And, most daringly, the three adopted a policy that said that all teachers in the system would take a national test before the end of the school year and that the board had not yet decided what could be done with the scores but that the scores should be grade-level normed.[27]

When the news got out, their action precipitated a huge reaction among teachers, staff, and board and also in the community at large. Everyone seemed to be screaming in pain or anger. Berger, Cox, and Gilliard joined together to force a special meeting of the board. The issue was simple: Who had political power?

At the special meeting on April 16 Campbell summarized the legal issue and Pittman's order. Based on his research, Campbell said, the nonvoting chair (Dan Alexander) could not use his presence to constitute a quorum, as he had done. Campbell advised that the board meeting of April 11 was not illegal per se, but the actions taken were without force, because the board did not have a quorum.[28]

Alexander defended himself. Pittman had wanted the board to be effective. The April 11 meeting was a regularly scheduled session, and the board had a long agenda to work through. Cox's last-minute failure to attend had made the board ineffective. He (Alexander) was an elected member as well as president, and, he continued, Pittman would not want to allow one of the two new members, who were on the board as a result of Pittman's ruling, to keep the president from ever having an opportunity to vote or take part. Alexander wanted Pittman to decide the issue.

Gilliard moved to set aside all the actions taken at the April 11 meeting. Alexander would not accept the motion, ruling it out of order. Because Gilliard's motion was not on the agenda, bringing it up out of order required the board's unanimous consent.

Alexander recognized Hiram Bosarge, who proceeded to read Title 16, on education, from the Code of Alabama, 1975. A filibuster had begun. He read page after page, with Berger, Cox, and Gilliard interrupting from time to time with points of order or parliamentary privilege. Alexander and Bosarge would not budge.

Alexander wanted his right to vote reestablished. He wanted the board to take the issue to Judge Pittman. Until the board did this, he made it plain, the stonewalling would continue. Bosarge read twenty pages of the Alabama Code during the two-hour standoff. Finally, Gilliard moved for and got adjournment.[29]

The next night it was more of the same. The board met before a packed audience and had to restrain residents at times. Gilliard and Alexander squared off once again; each restated his position: Alexander wanted the board to affirm his powers—to vote, to be part of the quorum, to participate— and the court to weigh in if need be; Gilliard wanted to overturn the actions of April 11, especially the teacher-testing policy, and he wanted to beat Dan Alexander.

Gilliard moved to reconsider actions taken on April 11. Alexander ruled the motion out of order; according to the rules, only those who had voted on the prevailing side could move for reconsideration. Gilliard moved to amend the agenda to specify "*consideration* of all items taken up on April 11." Alexander called for a vote: Bosarge voted no. Alexander said the motion failed to meet the criterion of unanimous consent necessary to amend the agenda.

This provoked a discussion of how that rule could be changed. Alexander made it clear that rules could not be changed easily. Back and forth, up and down. They continued to spar. Finally, they began to go through the printed agenda of that night's meeting, which was in fact the same as the agenda for the April 11 meeting. Hammons presented the first item again. Gilliard moved to adopt it. Alexander ruled Gilliard out of order. Alexander recognized Bosarge, who said he intended to read the Alabama Code into the record.

Before and during Bosarge's recitation, however, the board members discussed the effects of the stalemate on the system, teacher testing in general, and how they could end the stalemate. Bosarge read through page seventy-two of the code, and the board adjourned at 1:05 A.M., still deadlocked.[30]

Later that day U.S. District Judge Virgil Pittman, responding to the plaintiffs in *Brown v. Board,* issued a restraining order blocking the effect of all the school board had done at its April 11 meeting. According to Pittman, those actions were poisoned because the board did not have a valid quorum.[31] Once again the federal government had come to rescue or to thwart, depending on who was telling the story.

By April 25 the dust had settled. When the board met, Alexander was not present, deliberately, people thought. Gilliard assumed the chair, and Berger moved that item 24, the teacher evaluation program, be taken up first, out of order. Berger, Gilliard, and Hammons commented favorably on the thorough job done by the joint committee of staff and community in preparing the teacher evaluation plan.

Alexander arrived and took the chair. He commented on how totally he supported an evaluation program because he thought that instruction could only be improved in this way. He stated that he had received another note that was written by a teacher and contained numerous errors. The name did not appear on the list of teachers who needed enrichment or were being terminated. Gilliard retorted that the system was going to produce results faster than expected.

On a vote of 3-0-1 the board approved the new teacher evaluation system— Berger, Gilliard, and Bosarge voted yes, and Cox abstained. The board went through other items from the infamous April 11 meeting too and discussed them briefly. They reversed all the April 11 decisions. They had cut Sampson's hair.[32]

Education reform was on the governor's mind too. Fob James opened his legislative initiative in 1979 with a priority on education. He asked the legislature to fund 320 new kindergarten programs across Alabama where they did not then exist. He wanted funds to help local officials develop new programs to meet the special needs of school districts where students tested substantially below average on the newly mandated state proficiency exams.[33]

Discussion

During these crucial years the Mobile school board was divided by personality, to be sure—clashes occurred frequently in more or less noticeable ways between Berger and Alexander, Gilliard and Alexander, and Cox and Gilliard. Nevertheless, old metanarratives of racial difference conditioned interpretations of unfolding events.

Both new black board members, Norman Cox and Robert Gilliard, were well educated and had a lot of experience with whites, but when they took their seats, they brought with them a deep suspicion of white people in power. Their black neighbors told story after story that merely elaborated the whites' age-old use of politics, procedure, and law to cheat black people out of the good things in life. Testing for teacher competence looked like just another attempt to steal from blacks, and the two board members would have none of it.

Among many whites, the basic story was the inability of black people to achieve at a high level, because of their genes, family values, or lack of individual effort. What was to be done? Dan Alexander rejected white guilt and the paternalism of the old regime and substituted the values of the competitive market. He insisted on high academic standards, equal resources, and the responsibility of each person to work hard, be disciplined, and accept her just desserts.

Alexander was the pivotal figure. He was politically ambitious, street smart, and highly determined. He admired Huey Long and fashioned himself as another of the South's populist saviors. He did not use the language of racism. His use of the language of individual responsibility appealed to the religious fundamentalists who worried about the decline of moral values, to libertarian conservative ideologues who believed that government was inefficient if not altogether ineffective, and to hard-headed businesspeople who wanted to turn a profit in a competitive economic setting. White racists might read into Alexander's program white ascendency as much as many blacks did, but they too were handicapped in the political contest by the absence of racial language. Alexander talked about individual effort and about how the school's professional staff had let too many people down.

Alexander offended professional educators and sought to snatch power and privilege from them. They, along with black leaders, were his continuing antagonists. So when teachers, black leaders, and the press, both broadcast and print, demonized Alexander to a wider public, his personality, ambition, and political agenda polarized the county's attentive citizens. Stories about the meaning of board members' confrontations and Alexander's media antics became standard fare around family dinner tables, along with the chicken, potato salad, and beans.

Some constructed Dan Alexander as a madman, some a racist, some a savior, some a hard-headed politician. But Dan Alexander repeatedly told a story of educational failure and racial inequality, phrased in terms of personal inadequacy, and created a melodramatic atmosphere that made people take notice and respond. He told a better, more compelling, and more insistent story about these things than his opponents, and Alexander did it all before Ronald Reagan became president and made the Mobilian's claims legitimate in the eyes of the whole nation.

8. Grandstanding

As 1980 began, the Mobile County public school system had ninety-one schools and 60,931 students, 11,494 fewer than in 1970, whereas 11,314 students were enrolled in private schools. Moreover, even a cursory glance at enrollment figures showed another pattern of white flight, generally from heavily black city to suburban schools with fewer black students. For example, at Nan G. Davis Elementary School in the older suburban community of Theodore, 627 whites and 170 blacks attended in 1970–71; in 1978–79 the school had 914 white and 125 black students, or nearly 300 more whites and 45 fewer blacks. At suburban Grand Bay Elementary School during the same period the figures show that white enrollment increased from 650 to 926, while black enrollment increased from 154 to 168. Once predominantly white elementary schools in the city, like Old Shell Road and Mae Eanes, lost whites. Old Shell, for example, had only 68 whites in 1978–79, and Mae Eanes, which had 903 whites in 1970–71, enrolled 452 nine years later.[1]

Lawsuits lingered from the 1970s. In January 1980 Lottie F. James won a suit against the school board in U.S. District Court. The school board had denied James tenure in 1978 on the ground of professional incompetence. She was awarded $200, legal fees, and court costs, and the court ruled that the word *incompetence* was to be expunged from all records in the system pertaining to James and, by implication, to all teachers.[2] Soon after that the board dropped dismissal proceedings against seventeen teachers.[3] Three other teachers won a state court case against the school system, which was compelled to reinstate them as teachers and issue back pay. The three had refused to sign contracts for the 1978–79 school year because the contracts had provided for competency testing.[4]

* * *

By 1979 Dan Alexander was extremely frustrated. The school system's staff did not prepare the teacher-termination cases as quickly or as thoroughly as he expected. He was forbidden from naming publicly those he felt were incompetent because that would violate Alabama state law.[5] He still had no vote on the school board. Not surprisingly, he searched for a political future elsewhere.[6]

He came increasingly to believe that his future lay outside Mobile. In September 1979 he formed the Taxpayers' Education Lobby (TEL) with the goal of a statewide and then perhaps nationwide organization to challenge the stranglehold that teachers had on education policy. Individual taxpayers would contribute nominal dues to the organization, but collectively, Alexander explained, they would have great clout. Naturally, Alexander was its leader. One of his first acts was to condemn the Alabama Education Association (AEA) for permitting its members to chant in protest during Gov. Fob James's State of the State address. The teachers had shouted, "Education wants in!" while standing outside the legislative chamber when there were not enough seats for them inside. Alexander accused AEA of "yanking teachers from their classrooms for political power plays." He called for a "counter force" against the AEA, namely, his own lobby, "which is truly dedicated to a better quality of education rather than just more dollars for teachers."[7]

A small coterie of Alexander's conservative Mobile friends—the lawyer Jim Wood, the marketer Jean King, the pollster Jack Friend, and the Republican activist Grady Lloyd—helped him to put TEL together using $15,000 Alexander borrowed from a bank. They placed ads and used various lists to call people they thought might join, but after three months TEL had only 138 members. Alexander was disappointed and wanted to shut it down, but Lloyd told him not to do that. Instead, he would call Richard Viguerie in Washington, D.C., to see whether he might help. It took months for the connection to bear fruit, but an appointment was eventually set up for April 1980.[8]

When Alexander got to Viguerie's office, the two hit it off immediately and soon agreed that Alexander should take his organization to the national level. Viguerie introduced Alexander to people at the Heritage Foundation, a conservative think tank; to Howard Phillips of the Conservative Caucus; and to Paul Weyrich, godfather to many conservative intellectuals in national affairs. These were the same people who had helped Jerry Falwell to launch the Moral Majority just six months before. By July, Alexander had formed his new national organization. Save Our Schools (SOS) became a national player, one with local roots, in the conservative political movement.

The trips to Washington left Alexander's head swimming, but these political strategists clearly needed him to lead a national organization dedicated to changing America's public schools. Through his contacts he began to realize that the failure of public education had accelerated the moral decline of American society.[9]

Personal Issues and Public Spectacle

Early in 1980 Alexander let it be known that he had recently begun to carry a gun. He claimed that his life had been threatened because of his stand on teacher testing.[10] He spoke to local law enforcement officials, and they told him that "I would be wise to protect myself." Hiram Bosarge followed suit: "We've been getting threats on the telephone. They say they want me to vote a certain way." The two men believed that they should not have to pay for the guns for themselves because school board issues had brought the trouble, so they got John Sloke, director of security for the schools, to requisition personal firearms—a .22-caliber derringer for Alexander and .357 Magnum for Bosarge.[11]

The other board members asked the state attorney general to render an opinion about the board's liability should there be a mishap. When someone complained that teachers who were threatened had no school-supplied guns, Alexander half seriously replied that the board should also buy weapons for threatened teachers.[12] In March, Attorney General Charles Graddick announced that the school board could not properly buy weapons for its members.[13]

Alexander could not leave teacher testing alone. At a meeting of the Foley Rotary Club he read letters written by teachers with master's and bachelor's degrees who used incomplete sentences and frequently misspelled words. He wanted parents and taxpayers to become more active in education for the children's sake. He also announced that he would not run again for the school board. He said he could do more for education by energizing the Taxpayers' Education Lobby, which hoped to send representatives in favor of education reform to the state legislature.

Alexander said that the school board was in a unique and difficult position on teacher testing. He publicly complained that Norman Berger had failed to vote properly, because he had been elected by the whole county and a clear majority of its citizens favored teacher testing. Gilliard and Cox had voted against teacher testing too, but Alexander did not much criticize them because, he said, the two had been elected only from predominantly black districts and did not represent all the people.[14]

Alexander sought to shape the perceptions of others, and he was good at it. He told stories. He interpreted events. But his actions also prompted others to do the same thing. Board meetings became spectacle, and the board's conflicts became contests of stories.

On February 26, only hours after Alexander was hospitalized for gall bladder surgery, Robert Gilliard called a press conference to talk about school board issues, almost all of which were matters on which he and Alexander differed sharply. Acting as board president while Alexander was incapacitated, Gilliard first took issue with the statements that Alexander had made, that the two black members of the board did not represent all the county's citizens. Gilliard said, "Mr. Cox and I have never done anything to indicate we are only interested in the districts from which we were elected." Gilliard restated his opinion that testing was directed at black teachers.[15]

Gilliard's press conference irritated Berger. The next day, at the February 27, 1980, meeting of the board, he criticized Gilliard for allowing himself to appear as if he were speaking for the board. Berger said the board's policy permitted members to respond to reporters' questions so long as members made it clear that they spoke only for themselves. Gilliard, on the other hand, had called the press conference himself and had his own personal and political agenda.

Then the board took up teacher competency once again. Alexander had stimulated yet another discussion of testing when, some days before, he had advocated taking the issue directly to the people via referendum. At that time Berger had said he would bring a motion calling for the referendum. When he did so, at the February 27 meeting, the motion provoked more anger. Alexander was still recovering and therefore absent, so Ruth Drago took the lead. In Alexander's stead she accused Berger of bad faith. The resolution that Berger had brought to the board was a farce and a sham, Drago asserted. Berger had promised to amend Alexander's original idea to delete mention of a specific test and to recommend that the question of teacher testing go to referendum. Berger's motion called for a referendum to decide whether teachers, principals, and education specialists should be tested and did not mention a specific test. The balloting, though, was to be held at school buildings, which were not always the usual polling site, and would not be part of the regular election ballot in any case. By delaying board action, Berger had missed the opportunity to get the questions on the regular March 11 ballot, and Drago charged that he had done so deliberately to frustrate Alexander's intent. Berger, she said, was simply making a determined effort to keep the citizens of Mobile from expressing their forthright desire to test teachers.

Drago reminded board members (and the public) that they had been told repeatedly that a competency test used to fire teachers would not hold up in court. That was why the board had developed a formal evaluation process the year before to weed out inadequate teachers, only to discover recently that the process had not generated enough material in the files to terminate any-one. A literacy test could strengthen the board's position in those cases, Drago said. That's what they needed. In the five years that they had been talking about tests, five illiterate teachers would have damaged 750 children, Drago insisted. A literacy test would prevent that abuse. Berger was preventing the institution of a test by bringing proposals designed to distract and delay.

Berger responded that he had consulted a lawyer who had said that he would have trouble defending teacher testing. Because Berger could not ask the people of Mobile to vote on anything that had questionable legal stand-ing, he had brought his motion. Moreover, he was a layperson, and he had not known that time was a factor in getting something on the March 11 bal-lot until it was too late.

When the vote came, only Berger voted aye. Cox and Gilliard voted against the measure because they saw it as antiblack. Drago and Bosarge, proponents of testing and allies of Alexander, would not vote because Berger had stacked the deck against testing—a referendum held at schools on any day other than the regular election day would not attract ordinary voters; as a result special interests would carry the day and foreclose the issue.[16]

The in-fighting on the school board would continue. At a special meeting of the board on March 12, Alexander sought to impeach the validity of the parent-plaintiffs' standing in the *Birdie Mae Davis* case. He called for a vote on a motion "to instruct the law firm to file a motion challenging the lack of the plaintiff class or asking that the plaintiff class in the *Birdie Mae Davis* case, as represented by Mr. Blacksher, be identified." If the court ruled that the plaintiffs were not identifiable, Blacksher, the NAACP lawyer, would have no grounds to negotiate on their behalf. Indeed, if the plaintiffs were not repre-senting a certifiable "class," they could not sue on its behalf, and the suit would end.[17] Alexander also argued that because the goal of desegregation had been met, the lawsuit had become a burden to the people in the county.

Alexander wanted Gilliard to recuse himself because he represented the NAACP, which was behind the original parent-plaintiffs. Gilliard accused Alexander of representing the Taxpayers' Education Lobby. Polite words did not mask the hard feelings. On the motion to challenge the standing of the parent-plaintiffs, Bosarge, Drago, and Berger voted aye, and Cox and Gilliard voted no. It was another vote along racial lines.[18]

On March 14 Alexander sent a letter to the Alabama Ethics Commission, asking for an advisory opinion on the propriety of Gilliard's dual roles as both school commissioner and president of the local chapter of the NAACP.[19]

Alexander's action was prompted by Gilliard's vote against seeking the identity of the plaintiffs in the *Birdie Mae Davis* case.

Alexander later acknowledged that his letter to the ethics commission was a carefully timed ploy to keep Gilliard from voting on important aspects of the *Birdie Mae Davis* case. Originally, the motion to seek the identities of the plaintiffs had passed 3-2, but two days later Berger decided to call for reconsideration.[20] Berger's more tempered solution was to talk about the desegregation case with Judge Brevard Hand, in the belief that dialogue among the major political players would preserve the school system's gains.[21] Alexander, well aware that Berger's change of heart also meant a new decision on the legal challenge to the plaintiffs' standing, released a copy of his letter to the state ethics committee. This maneuver allowed Alexander to refuse to accept motions regarding the court case until the state ethics committee wrote an opinion on the Gilliard matter. Alexander's hope was that if Gilliard could not participate in the *Birdie Mae Davis* case, as president of the board Alexander would be able to vote to break a 2-2 tie on the issue.[22]

Gilliard fired back that Alexander was launching a "personal attack" on him and contended that he could represent both the schoolchildren of Mobile and the NAACP in school board meetings. During another heated school board meeting Gilliard accused Alexander of denying him his constitutional rights.[23] For Gilliard the overarching goal of the *Birdie Mae Davis* suit was "total desegregation," a valid and important goal that he would not abandon.[24] Gilliard received support from the Interdenominational Ministerial Alliance, which wrote a letter of its own to the ethics commission. The alliance claimed that Gilliard had "shown no bias when called upon to make decisions" as a school commissioner and was thus the victim of an "unwarranted verbal and written attack."[25] The ministers accused Alexander of "doing his level best to pull down as many people as he can into a cesspool of racism and demagoguery."[26] In another attempt to turn the tables on Gilliard's attacker, Julius E. Williams, president of the alliance, inquired whether Alexander was violating the ethics law by representing the Taxpayers' Education Lobby and the State Podiatry Association.[27]

Alexander responded with stories of bureaucratic inertia, noting that the *Birdie Mae Davis* case simply delayed needed school construction.[28] The court had to approve all county school construction, a point not lost on black or white parents who wanted immediate rehabilitation of dilapidated classrooms. In Mount Vernon town officials and parents boycotted school to protest the lack of adequate facilities.[29] An editorial in the *Mobile Register* expressed frustration over the *Birdie Mae Davis* case and added that "each time the board decides to replace a broken window pane, court approval must be sought."[30]

Alexander finally took his case directly to the public with an April 6, 1980, letter to the editor of the *Press*. In it he argued that Gilliard truly had a conflict of interest. More important, Alexander said, "I am deeply distressed that a recent letter to the editor inferred that I was racially biased. . . . It is a sad commentary on our times that any time a white elected official takes issue with the black leadership, the cry of 'racism' and 'bigotry' arises from certain segments of our citizenry. The truth is that most of the time these are legitimate issues being raised—and instead of proper responses, the public sees nothing but a smokescreen."[31]

The Alabama Ethics Commission ruled in late April. The commission found that Gilliard did not violate the ethics law by voting against the motion requiring the parent-plaintiffs to specify the categories of people they purported to represent in the *Birdie Mae Davis* suit. Similarly, the commission found that Alexander could remain as a lobbyist for the Taxpayers' Education Lobby but would have to comply with ethics laws pertaining to lobbyists. The favorable rulings for both school board members did not remove the hard feelings between them. Gilliard stated: "I must conclude that his actions in this instance give further proof that he has a deep-seated racist attitude."[32]

As for the case itself, Judge Brevard Hand called for certification of the identity of the plaintiff class, required the plaintiffs to show cause why the case should not be dismissed, and later allowed intervenors to play the role of plaintiffs.[33] Perhaps more important, he scolded the Mobile school board for neglecting the interest of the children in favor of "political gain" and "personal advantage."[34] The Mobile public also seemed weary of school board bickering. An editorial in the *Mobile Press* and *Register* declared that "we hope that students will not use the commissioners as examples" and ominously admonished that "none will be held blameless" in the fall elections.[35]

As was often the case with desegregation lawsuits, another year would pass before progress was made. Robert Campbell, the school board's attorney, had long held that the school board had worked in good faith to discourage segregation and eliminate racially identifiable schools. Campbell also expressed apprehension about additional white flight that would be spurred by another desegregation decision affecting the county. In November 1981 representatives of the black plaintiffs finally agreed to compromise and approved an interim consent decree. The decree called for the establishment of a professional observation team (appointed by all the parties to the suit) to examine Mobile's educational programs and then report findings on racial equity. If both sides could not reach agreement after the team presented its findings, the court would take up the case once more.[36]

City of Mobile v. Bolden

On April 22, 1980, a sharply divided U.S. Supreme Court announced that it had reached a conclusion in the case of *City of Mobile v. Bolden,* one of the most significant and controversial vote dilution cases of the latter half of the twentieth century. The *Bolden* decision meant that black voters challenging the at-large election of Mobile's city commissioners would have to prove that voting districts and methods had been fashioned with *racially discriminatory intent,* regardless of the actual outcomes of the at-large elections. Because the plaintiffs had not proved during the original trial that this had happened, the Court ruled that Mobile's at-large method of electing commissioners did *not* violate the constitutional rights of black voters.[37]

The history of the *Bolden* case was an interesting one. In 1976 U.S. District Judge Virgil Pittman had ruled that Mobile's sixty-eight-year-old city commission form of government unconstitutionally diluted the voting strength of African American residents.[38] Pittman had therefore mandated a remedy: a mayor elected at-large along with nine council members from designated single-member districts.[39] The Fifth U.S. Circuit Court of Appeals upheld the decision in 1978. Later in 1978, in *Brown v. Moore,* Pittman had determined that the at-large method of electing school commissioners was also unconstitutional and ordered that Alexander be made a nonvoting president of the board to make room for two new commissioners elected from single-member, majority-black districts.[40]

The local reaction to the Supreme Court's *Bolden* decision was predictable, because it preserved traditional white ascendency. Most city officials rejoiced, Mobile's three white commissioners expressed relief, and a few city employees suggested a city holiday.[41] In responding to the decision, city officials framed the ruling in terms of the "public good." Public Safety Commissioner Robert B. Doyle Jr. crowed, "I'm tickled to death with it, and I feel the whole United States is going to benefit from it."[42] Public Works Commissioner Lambert C. Mims added, "I think the people have won a victory. I think the local government should be in the hands of the local community. I think it's been a victory for the entire country, for all people from coast to coast."[43] An editorial in the *Mobile Press* and *Register* opined that by not allowing Mobile to become "Pittmanville," the Supreme Court "struck a major blow for citizens in local governments to continue deciding which form of government they prefer."[44]

The civil rights community, by contrast, was dismayed. Blacksher referred to the Supreme Court decision as "the biggest step backwards in Civil Rights to come from the Nixon Court."[45] In July the Justice Department agreed with civil rights proponents, claiming that the city commission electoral arrangement discriminated against blacks, even under the Supreme Court's new standard of proof.[46] The Justice Department joined in the suit against the school board, again citing unfair electoral arrangements.[47]

Unfortunately for both sides, the Supreme Court's decision did not address all relevant issues at hand. Mobile had postponed its municipal elections for three years because of its pending case.[48] Many officials were therefore unsure when the next municipal elections should take place. Moreover, in the companion case involving the Mobile school board (*Brown v. Moore*) the Supreme Court had vacated a lower-court order against at-large voting and had remanded it to the appellate court in light of the *Bolden* decision.[49] As a result the Court had not addressed the validity of Mobile's recent school board elections. Squarely in the middle of the dispute were Cox and Gilliard, both of whom had been elected under the now-vacated lower court order to change to district elections.[50]

Board Conflict

Although the vote dilution case involving the city commission appeared to be settled, the school board vote dilution case was very much up in the air.[51] Many felt that *Brown v. Moore* should be decided in exactly the same manner as *Bolden*. Alexander, who was attending a San Francisco convention when the *Bolden* ruling was handed down, argued that because of the Court's refusal to strike down at-large elections for the city commission, a real possibility was that at-large elections (instead of single-member districts) would be valid in school board settings as well. Alexander's new line of reasoning was that Gilliard and Cox, elected from single-member districts, were no longer valid members of the school board.[52]

Many observers attributed Alexander's arguments to his understandable resentment at being stripped of his voting power by Pittman after Cox and Gilliard became members of the board.[53] Black leaders called Alexander's comments irresponsible and noted that "they could easily serve to ignite a tense situation."[54] Black sentiment was that Alexander's only real concern was to establish an all-white school board.[55]

Hoping to get a speedy ruling from the courts, Alexander shifted from rhetoric to action. On May 7 he moved to strip the votes of the two black commissioners, arguing that "it is absolutely ludicrous to . . . let anyone vote whose vote might not count when the final cards are played."[56] Drago and Bosarge supported Alexander's motion, while Berger abstained. Gilliard and Cox left the board table outraged and called Alexander's action illegal. Both

Gilliard and Cox pledged to fight for their seats, ensuring that Mobile's school board would again be embroiled in controversy.

The board remained in a state of confusion for much of the summer. On July 25 Pittman again frustrated Alexander and his friends when he again denied Alexander voting privileges and ruled that Gilliard and Cox would continue to enjoy all the privileges of office.[57] Moreover, Pittman declared, the single-district election, not the at-large election desired by Drago, Bosarge, and Alexander, would proceed as scheduled in September.[58]

The political repercussions were clear. Because school board members' terms were staggered, and candidates had to live in the district from which they were seeking election, Alexander, a District 2 resident, would not be able to run for the board until 1982, the year that Pittman had set for the District 2 election in *Brown v. Moore*.[59] And although Alexander's ally, Drago, could still seek election in the upcoming District 5 election, Alexander himself would cease to be a school board member in November, unless a higher court stepped in to overrule Pittman's injunction.[60]

Not to be outdone by what he referred to as "the most inept federal judge," Alexander, backed by Drago and Bosarge, responded immediately, instructing the board's attorney to file a motion for reconsideration of the decision and a motion asking Pittman to disqualify himself from the case.[61] The board again dismissed the notion that its motives were racial. Bosarge contended that he had "nothing against blacks" but was upset that Pittman "took away my right to vote for whomever I wanted for President of the board."[62] Others also bemoaned what they viewed as a judicial usurpation of power. A *Mobile Register* editorial claimed that Pittman was again attempting to establish a role of "absolute dictator."[63] For more than a generation now the federal government had been portrayed as the oppressor of decent southern people.

As the summer of 1980 heated up, so did the rhetoric. Many African Americans were angry about Alexander's aggressive attempts to rid the board of Gilliard and Cox. At a late July school board meeting a citizen from a predominantly black area warned the commissioners to leave their representatives alone.[64] Policy makers also sounded off. Gilliard referred to Alexander as "the most impatient racist" he had ever known.[65] State Rep. James Buskey remarked that "the only difference in the philosophies of Dan Alexander and the Ku Klux Klan is the difference in what they believe in wearing in meetings."[66] Alexander fired back that "all they know to talk about is racism" and contended that the Black Legislative Caucus "figure[s] they've got a federal judge who'll give them anything they want."[67] The newspaper *Inner City News* condemned all whites, noting that those who remained silent during Alexander's "anti-black" campaign were as guilty as those who openly supported Alexander.[68] The black residents of Mobile were indignant that a city's white population would "spend long hours of work" to get rid of "the only blacks to ever serve on the Mobile County Board of School Commissioners."[69] Perhaps the greatest show of political solidarity occurred in late July when a mostly black crowd assembled to listen to members of the Congress of Community Organizations. In a tone reminiscent of an earlier civil rights era, Buskey warned that if justice was not served in the case, the matter of school commission elections might be taken to the streets.[70]

As the various factions battled rhetorically, the school board remained paralyzed, waiting anxiously for the Fifth U.S. Circuit Court of Appeals to rule on the validity of Pittman's latest decisions. In August several school board meetings were canceled; the superintendent assigned acting principals and assistant principals to fill vacancies in Mobile schools without the participation of the school board.[71] During the impasse Superintendent Abe Hammons struggled to expand the kindergarten program despite the policy paralysis. He proposed to increase kindergarten classes from twenty-five to thirty pupils but to give each teacher a classroom aide. His plan would allow two thousand more students to enroll than in 1979, but parents and teachers rejected it.[72] Alexander seemed quite willing to slight policy matters to force the judiciary's hand, noting that he did "not want another meeting to pass until my vote has been redeemed."[73] *Redeemed* was an unfortunate word choice: Black observers connected it to the Redemption, the period in the 1880s when whites reclaimed political power in their communities after Reconstruction and established hateful Jim Crow segregation.

In late August Pittman again rejected the school board's motion to reconsider his decision about at-large elections, which meant that the District 5 school board election would be held as scheduled.[74] Although Drago's opponents used the bickering on the school board as an election issue, she won the District 5 election.[75] Despite her victory she insisted that the appellate court should reverse Pittman's ruling and seat her as though she had been elected at large.[76] (This would also allow Alexander to remain on the board, instead of being forced to leave in November.)

In October, Pittman set a date—March 1, 1981—for a new trial in the *Brown v. Moore* case, which now was known as *Brown v. Board of School Commissioners,* but he did not restore Alexander's right to sit on the board.[77] A few days later the appellate court overruled Pittman's July order, declaring that Alexander could keep his seat on the board while the *Brown* case was being decided. Alexander was understandably ecstatic. At a press conference at the Mobile Municipal Airport, he expressed great excitement about the extension of his term and referred to the abuse of judicial power.[78] Asked whether he felt that an end was in sight for *Brown*, Alexander noted, "We will just have to wait for the next trial," a statement that was becoming an increasingly popular refrain for Mobile politicians.[79]

In November, Ronald Reagan was elected president. Both in his campaign and during his administration, Reagan attacked special privileges for blacks.[80] Many critics accused Reagan and the Republican Party of practicing the politics of racial division, dividing the Democratic Party from its traditional base among working-class whites through his attack on busing and other forms of affirmative action. Reagan successfully identified "big government" in Washington with the interests of racial minorities. In Mobile, Alexander and other conservative activists had already laid the groundwork for this theme. Clearly, the core of Reagan's coalition throughout the 1980s was working-class whites mobilized by his populist appeals, although his policies rarely benefited them directly.[81]

The cynical view of Reagan as the purveyor of racial sentiments for partisan gain persisted in many liberal and academic circles, but others argued that Reagan sincerely believed in color-blind justice and that federal affirmative action policy had strayed far from the original intent, to guarantee equal employment and educational opportunity.[82]

Alexander Moves On

The Taxpayers' Education Lobby celebrated its first birthday belatedly in January 1981, and Alexander was committed to seeing it flourish. Occasionally, his spontaneity and desire to promote his organization would raise critical scowls. In January, for example, he traveled to Louisiana to defend Richard Lee, a state judge. Lee had defied the orders of a federal judge by escorting three white girls to an all-white school in rural Buckeye instead of enrolling them in a predominantly black school as specified by the desegregation plan.[83] Alexander's defense of Lee prompted some critics to argue that he had "finally found a schoolhouse door to stand in," alluding to Alexander's stint as a campaign worker in the George Wallace machine.[84] Alexander drew parallels between himself and Lee, saying that "I, of all people, know how lonely it can be when you take a stand on some matters."[85] Whatever his motives, there did seem to be a publicity payoff—*Reader's Digest* quoted Alexander in its January 1981 article about local attempts to establish teacher competency testing.[86] Indeed, the idea of testing teachers was becoming a political "hot button" across the South.[87]

Despite Alexander's occasional lapses into racial rhetoric, the internal racial conflict on the board appeared to be decreasing in the early months of

1981. The tense moments that seemed to characterize the previous year were rare. At the very least, Mobile newspapers were not filled with ubiquitous personal attacks, and on some matters the school board members even managed to agree. They were able, for example, to defuse the potentially difficult issue of white/black faculty ratios by complying with the requirements of the U.S. Office of Civil Rights.[88] In addition, much of the focus on race was centered not on Mobile's schools but on the state's system of higher education. In January 1981 the U.S. Department of Education declared that Alabama had four months to end a "dual system" of higher education or face a cutoff of federal education funds.[89] In other words, the universities in the state had not done enough to advance integration and had thus remained virtually "one-race schools."[90] This issue occupied a prominent role on the state's education agenda throughout the year. Another reason for the Mobile board's reduced intramural conflict may have been the conflict emerging from outside. On February 14 William Hanebuth, director of the Mobile County Education Association (MCEA), chastised the board for its alarming rhetoric concerning state budget cuts in education. School board members, according to Hanebuth, had prematurely asked the courts to decide whether they could cut employee salaries in response to the budget cuts.[91] Instead of "ranting and raving," Hanebuth declared, the board should "calm down," take a good look at its own inefficient business operations, and stop living from crisis to crisis.[92] A week later the Alabama Supreme Court ruled from Hanebuth's perspective in deciding that the board had violated state law by failing to confer with the MCEA on education matters.[93] Alexander responded to MCEA by questioning the organization's claim to represent the majority of the local school system's employees.[94]

Brown v. Moore (Again)

The notion that the April 1981 trial in Brown might lack the confrontations of earlier rounds was dispelled on the first day. Alexander argued that his long-time nemesis, Pittman, the presiding judge, was incapable of being fair. Contending that the substance of Pittman's ruling was a foregone conclusion, Alexander extended his criticism not only to the plaintiff class but to the U.S. Justice Department and "the liberals in Congress" as well.[95] Alexander likewise questioned the court's timing in retrying Brown on school board elections before rehearing Bolden, the city commission case.

As the hearings began, both sides lined up a number of prospective witnesses. The plaintiffs in Brown tended to rely mostly on academic research. On the first day attorneys for Lila G. Brown and the Justice Department called three college professors to testify. Two history professors, Jerrell H. Shofner and Peyton J. McCrary, cited evidence that those who had fashioned Mobile's election process years before did in fact have an intent to discriminate and that one result was that it effectively prevented blacks from winning seats on the school board.[96] The social scientist Morgan Kousser testified the next day that at-large elections were at the heart of black educational inequality in Mobile. The sociologist Chandler Davidson's research of bloc voting patterns provided further evidence of whites' racial motivations.[97] Davidson claimed that white voters continually stereotyped black candidates.[98]

The school board countered Davidson's testimony by noting the success of black city council members Robert West and Bobby Emerson, both of whom had won at-large elections in small Mobile County municipalities. Davidson had testified that these elections were not significant and that they gave no indication of how Mobile voters would receive an African American candidate.[99] The school board also called witnesses of its own, most of whom were prominent politicians from the area. Former state legislators John M. Tyson Sr. and Mike Perloff contended that a qualified black candidate could beat a white opponent in a hypothetical election. Tyson suggested that racial tension was rare in Mobile, while Perloff identified a black former state representative—Cain Kennedy—as someone he thought would be elected to a judgeship the following year.[100] State legislators H. L. "Sonny" Callahan and Tommy Sandusky likewise testified against the professors' theories of racial polarization. Callahan and Sandusky argued that they were not opposed to single-member districts in principle, in that some years earlier they had supported a state measure that mandated single-member school board districts but that was later found to be unconstitutional.[101] Alexander followed up their testimonies with his own statement that the Mobile school board had in the past endorsed a single-member-district plan. Alexander argued that only the plaintiffs wanted this issue resolved by the courts, instead of settling it in the proper legislative channels.[102]

The dispute, then, centered on a simple question: How racist was the city of Mobile? The people who were following the courtroom spectacle had various opinions. The *Mobile Press* and *Register* adhered to a conservative line, stressing the financial burden of the proceedings. An April editorial referred to Pittman as a real-life "Six Million Dollar Man" and suggested that the legal costs of the proceedings were astronomical.[103] Another editorial pointed out that Kousser had received $35 per hour to testify for the plaintiffs.[104] Some editorials contained traces of anti-intellectualism. "We saw in Pittman's court last week a succession of what George Wallace used to describe as 'pointy-headed perfessers,'" one editorial announced, also claiming that the professors had burdened the court record "with a lot of yellowed newspaper clippings and much more unsubstantiated opinion."[105] Another rhetorical ploy by the editorial board involved questioning the knowledge of the professors and almost always enclosing the word *expert* in quotation marks in order to denigrate them.[106]

Black officials responded in various ways. State Sen. Michael A. Figures argued that the only black candidate acceptable to the dominant political elite would be a "white" black man. "They want somebody who's as close to white as he can be without being white. . . . They want a black candidate who thinks like them and that ain't fair."[107] Lashing out against a variety of officials, including Gov. Fob James and President Ronald Reagan, Figures suggested that the new racism was of a symbolic variety: "The view the press takes about racism is that it means 'I hate black folks.' . . . That's not what racism is. . . . When the political views you hold, the attitudes you have, impede the ability of black folks to progress, you're being insensitive to the traditional exclusion of black folks from the mainstream of American society. It has the effect of furthering racism. It doesn't mean you go to KKK rallies." Asked whether he thought Cain Kennedy would be elected to the bench during the next year's at-large elections, Figures said he thought that Kennedy would win but added that his election would not really counter the harsh reality, that African Americans in Mobile had limited political representation.[108]

It would take another year to settle the issues raised in the rehearings of both *Brown* and *Bolden*. In the meantime the board and city commissioners remained in office.

Competent Students, Incompetent Teachers?

Over the previous two years the news about student achievement had been relatively optimistic. In March 1980 the headline in the *Press* and *Register* blared "SCHOOL COMPETENCY SCORES 'FANTASTIC.'" Barton Academy administrators announced that 80 percent of the four thousand eighth graders had passed the reading competency test. Only 61 percent had passed the previous year—so the pass rate had increased by a whopping 19 percentage points. But still more striking were the mathematics results. Sixty-three percent passed the math portion, whereas only 35 percent had done so in the 1978–79 school year. Other grades recorded similar results. Ninety-two percent of the fifth grade passed the math test and 86 percent passed reading, whereas the year before only 68 percent passed math and 72 percent passed reading. The paper cited the highest- and lowest-scoring schools: Suburban Adams,

Azalea Road, Hillsdale, Scarborough, and Semmes had the highest pass rates, and inner-city Belsaw, Dunbar, and Mobile County Training scored lowest.[109]

The news remained upbeat in 1981. School officials reported that more students had passed the system's basic competency tests in 1980–81 than in the previous academic year.[110] Moreover, students' California Achievement Test (CAT) scores also increased.[111] For the first time since statewide testing had begun in 1966, Mobile County public school students had exceeded the national average.[112] Superintendent Hammons exclaimed, "We're excited about what's happened," and Governor James later remarked that the tests indicated "we are on the right track."[113]

Despite heightened student performance, many policy makers, especially Alexander, remained skeptical of the teachers' performance. In July 1981 the state announced the results of the first teacher certification tests, the tests given to those seeking to enter the profession. Although State Superintendent Wayne Teague expressed approval that 77 percent of the teacher candidates had passed the tests (a figure in line with that of other states) and praised the exam devised by the state, Alexander referred to the results as "concrete evidence" that many teachers could not pass an exam that tests for minimum abilities.[114] Sensing the opportunity to put teacher competency tests back on the agenda, he claimed that the results supported his earlier assertion that 25 percent of the state's teachers were incompetent. Moreover, Alexander argued, the Mobile system suffered in particular because it employed about eight hundred graduates of Alabama State University (ASU), a predominantly black university that had performed the poorest on the exam.[115] Indeed, only 14 percent of ASU students had passed the test. The two most successful schools, Birmingham Southern and Auburn University at Montgomery, saw 96 percent of their student teachers pass the tests.[116] Alexander vowed that the Taxpayers' Education Lobby would attend state legislative sessions until something was done about teacher incompetence, and he further suggested that the local school board would not be able to hear all the instances of teacher incompetence that should come before it.

The head of ASU's teacher education program, Dr. Gordon Bliss, claimed embarrassment over his school's scores, saying, "I thought my students would do much better than that."[117] The *Montgomery Advertiser* applauded his "no excuses" frankness and suggested that not relying on a "knee-jerk" reaction about cultural bias bode well for the school's future.[118] Alexander, however, in his normally aggressive fashion, argued that he *expected* African Americans to cry discrimination. Alexander thought it was time for black leaders to stop ranting about prejudice and address real problems.[119]

Alexander's attacks on ASU were relentless. On August 18 he declared that the state board of education should withdraw its approval of the teacher-training program at Alabama State University; then he extended this punishment to include any teacher-training program that saw 30 percent of its graduates fail the test.[120] In this sense Alexander hoped to avoid the charge of racism, given that both white and black schools would be affected by the new cutoff point.[121]

Opponents of teacher testing struck back. Paul Hubbert, executive secretary of the Alabama Educational Association, responded by calling Alexander a demagogue.[122] Levi Watkins, president of ASU, argued that "the tests showed very conclusively that blacks have not overcome the consequences of segregation" and that decades of underfunding could not be overcome overnight.[123]

In August the state board of education, meeting in Montgomery, effectively delayed a decision on a motion by board member John Tyson to adopt Alexander's suggestion to decertify teacher-training programs whose students failed to pass muster.[124] State board member Ron Creel felt that punishing these schools would be counterproductive, whereas the acting board chairman, Victor Poole, observed that the Mobile school board was the organization that had hired the inadequate teachers and principals to begin with.[125] Tyson's resolution later died on a tie vote.[126]

More good news for competency test opponents came in October. ASU students taking a second certification exam increased their pass rate from 14 percent to 35 percent. State schools superintendent Teague optimistically noted that although "ASU can't be pleased with the 35 percent passing rate, it can be pleased with the marked increase over the first series."[127]

Undeterred, Alexander again pushed for a referendum in Mobile. "All I'm asking is that the matter be put on a ballot," Alexander pleaded, "they can shut me up once and for all on the teacher-testing issue if the people decided teachers shouldn't be tested."[128] Alexander was so confident that residents backed teacher testing that he suggested that it be tied to the December referendum on a 5-mill property tax increase to finance schools. Alexander believed that people were more likely to vote for higher taxes if they knew they would be getting better teachers.[129] Opponents on the school board argued that until someone developed a competency test that could withstand the rigors of judicial interpretation, they would continue to vote against teacher-testing proposals.[130]

Opponents of teacher testing triumphed in December 1981, at least in the sense that Alexander's proposal did not make it on the ballot with the new tax. They also appeared to be prescient after three African American students asked the federal court in late December to prohibit the state board from administering the "homemade" test until it was found to be valid and fair for all groups. The plaintiffs complained that the tests penalized blacks because they had to acquire their education in racially segregated environments.[131]

As for the new tax itself, it failed miserably at the polls, despite the support of a majority of the school board and the *Mobile Press* and *Register*. The final count revealed a 3-1 edge for those who opposed the tax, a dangerous figure for a school board that was suffering through steep budget cuts.[132] Particularly disappointed with the outcome was Ruth Drago, the prime sponsor of the referendum on the additional tax. Alexander, by contrast, was indifferent; under his direction the next school board meeting did not even address the failed tax.[133] His overarching concern was teacher testing, yet another year had gone by and Mobile residents still could not vote on the issue. The more optimistic development for conservatives was that Alexander had drawn statewide attention to the issue. Gov. Fob James was now talking about teacher testing on a regular basis.[134]

In early 1982, while Mobile waited anxiously for the latest round of decisions in both *Bolden* and *Brown*, the school board became enmeshed in several issues. One involved the division of the Mobile public schools into two systems, one in the county and another for the city; implicitly, blacks would control one, whites the other.[135] The school board responded negatively to that idea.

Competency testing remained a heated issue, this time drawing sharper racial and cultural overtones than ever before. Black educators across the South took aim at the issue. Dr. Robert Clayton, director of marketing and planning at Talladega College, argued that the tests reflected the bias of American culture.[136] The rhetoric grew increasingly apocalyptic. Dr. Asa Hilliard, a professor at Georgia State University, claimed that standardized tests would "ultimately deprive black people of their opportunity for education," while Cordell Wynn, the president of Stillman College, argued that "the testing movement is a big game to put black colleges out of business."[137]

Alexander replied in similarly broad terms, tying poor teaching to the general decline of U.S. society: "First we have to discuss where we are in education and where we are product-wise. We're not giving as good an education to our youngsters as we did 10 years ago. Everywhere we look we see the decline of the quality of education. And it's not all the blame of the teachers. We live in a different society now. It's a more permissive and mobile society. And there are a lot more divorces and single parents now."

Despite their animosity toward teacher testing, many black leaders regarded it as an irreversible societal trend and therefore suggested that blacks receive better preparation for the exams.[138] The third round of testing seemed to confirm this philosophy, as the scores of black students showed improvement.[139]

The End of *Birdie Mae, Bolden,* and *Brown*?

Of the three lawsuits, the *Birdie Mae Davis* case appeared closest to resolution. In January 1982 the school board approved a plan for ending the litigation. Both sides agreed on the formation of a special citizens committee composed of ninety members from local parent advisory committees, twelve individuals appointed by the school board, and twelve individuals selected by the African American parents who had been the plaintiffs in the case. The committee was given wide latitude and considerable resources. Its purpose was to design a plan that created a unitary school system (not identifiably black or white). Although few rules were set beforehand, it was agreed that busing would be "employed only as a last result."[140] The U.S. District Court also chose two sociologists, Dr. Wilbur Brookover and Dr. James Mclean, to act as a "professional observation team" to oversee the progress of the committee.[141]

The state of the *Bolden* and *Brown* cases was considerably more confusing. It had been almost a year since anyone had examined the evidence in these cases. During the summer of 1981 Mobile had held elections under the existing rules (the three incumbent city commissioners were returned to office in at-large elections), and in a vote that split along racial lines the city's voters had defeated an effort to change the form of government.[142] Judge Pittman finally issued a decision on April 15 that reaffirmed his previous findings: Mobile's electoral arrangements for city and school commissions were originally established with the intent of discriminating against blacks and therefore had to be dismantled. According to Pittman, the black plaintiffs had indeed met their burden of proof: Mobile's at-large plan violated the Voting Rights Act of 1965 and the Fourteenth and Fifteenth Amendments to the Constitution.[143] This time around Pittman directed the state legislature (meaning the Mobile delegation) to develop constitutionally permissible electoral systems for Mobile's city commission and school board.[144]

Conservatives were outraged. At least in part they blamed a "liberal" Congress for passage of the Voting Rights Act of 1965 and the 1982 extension that set a "results standard" rather than an "intent standard" in determining discrimination.[145] Most of their venom, however, was directed at Pittman. In its strongest anti-Pittman editorial yet the editorial board of the *Mobile Press* and *Register* claimed that the judge was trying not only to supersede both Congress and the Supreme Court but was attempting to "thwart the will of a majority of the people of Mobile County by denying them their right to decide on forms of local government." "Pittman's inevitable strategy," the *Press* and *Register* claimed sarcastically, was the "appointment of himself as the non-elected, one-man legislative 'delegation' from Mobile County."[146] Alexander was characteristically aggressive. He chastised Pittman for the timing of the decision and labeled the judge a "gutless wonder." Alexander later referred to Pittman's decision "as the best argument I can think of for the election and recall of federal judges."[147]

The African American take on the case was different. State senator Figures sharply criticized the white leadership in the city: "These people are playing a very dangerous game and whether they know it or not, things are about to explode in their faces."[148] Carnell Davis's editorial in the *Inner City News* heralded Pittman as a "great judge" who would be "remembered by history."[149] For Davis and other black opinion makers, the central question of the case was a simple one: Should African Americans have a say in governing Mobile?[150]

Despite predictable reactions from both sides, it was not completely clear what the decision entailed. Pittman, for instance, had refrained from throwing out the present city commission.[151] To make matters more complex, there were differences between *Brown* and *Bolden*. In the city case the judge set a deadline of the summer of 1983 for the establishment of a constitutional government; in the school board case the judge mandated the installation of another electoral arrangement before the summer election.[152] Because Mobile's next city election was not until 1985, the ruling appeared to set up a special election two years before the regular election.[153]

One key question was whether Pittman's ruling was appealable. In the city's case Pittman indicated that because his ruling was not a final order, no one could appeal the case; moreover, he did not intend to make it a final order until the legislature had acted to change the form of government and establish single-member electoral districts. The judge also said that he would not cut short the terms of incumbent city commissioners.[154] That would mean that no new city election would take place before 1985. The black community was perplexed. According to this scenario, African Americans would be denied representation for three more years. Furthermore, because the ruling was not an order, no one could file appeal until September 1983.[155] Some black residents became concerned that white legislators might take a chance on the Supreme Court's reversing Pittman again instead of making a good faith attempt to restructure the government.[156]

One clear lesson emerged from the decision: It was not always easy to identify the winners and losers in Mobile politics. Interpretations controlled actions, and interpretations of events varied widely.

The late spring witnessed the reemergence of the teacher competency issue. (From 1980 to 1983, it is safe to say, the issue of teacher competency never died in Mobile—it only lay dormant at times during the heated decisions of *Brown* and *Bolden*.) Part of the reason for the renewed emphasis was the negative media attention that was focused on Alabama State University after the school's failure rate on the teacher-licensing test increased the fourth time the test was given. Statewide, 81 percent of the prospective teachers passed the text, but only 30 percent of ASU's teacher candidates did so, down from 48 percent the third time the test was given.[157] In May the Alabama Board of Education waived temporarily the requirement that teacher candidates pass competency tests. Teachers who did not pass the test but met all other requirements could be given a temporary certificate for one year, with the chance for renewal in subsequent years.[158] To support his reasoning state schools superintendent Wayne Teague cited some problems with the testing material and suggested that it needed refinement.

The state board's decision was more than enough for Alexander, who demanded that Teague be fired. "It's just ridiculous," Alexander asserted. "We spent four years trying to get this test passed. . . . We've spent $37,000 in taxpayers' money giving four tests. And the failure rate each time was more than 20 percent."[159] Norman Berger responded more temperately, suggesting that questionnaires be sent to parents to determine whether they thought all Mobile teachers should be tested.[160] The *Mobile Press* and *Register* pointed to discrepancies between the state board's decision and the local board's decision on teacher testing, commenting that "fortunately, our local board seems at last to be headed in the right direction."[161] A month later in a 3-2 vote, the school board decided it would not ask the state board to grant temporary teaching certificates to individuals who had not taken and passed the Alabama Initial Teacher Certification Test.[162] The vote split along racial lines, with Cox and Gilliard again the odd men out.

Bad teachers apparently did not affect students: reports about student achievement scores were again optimistic. Throughout the spring and summer headlines across the state exclaimed good news—"A HAPPIER REPORT ON TEST SCORES" and "TESTS GIVE EVIDENCE OF STUDENT PROGRESS".[163] Mobile was no exception to this general trend. The average CAT scores for county public schools improved or remained stable on several different levels.[164] On average Mobile students also performed better in reading and math than the year before. Even schools previously at the low end of the scale made progress.[165]

Perhaps the improved student performance limited the political appeal of Alexander's Taxpayers' Education Lobby in Mobile and elsewhere in the state. It was no doubt difficult to swallow narratives about incompetent teachers when students seemed to be performing so well. Outside Alabama, however, Alexander's new organization, Save Our Schools, or SOS, as it became known, was flourishing. By the end of the summer Alexander had set up shop in Washington, D.C., and had more than fifty thousand people listed as fighting for his cause.[166] Alexander's "reverse" strategy (from national to local organization) appeared to pay dividends in terms of money and national exposure.

Morality Politics

Alexander attributed the dramatic rise of SOS to his valuable Washington connections, especially Richard Viguerie, the GOP's brilliant direct-mail strategist and "New Right" politico.[167] It did not take long for Alexander to surround himself with an influential Republican network, including powerful senators and executives of political action committees. As president of SOS, Alexander was invited to attend a Reagan White House gathering promoting voluntary prayer in school.[168]

Predictably, Alexander began to expand his political base. Whereas he once gave speeches geared solely toward teacher certification, now he offered sermonettes: "The Golden Rules of the Classroom" and "Love of God, Neighborhood, and Country." In August 1982 he remarked that "people are going to have to get off their apathy and start pushing for these things because we have gotten away from the basic things we used to do—not just the three Rs, but basic traditional American values."[169] Alexander's diatribes against Mobile's teachers were evolving into broad-based assaults on a new secular permissiveness running rampant in American society.

With political notoriety and media attention came enemies, and Alexander had more than most. In 1982, while the school board president attacked teacher incompetence and secular humanism, everyone else waged war against him.[170] The National Education Association described Alexander's SOS efforts as "a scurrilous campaign of fear."[171] In May, Paul Hubbert responded to Alexander's attacks on the Alabama Education Association with a counterattack. Hubbert claimed that Alexander's involvement with both the Tax Assessor's Office (which had had Alexander on retainer since 1971) and the Mobile County school board constituted a conflict of interest.[172] In June, Gilliard filed a lawsuit against Alexander that sought $100,000 in damages for failing to recognize Gilliard's votes on matters involving the *Birdie Mae Davis* case.[173] More conflict ensued when a majority of the board voted to hire a lawyer to represent Alexander at taxpayers' expense but denied financial support to Gilliard in the suit.[174] The board's logic was that Gilliard had not entered the suit with the board's approval and therefore did not deserve the same courtesy.[175] For many blacks in Mobile the board's decision was just another step in a long line of racist acts.

By the end of the year the attacks had become increasingly personal. In an exclusive interview in the black newspaper *New Times* in August, Gilliard branded Alexander a segregationist and racist.[176] During a November board meeting Alexander called Cox a jackass, and Cox replied, "You're a jackass yourself."[177] Most Mobile residents wondered whether political discourse could sink any lower.

More Conflict Over *Birdie Mae Davis*

At the beginning of 1983 many people hoped that it would be the year of educational problem solving. The committees (the 114-member committee had formed a steering committee) discussing the *Birdie Mae Davis* case had now met for nine months, and some people were optimistic that the desegregation battle would not have to see the courtroom again. *New Times* had suggested in September 1982 that its readers should monitor the committee closely, because its plan "could have the greatest impact yet on school desegregation in this country."[178] Few, however, were closely watching the committee's work, which was carrying out most of its deliberations quietly. As an increasingly greater portion of the committee's plans came to light during the winter of 1983, volatile arguments about *Birdie Mae Davis* returned to the Port City.

Malcolm Howell, chairman of the fourteen-member steering committee, had long touted the moderation of the plan that his group was formulating. He said that its main focus was attendance zones, not a more aggressive idea that might "turn the school system topsy-turvy."[179] The committee was avoiding potentially contentious ideas, like massive countywide busing for racial balance, which might threaten the success of already desegregated schools. In general, the committee felt that each public school in Mobile should have a black-white *or* white-black ratio of 75-25.[180]

In imprecise, general terms the plan appeared to be a compromise. As the steering committee released the devilish details involving about thirty schools, however, many Mobile citizens prepared to resist. Opposition came from a variety of groups. Predominantly white parents from west Mobile expressed anger about a busing proposal that would transport their children from suburban Hillsdale Middle School to the city's Booker T. Washington Middle School, about six miles away.[181] In a highly visible antibusing demonstration about twenty-five parents from Carriage Hill rode a rented school bus to Toulminville to protest the time and distance involved (about eight miles). Others were peeved about the steering committee's use of a desegregation consultant who was not local, Dr. Willis Hawley, of Vanderbilt University's Peabody College for Teachers.[182]

Perhaps the most visible opposition to the plan, however, came from the African American community, which strongly protested the closing of black neighborhood schools. In particular, the proposal to shut down Prichard Middle School, and transfer its students to the Mobile County Training School, drew much attention. John Smith, the African American mayor of Prichard, claimed that he would not stand idly by while black children were bused into other areas for the sole purpose of establishing acceptable levels of race mixing.[183] Smith noted that "people need to stop trying to mix the community and focus on quality education. It's not so much who you are going to mix us with, but whether all schools have the necessary resources."[184] George Langham, a black member of the steering committee, similarly asserted he would be vehemently opposed to any proposal to close a school in a black community.[185] Langham added that establishing magnet schools in the black community to draw white students was an absurd idea.[186]

The opinions of Smith and Langham revealed the changing politics of desegregation. The black leadership in Mobile no longer advocated the "integration-at-all-costs" philosophy championed by the NAACP but instead questioned a desegregation policy that seemed to heap most of its costs on African Americans. Charles W. Porter of *Inner City News* wrote: "Questions which SHOULD be circulating in the black community are: At what point do we take a stand on letting our children bear the heavier burden of busing. After the long ride, . . . then what? . . . What will be the impact (academically, emotionally, culturally), etc. on our children?"[187] An earlier editorial in *Inner City News* asked a question that was brief and to the point: "Is desegregation worth it?"[188]

Blacks had abandoned the old story of integration. They did not need whites in order to learn effectively; the majority culture need not be imposed in order for black children to succeed. Black children needed resources and community-based schools.

The complaints by black leaders foreshadowed the problems that the steering committee would face when it revealed its plan to the citizens' committee in March 1983. Seventy-four percent (84 of 114) of the citizens' committee showed up and, after deliberating for several hours, fell short of the two-thirds majority they needed to pass the plan on to Judge Hand.[189] Bobby Shrum, who chaired the citizens' committee, was not surprised: "The closer we got to the end, the more I doubted we would agree on a plan. . . . I kept hearing them (committee members) say 'don't mess with my kids' and 'don't mess with my school.'"[190] After spending a year trying to agree on a solution to *Birdie Mae Davis,* the committee could not reach agreement.

More Board Squabbles

An article in the February 10, 1983, edition of *Mobile County News* exclaimed, "Dan Alexander is on the move," and went on to highlight the school board president's national activities.[191] Most observers agreed that Alexander was looking for bigger and better political offices. Bill Sellers, a reporter and columnist for the *Mobile Press* and *Register,* argued that Alexander was so adept at playing the role of the people's martyr that he might land in Congress. Sellers astutely noted, "George Wallace might still be a circuit judge in Barbour County had he not arranged to get himself held in contempt some 25 years ago by another federal judge who was considered unpopular."[192]

Many people thought that Alexander was using Wallace's tactic of whipping up public discontent for political gain. That story certainly helped to explain the incredibly rancorous proceedings that characterized school board meetings in the spring of 1983.

In March, Cox proposed that the board alter its policy on political activities so that school board employees could serve in the state legislature. Alexander in turn refused to allow a vote because, he said, it was not in the interests of the taxpayer. When Cox objected, Alexander warned that "if you don't like the way I'm running the meeting, go back down there to your judge and get me removed as chair."[193] Commissioners Cox, Bosarge, and Gilliard left the meeting in protest, leaving eleven items on the board's agenda unfinished.[194]

Political in-fighting was so endemic to the board that simple administrative matters turned into epic political struggles. Whether to reappoint Abe Hammons as superintendent was a case in point. The board failed to muster a quorum for at least two scheduled school board meetings. Some cited this failure as a calculated plot by the three board members who did not want to renew Hammons's contract (Cox, Gilliard, and Bosarge).[195] As a result his contract was in limbo during a crucial time for the administration of the school system. Judge Hand, sensing that the school board would never overcome its political differences long enough to make a reasonable decision, again intervened and barred the school board from firing Hammons before his contract expired on June 30.[196] Hand cited reasons of stability in his order and suggested that Hammons's departure would "simply cripple efforts" to end the *Birdie Mae Davis* case.[197]

Alexander, although a supporter of Hammons's, urged the board to appeal Hand's order and claimed that the school board, not a federal judge,
should choose the superintendent.[198] Apparently, members of the board
wanted decision-making power, even though their bickering effectively prevented them from ever exercising it. The irony was not lost on the editorial
board of the newspapers. The *Press/Register* cited the board's "disgraceful
spectacle" and "cat-and-mouse political maneuvering," actions that could
only lead to a further loss of confidence in the city's educational system.[199]
"It seems to us," the editorial continued, "that the board is unwilling or incapable of hiring or rehiring anyone—black, white, or anything else."[200]

The cat-and-mouse game continued. On June 30 Judge Hand suspended
his earlier order and gave the board fifteen days to decide whether it wanted
to renew Hammons's contract. The school board then voted 3-2 not to renew his contract but to retain his services through the middle of July.[201] To
the chagrin of board members Hand then reinstated Hammons as superintendent. Ironically, the federal court's micromanagement of the school board
was now offensive to black leaders. The second reconstruction of the South
had come to this.

Outraged board members who had voted against Hammons claimed their
reasons for doing so were legitimate. Cox argued that the superintendent
"hasn't been fair to minorities," while Bosarge cited severe budget problems
during Hammons's reign.[202] Allies of Hammons, most notably Norman Berger, defended the superintendent's record on minorities and said that the
budget problems were mostly the fault of the school board.[203] The majority
of the school board still insisted on appealing Hand's order to retain Hammons and, in a more aggressive move, ordered the superintendent to "vacate
the premises" of Barton Academy.[204]

Not to be outdone, Hand ordered commissioners Bosarge, Gilliard, and
Cox to appear in court to justify their demands that Hammons leave Barton
Academy. If they could not offer proper justification, the judge warned, he
would hold them in contempt.[205] Faced with the threat of steep fines, the
school board voted to rescind the order for Hammons to leave.[206] The board
then voted to hire Assistant Superintendent Larry Newton to replace Hammons, just in case the appellate court overturned Hand's order. In September the school board, citing "extra judicial discussions" between Hand and
Hammons, filed a complaint with the federal judicial review commission,
claiming that the judge had engaged in inappropriate behavior.[207] Hammons's attorney responded in October with a motion in federal court that
sharply criticized the board. Declaring that "my hired help ain't talking about
me like that," Alexander encouraged the other board members to file an offi-

cial letter of reprimand against Hammons.[208] At the end of 1983 the conflict had still not been resolved.

The Hammons case showed that in the hands of the Mobile school board, a seemingly perfunctory matter involving replacement of an official turned into a monthslong political ordeal, complete with judicial maneuvering and courtroom drama. Some observers described Hammons's ordeal as "essentially political."[209] An African American newspaper labeled the motivation for trying to retain Hammons as racist, because Gilliard and Cox had been at the forefront of trying to get Hammons removed.[210] Clearly, Mobile's major newspapers were fed up with the board's grandstanding. Whether the public would adopt the same perspective remained to be seen.

As the fall school board elections approached, several of Mobile's newspapers seemed intent on fostering an anti-incumbent mood.[211] Certainly, the school board was susceptible to a such criticism, as its political divisions had forced it to postpone or ignore a number of fairly important policy items.[212] Headlines about education issues had been negative throughout the summer. The *Mobile Press* headline over a story citing a consultant's findings said, "SCHOOLS MORE SEGREGATED NOW" than in 1973; a *Mobile Register* article indicated that a higher percentage of the county's public elementary students had failed in 1983 than in 1982.[213]

Unfortunately for voters who wanted to throw the rascals out, they could dispose of only one school board rascal—Norman Berger. The reasons were complex. In June the Eleventh U.S. Circuit Court of Appeals, created in 1980 when the Fifth Circuit was split in two, had upheld Pittman's ruling against at-large elections, and Pittman had later ruled that only two board seats from single-member districts would be up for grabs in the fall—those for District 1 and District 2.[214] The school board petitioned the Supreme Court to delay the election but lost.[215]

Although Berger decided to seek reelection to the seat for District 1, Alexander at the last minute chose not to seek office again in District 2. In typical Alexander fashion he blasted the judiciary at a press conference: "I cannot in good conscience seek office in an election which is taking place solely because of a federal court order."[216] Alexander also noted that he was eyeing higher political office, specifically Alabama's District 1 seat in the U.S. House of Representatives.[217]

Kenneth W. Canton, who made teacher competency testing one of his major campaign themes, soundly defeated Berger in the Democratic primary.[218] Canton in turn was defeated in the general election by Republican Howard "Chipper" Mathis III, who argued that "cleaning up the school board" would be one of his top priorities.[219] In District 2 Judy McCain edged out Bill Winters in the Democratic primary and defeated William E. Buckley in the general election. The new board consisted of Cox, Gilliard, Drago, McCain, and Mathis.[220] Both winning candidates (as well as all the other first-time candidates, for that matter) called for a unified school board "that directs its money and energy toward the school room rather than the courtroom."[221] A week after she assumed office, McCain was elected president of the board. She said that she hoped the board "will be more peaceful and tranquil than in the past."[222]

Alexander's Legacy

What would the school board be like now that it would not be dominated by Mobile's most colorful personality? Black leaders spoke of a peaceful new era. An editorial in *New Times* referred to Alexander as the black community's "arch antagonist" and noted that "the school system and the community will certainly be better off with the absence of his rambunctious, often racist, and usually self-promoting, self-serving, opportunistic behavior."[223] State representative Buskey said that Mobile County "deserves much more than what Commissioner Alexander gave to it."[224] Conservatives, by contrast, bemoaned the loss of an aggressive leader who would fight for the New Right's interests. One Mobilian resident declared "so long to a magnificent gladiator and knight. A heart-felt thanks is bid to Dan Alexander from those of us who know."[225]

Alexander said that his greatest accomplishments included requiring board approval of policies regarding student testing, promotion, multiple diplomas, and Mobile's reading program.[226] Alexander added that the reading plan had increased student test scores by two and sometimes three grade levels.[227] However, it was not clear whether Alexander and his conservative allies had won the big battles during the preceding four years. Certainly, his side had lost the judicial debate between at-large versus single-member districts. The 1983 elections were testament to that.

But there were other examples as well. In the twenty-one-year-old *Birdie Mae Davis* case, after the committee had failed to work out a solution during the summer, the district court considered the suit yet again in October 1983. The parent-plaintiffs still were hotly contesting the school board's most strident argument—that Mobile County already possessed a racially unitary system. As the year ended, the end of the *Birdie Mae Davis* case was nowhere in sight. Presiding Judge Hand remarked to the endless parade of expert witnesses for both sides: "It's been entertaining listening to academe who can't agree on anything."[228] Clearly, he would not be making a ruling anytime soon.

Finally, what could be said of Alexander's favorite issue, teacher testing? Local and state political opinion appeared to be in Alexander's corner. But again the courts would intervene. On August 10 U.S. District Judge Myron Thompson forbade the county school board from using the National Teacher Examination (NTE) in the selection, employment, and reemployment of teachers.[229] In addition, Thompson ordered that the board rehire all teachers whose contracts it had failed to renew because the teachers had not scored at least 500 on the test.[230] When the board attempted to get around the order by hiring the teachers as substitutes, Thompson threatened fines and imprisonment.[231] The school board relented. Even more bad news for testing advocates emerged in November—the Educational Testing Service decided to ban the use of the NTE for the purposes of weeding out incompetent teachers.

Discussion

Dan Alexander lost most of the battles he fought. U.S. District Judge Virgil Pittman overturned the at-large electoral system that Mobile County had used for decades and imposed a single-member-district scheme so that blacks would be guaranteed political representation. Pittman's decisions also rendered Alexander voteless on the board. When Alexander resisted and schemed to thwart Pittman's power, the judge promptly slapped him down again. Alexander and the board majority could not even fire a superintendent without Pittman's approval. Alexander and his allies tried to identify and remove incompetent teachers, and the courts prevented that. Nevertheless, these setbacks allowed Alexander to fashion a powerful narrative in the public mind: The heavy hand of the federal government was unjust.

Black board members and community leaders were deeply suspicious of Alexander and complained at every turn. Alexander and his backers used student and teacher testing against blacks, they said, and that was racist. The tests were biased, they argued. And they regarded anyone who frustrated black progress as a racist, not just Klan members.

Alexander was frustrated and he showed it. Board debate all too often became political spectacle. Increasingly, though, Alexander was moving away from leading the school board to working as a conservative advocate and lobbyist through his creation, the Taxpayers' Education Lobby, and later the Save Our Schools organization, which he had created under the tutelage of national New Right strategists like Richard Viguerie and Paul Weyrich.

What is crucial to note is this: Alexander lost political battles in Mobile, but he won the narrative contest. He shifted the ground of public debate among whites, and even among many blacks, away from dogged racist resistance and toward significant change. He embraced a new story of what it meant to be southern. The old story legitimized social and economic inequality through references to blood, family, and place. The new story celebrated individual achievement, not traditional social hierarchy, as the foundation of social justice. If the community held high standards for every child, it would raise the competence of a whole generation. Competition was good. Special treatment of blacks—whether of students, teachers, or traditionally black universities—was not desirable because special treatment led to incompetence and ultimately social decay.

Alexander was able to make this argument stick for two reasons. First, his metanarrative was America's foundational story, so it trumped all the others. If everyone got the same treatment by government, that was fair, but guaranteed results were not American and not fair. Also, Alexander did not make an easy target for black leaders because he avoided old-fashioned race baiting. He did not allude to the old metanarratives of genetic black inferiority. He rarely proposed, justified, or countered policies by using words that had been identified with the old racist hierarchy, nor did he cite paternalist arguments that had so often been used in the past to explain the black exception to universal norms. Instead, Alexander's words countered that notion by implicitly assuming that blacks could compete if they were held to the same standard as whites. Moreover, he did not use racist language publicly himself nor did he countenance it in others, even when provoked by black leaders' charges of racist intent.

The synergy between Dan Alexander, neoconservative activist, and Ronald Reagan, national conservative leader, was obvious. Reagan argued individual merit too. Indeed, the Reagan administration regularly attacked affirmative action in all its manifestations. The ascendency of Reagan nationally and the New Right locally depended on the energetic articulation of its ideas by men like Dan Alexander.

PART 3

Inequality and Cultural Change

9. Narrative Closure

LOOKING BACK at Mobile's history, it is clear that desegregation lost its hold on the public imagination in the mini crisis of 1982, when blacks and whites, city and suburbs struck a Faustian bargain. Judge Brevard Hand had ordered the formation of a citizens' committee to study the problem of continuing racial inequality in the schools, and it hired Dr. Willis Hawley, a nationally known desegregation expert from Vanderbilt University; Hawley pressed the committee to move toward integration. Hawley believed that the method preferable for achieving integration was countywide busing for racial balance, with a target of a student body that was 40 to 60 percent black in each school, because it was the best hope for extensively equalizing resources and social status. As Hawley's proposals circulated, black and white parents became agitated. Word spread quickly in both communities, from committee members to parents to grandparents to friends to neighbors. In the end, the steering committee rejected Hawley's ideas and sought merely to rezone some schools and to build others in order to create somewhat more integrated settings and, most important, to consider 20 percent of *either* race sufficient to call a school desegregated.

Even the modest proposals that the steering committee had developed were threatening to some people, and the full committee voted to reject them. People on both sides wanted to protect their children and community schools. Whites, especially, noted that the arguments were now the same across the racial divide. Blacks wanted resources, not the burden of busing.

Following that emotionally charged period, issues of school desegregation largely disappeared from public debate. The *Mobile Press* and *Mobile Register* began to reduce coverage of school and race-related issues. Alexander's leave-taking aided that editorial decision. And within a few years Ruth Drago, like Hiram Bosarge, would disappear from public view, replaced by other white board members who had less interest in direct confrontation with black board members and activists in their communities. Behind the scenes lawyers for the two sides, with the school board and senior staff in tow, began a long, intermittent, and largely secret process of negotiating solutions to lingering issues connected with *Birdie Mae Davis,* particularly the then-stalled school construction program. Progress, however, was slow and conflicted. James Blacksher, the white civil rights lawyer who represented the plaintiffs, lost standing within the black community when some there thought that he was too willing to surrender black-area schools for the sake of greater integration elsewhere.

* * *

Ronald Reagan knew that busing was highly unpopular, and he made it a part of his campaign strategy. The yellow school bus had come to symbolize the excessive social engineering that liberals (read Democrats) had embraced. In 1977 Reagan told the American Conservative Union that he wanted to "combine the two major segments of conservatism into one effective whole." That is to say, he wanted to unite social conservatives, who cared about things like busing, with economic conservatives, who wanted low taxes and open markets, in "a new and lasting majority."[1] The 1980 Republican platform condemned the use of "forced busing of school children to achieve arbitrary racial quotas."[2]

Reagan appointed Bradford Reynolds to head the Justice Department's Civil Rights Division and made him the point man for an attack on all affirmative action policies established by the Democrats and the courts. Reynolds argued that magnet schools were the most appropriate way to foster desegregation. Magnet schools, organized around special themes like science or the performing arts, would appeal to parents who would otherwise chafe at sending their child across town on a bus. By 1988 the United States had five thousand magnet schools, four times more than in 1980.[3]

Voluntary Approach to Desegregation in Mobile

In Mobile, Judge Brevard Hand pressed the parties to bring *Birdie Mae Davis* to a conclusion. Indeed, after a fairness hearing, on March 27, 1986, he found that the district had achieved unitary status in four areas: facilities, transportation, extracurricular activities, and faculty assignments, but he also found that the system was not fully unitary in two areas: assignment of principals and students. He ordered the board "to eliminate, to the extent practicable, any remaining vestiges and effects of the prior dual, segregated system of education," and his order prompted movement and another round of negotiations between the parties.

On November 22, 1988, the parent-plaintiffs and defendant school board filed a joint agreement for the court's approval; the whole scope of this agreement was to be a "voluntary approach to desegregation."[4] In it the plaintiffs insisted upon more resources—for both building and program upgrades—rather than more integration. In order to remove all vestiges of the old forbidden discriminatory system, the school board agreed to several points on which the parent-plaintiffs were adamant: (1) establish magnet schools in hard-to-desegregate areas, (2) renovate black-area schools, (3) develop and implement programs to strengthen instruction and improve educational outcomes for students, (4) assign teachers and other staff on a racially proportional basis in all schools, and (5) monitor the interschool transfer policy and effects so that it could not be used to undermine desegregation.

A central piece of the magnet school agreement was strengthening the program at LeFlore High School, the new facility built to assuage Toulminville residents. LeFlore's magnet-school-within-a-comprehensive-school was to be made into a full-day program with many more advanced placement and honors courses, some of which had to be unique in the system, and transportation was to be provided to students on the same basis as nonmagnet students (if any children from a neighborhood were bused, all would be bused to whatever school they attended). Six other magnet schools were planned so that all grade levels would be covered, and some of these schools would have academically advanced programs. The student body of each magnet school was to be racially balanced. The magnet school package allowed all parents limited choice in the schools that their children attended, and it pleased advocates of black-area schools to have greater resources poured into their neighborhoods.

The board agreed *not* to build the long-proposed high school at Eight Mile but instead to completely refurbish and landscape Blount.[5] Moreover, the board agreed to create an altogether new comprehensive curriculum for the school, with an appropriately new faculty to make it work. The board, the parent-plaintiffs, and the community all implicitly recognized that Blount would be overwhelmingly black, but everyone accepted that the added resources would please the community and support students, black or white, who chose the school.

In addition, the agreement stipulated that the school board would assign top priority to rehabilitating the physical plants of all facilities in the inner-city black neighborhoods to a standard at least as high as that of any other facility in the system. In an effort to show its continuing support after the first round of construction, the board further committed "that 60 percent of all renovations funds (but not less than $1.2 million per year) will be applied in schools with a majority black student body or in schools designated for magnet programs." The parent-plaintiffs wanted more money directed at black students in other areas too, particularly those who attended neighborhood schools in black communities; the decree specified that these schools would receive "priority for additional resources and programs designed to enhance their academic quality and effectiveness," and "first priority in securing and retaining talented, high-quality, effective professional educators."[6]

Just above the signatures of the attorneys on the consent decree came this pregnant sentence: "Four years after final approval of this agreement by the Court, if the agreement has been implemented in accordance with its terms, the undersigned parties shall jointly move for dismissal of this case."[7] Judge Hand approved the consent decree on January 13, 1989.

In 1982 the community had rejected busing for racial balance designed to equalize interracial contact. Now the parent-plaintiffs and the school board had chosen to use money and voluntary desegregation to remove the lingering effects of Jim Crow, and the court had agreed.

In 1990 Hazel Fournier was elected to the Mobile County Board of School Commissioners. She was the first black woman to serve in that capacity. She had been a teacher and had retired from the Mobile school system as assistant superintendent. Later she was joined by David Thomas, the other black representative on the board, who had replaced Joseph Mitchell when he became a state legislator. Fournier was a particularly knowledgeable and vigilant protector of black interests on the board. Nevertheless, she was elected its president with white support as the ultimately successful negotiations to end the *Birdie Mae Davis* case were under way. The *Mobile Register* intended no irony in endorsing her reelection bid in 1996: "As president of the board, Mrs. Fournier has shown that she is capable of building consensus on these and other difficult topics."[8] Older citizens of both races could not help but remark on the changes in the newspaper and the community during the past thirty years. It was as if a truce had been declared.

Fournier herself had doubts. The truce was little more than the reemergence of the old conservative mentality: maintain order and offer compromises but justify the hierarchy of social class. This time the conservatives justified the status hierarchy in terms of individual effort rather than biological necessity.

* * *

In 1993 and at other times Judge Hand inquired about the progress being made toward a consent decree. In 1996 he warned, "You're going to have to stand on your own two feet sooner or later, not on mine. They're getting old and I'm getting tired."[9] He was prompted by recent rulings of the U.S. Supreme Court, which "directed federal District Courts handling school desegregation suits such as this action not only to require school authorities to disestablish all vestiges of the prior dual system to the extent practicable (thus achieving 'unitary status') but also to restore full control over the operation of even formerly dual systems to local authorities as soon as possible, so long as the effects of the prior segregation have been ended insofar as practicable and so long as the school system has committed itself in good faith to the operation of the system free of racial discrimination."[10]

In 1996 the *Birdie Mae Davis* case appeared finally to be at an end. To mark the occasion Brett Blackledge began to work on a series of articles for the *Mobile Register* that assessed the results of thirty years of school desegregation. Blackledge's reports painted a picture of sharp contrasts between blacks and whites, between hopes and realities. He found, for instance, that while blacks made up nearly half the student population of Mobile, they occupied only 15 percent of the spots in intellectually gifted programs. On the other hand, they made up 74 percent of the enrollment in classes for children labeled moderately or mildly mentally retarded. Blacks also constituted 68 percent of those students who left high school without a diploma.[11]

Blackledge interviewed many current leaders for his report. Fournier reminded him that the Mobile board had used biological arguments about black inferiority in 1963, and she said, "That mentality to some extent still exists." On the other hand, Albert Lowery, the black principal of Shaw High School, noted that while relatively few black students were taking advanced placement courses at his school, all students had the opportunity to sign up for them. Most black students, he said, simply did not take up that challenge.

There, in adjoining paragraphs in Blackledge's report, the metanarratives clashed: Fournier made the claim of continuing white racism based on wrongly held notions of innate difference, while Lowery implied that inequality continued because blacks simply did not work hard enough. In the conflict among metanarratives, experience mattered. Blacks now had power and responsibility within the system, certainly far more than twenty years earlier, when Dan Alexander, Robert Gilliard, and Norman Cox had first clashed, and they were disciplined by their experience. Sallie Johnson, a black woman who directed the school system's special education program, agreed that far too many children were being classified as intellectually challenged, "but I really don't think there is racism in those figures, [instead] I honestly think it's an attempt by teachers to help students who need remediation through special education."[12]

The 1988 consent decree had created magnet schools in predominantly black inner-city areas in order to attract white students voluntarily. These special schools enrolled only about 6 percent of the county's students, but they were among the most integrated. The system created attractive programs and recruited extensively because the court decree said they had to be integrated or closed. Old Shell Elementary and Dunbar Middle became centers for the creative and performing arts; Chickasaw Elementary and Clark Middle offered a special science and math program; and Council Traditional and Phillips Academy offered academically advanced curricula.

White parents frequently complained that their children were put on waiting lists for the academic magnets when less-qualified black students were admitted. White parents also complained that their children sometimes were held on the waiting list until the school system found and enrolled a qualified black student in order to maintain the racial balance. For their part, some black parents said the academic magnets were a revolving door. Nearly one-third of Phillips Academy's 783 students failed a grade in 1997–98, and most of those who flunked out were black. Other black students had to be recruited in order "to keep up the numbers."[13]

LeFlore remained a problem. The magnet program there, a school-within-a-school first begun in 1981 and extended in 1989, enrolled five hundred black youngsters each year and produced as many graduates with advanced diplomas as all the other high schools combined, but only 17 percent of LeFlore's students were white.[14] LeFlore's special programs could not overcome white people's identification of the LeFlore campus as the symbolic core of the African American community.

What about racial balance? "The system's 85 campuses remain among the most segregated in the country," wrote Blackledge. "The system is the second most segregated in the country when compared to 44 others of similar size. Only the Fulton County, Ga., system outside Atlanta is more segregated," the *Register* reported.[15] Blackledge summed up his findings this way: "The fact remains that after three decades of court-ordered desegregation, the black educational experience in Mobile County doesn't measure up to the white experience."

Many black parents complained that the racial disparities proved that the system continued to treat black students differently from white students, but those parents seemed to be fewer and their feelings less intense than decades earlier. White officials argued that racism had nothing to do with different patterns of performance; instead, they said, the disparities were the result of social troubles that school could neither control nor resolve: "It's up to students and parents to take advantage of those opportunities."[16]

Narrative Shift

The real world affected the interpretations of the statistics that people offered. Clearly, disparities existed between black and white students' experiences and performance, and family economics may have been the reason for some of that difference, but some African Americans, including Hazel Fournier, still blamed whites for the continuing differences in student performance. She said the system had made the unfair assumption that black children could not learn. Continuing racist assumptions and conduct lay behind black failure, she implied, and that warranted continuing court intervention.[17]

Another black citizen, the Reverend Jesse McDaniel, a plaintiff in the *Birdie Mae Davis* case, said that desegregation was no longer the issue for the schools; instead, "we need to assure students that wherever they are, they will have equal treatment, and show them that their needs will be addressed—addressed as a person rather than as a race." He did not say, but one could hear the narrative of individual challenge and individual achievement shadowing his words.[18]

Dan Alexander had aggressively and persistently raised a counternarrative in Mobile—discipline, standards, and individual effort pay off—to challenge the story of persistent white discrimination as the primary explanation for the manifest differences in students' performance. And, despite his absence from the Mobile scene, the rhetoric of individual responsibility had ascended. Magnet schools for ambitious students of any race were a natural extension of Alexander's message.

What had become of Mobile's principal agitator and narrator? Alexander's Save Our Schools organization quickly became a national force as it pressed the conservative agenda in education. SOS had tens of thousands dues-paying members, and it published and distributed about 200,000 copies of *Who's Running Our Schools?*, a screed attacking the National Education Association, which SOS claimed was a sinister political force controlling education policy in Congress and the states.

Alexander built a direct-mail empire so that he could bring ideological counterforce to bear in school boardrooms and legislatures across the land, but that effort was stymied on December 11, 1986, when he was convicted in federal court of extorting kickbacks on school contracts from 1977 to 1984. He served four years in a federal prison. During those years his wife continued to build his mailing list, and in 1992 Alexander founded the Seniors Coalition as a counter to the American Association of Retired Persons (AARP), which he and other conservatives regarded as too liberal and too powerful on issues like Medicare. Although the Seniors Coalition had only one million members to the AARP's thirty-three million, the Seniors Coalition became a respected conservative lobby in Congress. Alexander's involvement in the new organization was problematic, though, and a new board of directors purged him, only to be deposed themselves when Alexander struck back. After that, given the tumult, Alexander's role became anomalous.[19]

"Racial discrimination has declined," wrote Clarence Page, whose syndicated column appeared in the *Mobile Register*. He asked, "Has the time come for us [blacks] to stop viewing ourselves as outsiders?" Many blacks, he countered, were pessimistic. Middle-class blacks, especially, had to deal with the sting of racism daily because they were swimming in the predominantly white mainstream. They had jobs in big law firms but were not senior partners. He quoted one young lawyer who was attending a 1996 regional meeting of the Urban League: "I seriously question your premise that racial discrimination has declined. . . . I don't think we've made progress. Discrimination has only become more subtle." Page cited a Yankelovich Partners survey of twelve hundred black American adults: More than half said things were getting worse, and about half believed that race relations will "never be better than they are." Nonetheless, Page quoted Jesse Jackson: "No one can save us, for us, but us." The survey data supported Page's assessment. Nearly half the national sample agreed that "the failure of blacks to take full advantage of the opportunities available to them constitutes a greater problem than discrimination by whites." Only a third disagreed with that assessment.[20] Page's point: Middle-class blacks must try harder to break through to the top despite subtle racism.

Birdie Mae Davis Ends

Civil Action No. 3003-63-H, better known as the *Birdie Mae Davis* case, came to an end on March 27, 1997, but not without some final spasms.

Features of the 1989 consent degree had been put into place later than planned because of cost overruns and construction delays, and the parent-plaintiffs were reluctant to join the school board in asking that the suit be formally ended until the board had delivered everything it had promised. In 1996 white members of the board finally had the political will to force the issue. Even then, members of the plaintiffs' group tried to thwart the move.

Judge Hand dismissed the case outright, but in an effort to shape the future, Robert Campbell, the lawyer who still represented the school board, and Greg Stein, appearing for the parent-plaintiffs, brought another, separate agreement that for three years the school board would continue to (1) operate magnet schools in an effort to racially balance predominantly black schools, (2) enforce school attendance zones, (3) commit equal educational opportunities and funding to all schools, (4) make sure each school had at least one black administrator, and (5) establish an advisory panel of plaintiffs' representatives who would keep tabs on the school system.[21] But even if the school board failed to comply with any of these points, no one could reopen *Birdie Mae Davis;* complainants would need to bring a new, separate action to seek relief.[22]

The Justice Department agreed to go along with ending the case but reiterated that the school board's good-faith efforts to end the vestiges of the dual school system were what closed the case.

Some plaintiffs complained that desegregation goals, like reaching racial balance at each school, had not been met and that Stein had not fairly represented the plaintiffs. Stein said he had found it impossible to gain a unanimous decision from the plaintiffs' group, and he was supported by the NAACP Legal Defense Fund's Norman Chachkin of New York.[23]

Debi Ogle, PTA president at Baker High School, believed that ending court intervention in the schools, through the *Birdie Mae Davis* case, would be desirable: "You know what? Our children segregate themselves anyway . . . whether it's according to the music they listen to or who they sit with at lunch. . . . I think we just need to treat everybody as equal and go on about the business of educating our children and teaching them to read."[24] Her voice echoed others' sentiments: Subcultural separation was acceptable because the kids themselves wanted it. Cultural assimilation was out, and the "garden salad" of America was in.

Hazel Fournier hoped that the end of *Birdie Mae Davis* would lead to greater financial support for the schools by taxpayers. "I think the building program brought us together," she said.[25] Mobile still had a huge need for more and better school buildings, yet every time board members sought to raise taxes for schools, all they heard about was the waste of money in the *Birdie Mae Davis* case.

But even after the thirty-four-year effort to desegregate the schools, Fournier could not let go of her suspicions. She believed that blacks could not trust the school system to treat black children fairly, and she lamented that the parent-plaintiffs no longer had an opportunity to prove that the legacy of Jim Crow segregation remained embedded in the obvious disparities between the races in the schools. She pointed to the distrust apparent in recent disruptions, including picketing of schools, boycotts by students, and the public protests of black ministers. Had Mobile not fought so hard against desegregation, blacks might have been able to trust, but they could not yet do so. Despite meeting the letter of the law, Fournier noted, the school system failed black children by its historical defiance and continuing indifference. As one sign of her suspicion of whites, she proposed that the school board require a supermajority of four of the five board members for all major decisions in the future.[26]

The supermajority idea for school board decision making had been floated for some time because most major decisions, including those leading to the end of *Birdie Mae Davis,* had come on votes of 3-2 along racial lines. Fournier claimed that the supermajority would be more inclusive and would go a long way toward forcing a spirit of compromise. As it was, she said, she and the other black board member were often "not heard" by white board members, who courted the votes of their black colleagues only in matters involving land sales, which required a four-member affirmative vote. White board members opposed the idea of a supermajority, and Judge Hand refused to make a change in voting rules a part of the *Birdie Mae Davis* settlement.

When the final agreement negotiated by Stein and Campbell came up for approval by the school board, it passed 3-2 along racial lines.[27] Later Campbell announced that no one had appealed by the May 9 deadline and that *Birdie Mae Davis* was finally over.[28] The case had consumed more than $800,000 in lawyers' fees.[29]

Reporter Brett Blackledge interviewed Ollie Mae McDuffie, the mother of Birdie Mae Davis, about the original grievance and the case. Back in March 1963, when black parents sued Mobile County's segregated school system seeking relief, she had articulated the goals simply and clearly: "So that my children and all other Negro children similarly situated will be able to obtain assignment to, and education in, the public schools of Mobile County without regard to race or color." For her part, in 1996 McDuffie said, "I feel like when they started this, that's what they wanted to do."

Blackledge concluded: "The goals of desegregation remain the same today, although the methods to accomplish them have changed. What was once a fight for integration has evolved into a battle for equity as black plaintiffs have shifted from improving the racial balance at schools to improving their own neighborhoods' schools. . . . The fight for desegregation in Mobile County is coming back to where it began in 1963: ensuring that schools serving black students are as good as those serving white students."[30]

Black leaders were in a fateful position—fighting for the proposition that separate neighborhood schools can be equal to white schools in the task of educating black youngsters in a competitive world. Beatrice Morse, an adviser to the court in the *Birdie Mae Davis* case, made plain her concerns: "I hope separate can one day be equal, because desegregation has never been equal."[31]

10. Redefining the Problem of Racial Inequality

THE UNITED STATES seems always to have had a "race problem," but the nature of the problem and its solution have changed over time. By looking in detail at Mobile, Alabama, I have argued in this book that the race problem has been periodically redefined.

A redefinition of a social problem occurs when elite rhetoric and public opinion shift markedly from one way of interpreting societal concern to another. Theoretically, the shift in the intensity, direction, and focus of rhetoric and opinion may be occasioned by critical events (human-caused events such as lawsuits, elections, or civil disturbances) or by natural catastrophes like hurricanes or epidemics, which occasion intense, frequent, and focused interpersonal communication. Or the redefinition arises from incremental performance trends embedded in the real world, like the slow erosion in public services or the quality of life.[1] Theoretically, at least, redefinition also may be stimulated entirely by rhetorical games played among contending political activists, and those games may not correspond to reality in any significant manner.[2]

The historical narrative that I laid out in part 1 of this book shows that many whites in Mobile and elsewhere at one time regarded blacks as genetically inferior and that in the 1950s and 1960s blacks and liberal whites redefined the problem of racial inequality as the product of white racism. As I related in part 2, the problem was redefined yet again in the 1980s and 1990s. Increasingly, conventional wisdom said that blacks got fewer of society's benefits simply because they did not work hard enough or take advantage of opportunities when they arose.

The record also points to a corresponding shift in public policy. Separate-but-*un*equal public schools fit the notion of innate racial inequality. Busing for school desegregation, an assimilationist policy, emerged from the notion that white racism caused racial inequality. Later, school districts established magnet schools and other differential resources to accommodate individuals who want to work hard, whether black or white.

I have also suggested that the political culture of Mobile and the South underwent a general shift from hierarchy to individualism. A cultural shift would not have occurred if prevailing white opinion had redefined the problem of racial inequality wholly within a hierarchical context. If, for example, prevailing white opinion had moved from blaming contemporary white oppression to blaming the historical effects of long-ended Jim Crow discrimination for racial inequality, no real change would have occurred. Both explanations assume a white-generated racial hierarchy. But if the redefinition shifted the blame for racial inequality from white discrimination to inadequate personal effort by blacks, we have seen a marked cultural shift from hierarchy to individualism. Arguably, this significant cultural shift has taken place in Mobile.

In this chapter I ask and answer two general questions: Did the general public change its views in a manner that corresponds to activists' rhetoric with regard to the explanation given for continuing racial inequality and to the public policy designed to remedy it? And does any shift in public opinion confirm the importance of storytellers as agents of political and cultural change?

Scholarly Perspective

Social science scholarship guides this inquiry. It posits a two-step process of change: A "critical community" of intellectuals develops new ideas, and political activists pick up these ideas and use them in public discourse to reshape social norms and reconceive public policy.[3]

Critical communities of intellectuals, at think tanks and universities, seek to reconceptualize social problems. They do not seek specific outcomes so much as they attempt to influence the intellectual framework that people use to think about our world. Then, over time the ideas of critical communities become ideological frames, political orientations taken up by others.[4] The social movement, a loose coalition of local activists, uses the new ideas to win sociopolitical battles.

At a fundamental level politics is a contest about meanings. Whoever manages to construct the meaning of an event structures the pattern of our collective lives.[5] Mass media and social or political movements help to structure the interpretations that we make, but more important are citizens who actively engage in the interpretive process: "This debate is reflected in the mass media, but its true locus is in homes, schools, and workplaces. The movement in society is decentralized and without centrally controlled direction. Its prime activities are those that engage people in conversation or provoke them to new thoughts."[6]

Meaning making involves social construction. Schemata of interpretation that allow us "to locate, perceive, identify, and label" what happens are called frames.[7] Frames may be set by the mass media, but people actively construct meanings for themselves too and use media coverage as raw material to do this.[8]

The mass media and social movement activists frequently frame social problems for the publics, but whether these interpretations are congruent with objective indicators of system performance and how media and/or movement frames come to dominate an issue arena are always open to question.[9]

The Problem of Racial Inequality

Explanations for racial inequality vary considerably and have varied through time. Some people attribute inequalities to deficiencies in black people themselves. They cite biological inferiority, self-destructive cultural values, or lack of individual effort. Others see African Americans as victims of white discrimination or outright oppression, past or present.

While specific public policies seem inevitably to have followed from each explanation—as, for instance, separate-and-unequal public facilities from a judgment of innate inequality—this may not have in fact been inevitable. Shifts in the definition of the problem and any related changes in public policy are matters for empirical investigation.

Six statements, drawn from the six metanarratives that purport to explain why blacks generally seem to get less of the good things in life than whites, were included in both the National Election and San Francisco Bay Area studies in 1972.[10] In 1986 a Mobile study used the same questions, as did a second Bay Area study.

Table 2 shows the percentage of white and black respondents who agreed with the six explanations for black inequality in Mobile in both 1986 and 1994. Between 1986 and 1994 whites in Mobile show a significant decline in agreement with each explanation save one—blacks don't try hard enough; 60 percent made that response in 1986, whereas 67 percent did in 1994. In 1986 whites endorsed a confusing admixture of explanations, but by 1994 white opinion had crystallized. Few whites said that black inequality resulted from white discrimination (20 percent) or oppression (8 percent). Old-fashioned racist explanations diminished greatly; fewer whites in 1994 claimed that God

Table 2. Explanations for Racial Inequality in Mobile, 1986 and 1994 Surveys

	Percentage in Agreement			
	Whites		Blacks	
	1986 (*n* = 302)	1994 (*n* = 281)	1986 (*n* = 122)	1994 (*n* = 107)
1. A small group of powerful and wealthy white people control things and act to keep blacks down.	23	8	46	25
2. The differences are brought about by God; God made the races different as part of his divine plan.	40	27	51	25
3. It's really a matter of some people not trying hard enough; if blacks would only try harder, they could be just as well off as whites.	60	67	56	45
4. Generations of slavery and discrimination have created conditions that make it difficult for blacks to work their way out of the lower class.	49	20	62	40
5. Black Americans teach their children values and skills different from those required to be successful in American society.	39	26	25	15
6. Blacks come from a less able race and this explains why blacks are not as well off as whites in America.	22	8	42	22

Source: Data from author's files.
Note: The total (*n*) for each column includes "don't know" responses.

or biology compelled black inferiority. In short, whites seemed unwilling to excuse lesser black performance. Inequality was more often seen to be the result of insufficient individual effort and self-reliance. This pattern of responses signals an important cultural shift.

The black samples in the two surveys are not large enough to make detailed analysis possible, but two things are worth noting in table 2. Over time blacks show less agreement with all the explanations, but by 1994 both blacks (45 percent) and whites in Mobile most often cited the explanation that blacks are not working had enough. In 1986, 62 percent of black respondents attributed lesser black performance to the burden of slavery, but that explanation ranked second in 1994, with only 40 percent in agreement.

In Mobile one explanation for racial inequality increasingly stood out among both blacks and whites: In a competitive world many African Americans simply had not worked themselves out of their inequality. National data suggest the same movement; two items used in 1972 and in five recent National Election Studies (NES) also show a cultural shift.[11] The presentation and answer categories in the NES data were not the same in 1972 as later years, so a comparison between 1972 and 1986 is problematic. Nevertheless, the trends after 1986 are clearly congruent with the Mobile data. Figure 1 plots the percentage of those who agreed or agreed strongly with this statement

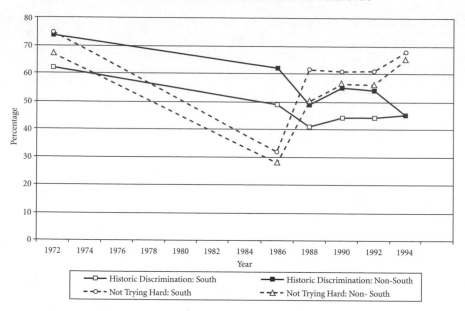

Figure 1. Explanations for Racial Inequality, Whites Only, by Region. (Data from National Electional Studies, Institute for Social Research, University of Michigan)

in national samples: "Generations of slavery and discrimination have created conditions that make it difficult for blacks to work their way out of the lower class." In 1972 most white Americans agreed that historic discrimination made it difficult for blacks to achieve equality. Support for this notion among whites inside and outside the South seems to have declined appreciably between 1972 and 1986. In 1986, 49 percent of white southerners and 62 percent of white nonsoutherners perceived that the burden of historical abuse handicapped black Americans. The two figures fell to 41 and 49 percent, respectively, in 1988 and then rose a little until they converged at 45 percent in 1994. The decline among white nonsoutherners—almost 20 percent—is particularly noteworthy. NES respondents were also asked to agree or disagree with this statement: "It's really a matter of some people not trying hard enough; if blacks would only try harder they could be just as well off as whites." In this case a sharp decline seems to have occurred sometime between 1972 and 1986, but what is most significant is the sharp rise between 1986 and 1988. In 1986 only 32 percent of southern whites and 28 percent of other whites agreed, but by 1988 the figures were 62 and 50 percent, respectively. The percentage agreeing increased sharply again between 1992 and 1994, and the southerners and nonsoutherners converged at 68 and 65 percent, respectively—a rise of more than thirty-five points in eight years in both regions. Nationally, the two explanations for black inequality had reversed positions in less than a decade.

Hypotheses

Public opinion data nationally and from Mobile clearly show that a redefinition of the American race problem occurred in the late 1980s or early 1990s. Americans moved away from "discrimination" and toward "lack of individual effort" as an explanation for racial inequality.

The theoretical issue is whether the shift was influenced by changes in the general public's lived experience, media portrayals of ongoing events, agitation by social movement activists, or some combination of these. An equally important theoretical issue is whether the public, as manifested in public opinion surveys, actually preferred a new racial policy, in this instance a new school desegregation policy to replace busing that was consistent with changes in abstract ideas about racial inequality.

Data

In this chapter I use three types of quantitative data—census reports, school performance indicators, and public opinion data—to answer fundamental questions about cultural change, problem redefinition, and policy consequences.[12]

County-level census data on postsecondary education and occupation provide objective measures of racial and system stress. I used data from the Mobile public school system—test scores, graduation, suspension, and dropout rates, and types of educational programs completed—to calculate indicators of school performance. Attitude data come from surveys of public opinion that I conducted in Mobile in 1982, 1986, and 1994. The surveys used random-digit sampling techniques for telephone interviews. Sample sizes were 666, 448, and 402, respectively, generating estimated sampling errors of about 5 percent. Data from each sample closely approximated known population characteristics.

Media treatment of racial issues required an analysis of both national and local sources available to Mobile residents. I assayed network evening news programs by using the index of the Vanderbilt Television News Archive; I counted all stories dealing with three public problems—busing, crime, and social welfare—from 1970 through 1995. I used the *Mobile Register*, a morning newspaper, to assess local media coverage. I randomly selected eight weeks from even-numbered academic years from 1980 through 1994—a sample of

390 days—and coded front-page news stories, editorials, opinion columns, and letters to the editor for focus and manifest or implied racial content.

Analysis

For decades the white South explained racial inequality as a natural occurrence: Inequality grew out of blacks' genetic and cultural inferiority, and, moreover, it was probably God's will. These terms justified the policy of racially separate schools, with diminished norms and resources. When the civil rights movement redefined the race problem in the South, it did so by asserting that whites' enslavement of and discrimination against black people had unfairly and unconstitutionally held them down. Over time the federal government imposed redistributive welfare, employment, and education policies in order to bring blacks successfully into the competitive arena. Busing for racial balance was supposed to raise black educational achievement without hurting white achievement and improve race relations.[13] Because busing was redistributive in terms of class and social status, it was very unpopular among whites.[14]

Historical Context

National and local trends and events intersected to stimulate changing views of why blacks do less well in the United States than whites. My model of cultural change requires national "critical communities" of intellectuals who analyze the status quo and offer a rationale for a new direction, and it requires local agents of change.

National Reacting to redistributive federal policies in the 1960s, a "critical community" of conservative intellectuals, given voice mainly in *Commentary* and *Public Interest*, reconceptualized racial issues as part of their broad-based critique of U.S. life.[15] What began as a critique of the ways in which social welfare policies were administered became increasingly a specification of the limits of social policy itself.[16] While the neoconservatives supported civil rights, they were not optimistic that civil rights laws and especially affirmative action policies would accomplish what liberals wanted. Neoconservatives saw racial issues as infinitely complex and beyond reformers' reach because of "the law of unanticipated consequences." Indeed, in *Beyond the Melting Pot* (1963) Nathan Glazer and Daniel Patrick Moynihan argued that the United States could not abrogate patterns of voluntary association and ethnic and tribal ties—precisely the factors that stood in the way of liberals' policy of integration.[17]

Social movements on the political right picked up and used a neoconservative intellectual critique of liberal welfare and social policy. Christian fundamentalists, libertarians, and racist groups, assembled as the New Right, all appropriated the intellectual work of neoconservatives to give better rationalization to their own ideologies. President Ronald Reagan disappointed the New Right when he failed to dismantle federal policies, but he legitimized many of its symbolic claims to a wider U.S. public.[18] Reagan spoke regularly about self-reliance, and he attacked all affirmative action policies, including busing for racial balance.

Local The historical narrative that I laid out in parts 1 and 2 of this book provides the context for the quantitative assessment that I undertake here. Public schools in Mobile County, as throughout much of the South, remained segregated in 1963, nine years after *Brown v. Board of Education.* In federal court hearings in November 1963, the Mobile school board's attorneys argued, through an expert witness who talked about brain sizes, among other factors, that persistent academic inequality was the result of blacks' innate inferiority. The expert said that the difference justified separate schools. The court approved a "freedom-of-choice" plan for 1964, and only seven black youngsters transferred to previously all-white schools. In 1965 thirty-two African American pupils, in a school district that had approximately thirty-one thousand black students, attended formerly white schools. Busing began by court order in 1971 immediately following the Supreme Court decision in *Swann v. Charlotte-Mecklenburg.* Protest by whites was vehement at first, but the schools settled into uneasy civility.

Two controversies—one in 1978–79, another in 1982–83—stimulated community activists to debate racially loaded issues and provided the events that allowed me to peg alternative views of the race problem:

1. In 1978 Dan Alexander, other white board members, and others in the community tried to establish competency testing of all students and teachers. They wanted no more "social promotions" from grade to grade; additionally, they wanted students to pass a proficiency test in order to obtain a high school diploma. Those who could not demonstrate mastery would end school with only a certificate of attendance. Proponents also wanted teachers—both existing staff and future hires—to be tested in order to demonstrate that they knew their material. Many blacks saw the move as a cynical attempt to purge black teachers and to punish black children. But in the rhetorical contest black leaders were constrained by U.S. cultural norms—after all, who could be against merit and competence? The proponents of rigorous testing appropriated the language of a competitive marketplace and con-

sequently put black spokesmen on the defensive without using the language of racial hierarchy. After much debate and many disputes that played out in the media, the antagonists reached compromises, but the notion of competitive achievement was ascendant. Neoconservative ideas found fertile soil in white Mobile and long predated Reagan's ascendency.

2. In 1982–83, after a year of study by a citizens' committee appointed by the judge, Mobile residents made an attempt to modify and extend the busing plan to the remote edges of the county, but that effort failed when fragile coalitions among whites broke up over perceptions of immediate self-interest. The expert hired by the committee was strongly assimilationist and an advocate of busing, and the controversy stimulated by his recommendations supporting racial balance in most schools was the last formal public discussion of the effects of busing by movement activists in the community. During the next ten years the school system made minor adjustments as it built new schools or remodeled old ones, but the system remained under a court-ordered busing plan.

Public Opinion and Busing Policy: Shifting Goals

National polls asking about desegregation of U.S. life—jobs, housing, intermarriage, and schools—have shown an evolutionary trend toward greater acceptance of minorities since the 1940s.[19] But open access and equal opportunity were one thing, busing quite another.[20] In Mobile in 1994, 74 percent of the white public and 36 percent of the black public opposed busing for racial balance.

As policy, busing was supposed to raise black educational achievement without hurting white achievement, and it was supposed to improve race relations as children learned more about each other. Table 3 lays out opinions about the affirmative goals of busing in Mobile. As answers to question 13 show, in 1994 white respondents were much less likely than in 1982 to think that busing helped black achievement; only 34 percent said it helped black educational achievement in 1994, whereas 48 percent had made that claim in 1982—a steady negative trend. The "don't know" category grew most noticeably. Stories of busing's success were not publicly touted, even by black leaders. Instead, many black leaders came to prefer and then proclaim that they wanted more and better resources devoted to black neighborhood schools, not simply more busing. Most of the shift occurred between 1982 and 1986, after busing was re-debated by school activists within the Mobile community and well before the 1988 consent decree that established the trade-off between less busing and more financial resources for black youngsters.

Table 3. Perceptions of Busing in Mobile County

	Whites			Blacks		
	1982	1986	1994	1982	1986	1994

Q13. Let's think about the racial situation in Mobile's public schools. In your opinion, has school desegregation increased the educational achievement of black youngsters, decreased their educational achievement, or has had no effect on educational achievement of black students.

1. Increased achievement	48%	39%	34%	54%	55%	56%
2. Decreased achievement	13	17	17	7	17	9
3. No effect	28	32	26	28	25	24
9. Don't know/no answer	12	13	23	11	3	12

Q14. What about white youngsters. Has desegregation of the schools increased their educational achievement, decreased their educational achievement, or has desegregation had no effect on white educational achievement?

1. Increased achievement	8	10	10	21	33	37
2. Decreased achievement	54	49	49	10	17	10
3. No effect	33	31	28	47	40	36
9. Don't know/no answer	5	10	12	22	10	18

Q15. Some people think desegregation of the schools has helped black and white children to understand and appreciate one another more fully, while some seem to think desegregation has created more racial prejudice and hostility among children. Still others say desegregation has had no effect on racial attitudes of students. What is your view? Has desegregation . . .

1. Helped reduce prejudice	59	46	40	68	61	63
2. Created more prejudice	18	25	30	10	19	6
3. Had no effect on student's racial prejudice	15	21	21	15	17	22
9. Don't know/no answer	8	9	9	7	4	9

Q16. What do you think is a reasonable goal for desegregation? Should schools be racially balanced, that is, about an equal number of black and white students, or should a school be considered desegregated if it has about 20 percent of *either* race?

1. About equal	25	26	41	68	62	69
2. 20 percent either race	48	53	37	18	30	13
9. Don't know/no answer	28	22	22	14	8	17

Q18. If you had a child who was included in a busing plan, would you prefer to send him to the school *nearest your home* or to a school farther away which had a *better program* for students with his interests and talents?

1. Nearest school	38	28	30	23	25	19
2. Better program	58	64	57	75	74	73
9. Don't know/no answer	4	8	12	2	1	8

Source: Data from author's files.

Most of the shift also occurred well before the sharp decline from 1986 to 1988 in whites' acceptance of the "burden" item in the national public opinion studies (see figure 1).

At each point in time, about half the whites said that busing hurt white achievement (see table 3, question 14), but other aspects showed change. In 1982, 59 percent said busing reduced prejudice, but in 1994 only 40 percent of white respondents made that claim (see question 15). Here again the major portion of the decline occurred between 1982 and 1986, a period in which activists were debating ways to revise and extend the county's busing plan. During the period that the data show that the problem of racial inequality was being redefined most sharply—1986–94—attitudes toward the goals of busing eroded more moderately.

The data suggest that more and more whites viewed busing as wasteful or counterproductive. Black attitudes were, however, rather stable over twelve years. Generally, black respondents believed busing did help black youngsters to higher achievement without hurting whites and that it did improve race relations.

Overall, whites did not like busing and increasingly said that it did not meet its stated goals; however, whites adjusted over time, moving away from a traditional hierarchical culture based on race and toward a cultural model of competitive individuals.[21] Questions 16 and 18 in table 3 mark this shift: In 1982 and 1986 whites preferred schools to be considered "desegregated" when they reached only 20 percent of *either* race as this would serve to minimize white exposure to blacks. But by 1994 many more whites preferred the racial population of schools to be about equal (see question 16). Thus whites seemed to accept racial balance as a norm embedded in the court's existing plan for magnet schools. Also, throughout the decade most whites said that they would choose a better program for their child, even if it was farther away, over a closer but less appropriate school (see question 18); this showed that busing as transportation to a better educational program was generally acceptable.

Whites accepted the idea of racial balance—and this signaled a symbolic triumph in the national government's second reconstruction of the South—but they thought that forced busing for racial balance was flawed. On the other hand, whites seemed to be saying that busing for educational programs was fine, as long as it was a parent's choice. Indeed, several black-area magnet schools had waiting lists for white students because the schools' special programs seemed so desirable, and the parents wanted the schools to provide bus transportation for them.

Generational Change

Age functions as a surrogate for desegregation experience among white people; generally, younger cohorts have experienced school and job desegregation more completely than older ones.

When I cross-tabulated age with the perception of busing's effect on white achievement, as I did in table 4, the result was striking. In 1982 and 1986 many younger whites—about 40 percent—said busing hurt white achievement, but in 1994 only 16 percent agreed with that sentiment. In 1994 fully 56 percent of respondents in the youngest age category said busing had no effect on white achievement. In all three surveys majorities of the two older age groups believed busing hurt white achievement.

Table 4. Perception of the Effect of Busing in Mobile on White Educational Achievement by Age Group (Whites Only)

	Percentage Responding				
	Increased	Decreased	Same	Don't Know/ No Answer	Number
1982					
Age (years)					
18–30	12	40	45	3	145
31–47	7	56	30	7	163
48+	6	65	25	5	166
probability = .0002					
1986					
Age (years)					
18–30	16	39	35	11	98
31–47	5	54	34	8	116
48+	10	54	24	12	94
probability = .0422					
1994					
Age (years)					
18–30	16	16	56	12	50
31–47	7	50	29	13	128
48+	11	64	14	10	111
probability = .0000					
Difference between 1982 and 1994					
Age (years)					
18–30	+ 4	−24	+11	+9	
31–47	0	− 6	− 1	+6	
48+	+5	− 1	−11	+5	
Loglinear goodness-of-fit statistics:	Chi-square	DF	Significance		
Likelihood ratio	117.2967	28	7.E–13		

Source: Data from author's files.

Table 5 looks at the cross-tabulation of age and whether the threshold of "desegregation" ought to be 20 percent of either race or equal numbers of blacks and whites. Between 1986 and 1994 white opinion in Mobile underwent another striking shift. More whites than in 1986 said "equal numbers" of blacks and whites should be the target of desegregation. What is especially revealing is that all three age groups shifted in the same direction and that the middle group shifted the most. Where 19 percent of the middle cohort said "about equal" in 1986, fully 46 percent made that claim in 1994, about the same level as the youngest group. Twenty years' experience with busing seems to have caused whites not to fear racial balance in schools—even though black students made up more than 40 percent of the student population in Mobile's public schools—as long as programs within schools re-

Table 5. School Desegregation Target in Mobile by Age Groups (Whites Only)

	Percentage Responding			
	About Equal	20 Percent Either Race	Don't Know/ No Answer	Number
1982				
Age (years)				
18–30	35	46	19	145
31–47	21	54	25	163
48+	19	43	38	166
probability = .0002				
1986				
Age (years)				
18–30	37	52	10	98
31–47	19	57	24	116
48+	22	47	31	94
probability = .0010				
1994				
Age (years)				
18–30	51	31	18	50
31–47	46	34	20	128
48+	30	42	28	111
probability = .0557				
Difference between 1982 and 1994				
Age (years)				
18–30	+16	−15	−1	
31–47	+25	−20	−5	
48+	+11	−1	−10	
Loglinear goodness-of-fit statistics:	Chi-square	DF	Significance	
Likelihood ratio	103.8803	20	.0000	

Source: Data from author's files.

sponded to individual needs and talents. Seemingly, a culture of individualism increasingly replaced a culture of racial solidarity.

Table 6 examines the relationship of age and the general explanations for racial inequality in Mobile. The pattern is consistent—agreement with the items varies with time across all age groups. For five explanations the percentage agreeing with the statements declined. With one explanation—blacks not working hard enough—all three age groups increased together. The youngest group, however, increased the most, and the youngest whites, more than any others, favored the "not trying" explanation for black inequality in 1994. Whites seemingly converged on one general idea of what mattered, and that view manifested a highly individualistic cultural norm.

Table 6. Agreement by Age Groups with Explanations for Racial Inequality in Mobile (Whites Only)

	White People	God	Not Trying	Historic Discrimination	Different Values	Less Able
1986						
Age (years)						
18–30	26%	40%	64%	53%	42%	18%
31–47	20	39	59	49	56	18
48+	21	44	70	48	53	33
1994						
Age (years)						
18–30	8	17	80	27	26	2
31–47	9	32	71	24	40	7
48+	10	35	77	18	40	14
Difference between 1986 and 1994						
Age (years)						
18–30	−18	−23	+16	−26	−16	−16
31–47	−11	−7	+12	−25	−16	−11
48+	−11	−9	+7	−30	−13	−19

Source: Data from author's files.

Reprise

The survey data show that white respondents in Mobile significantly changed their views of the "race problem" and corresponding public policy sometime in the 1980s and early 1990s. Many more whites came to believe that racial inequality was not the fault of whites and that blacks could work their own way out of the lower class. Whites also believed that busing failed to achieve its goals and preferred better programs over neighborhood schools. Whites came increasingly to support racially balanced schools for people with interests and talents like their own.

These attitudinal shifts are consonant with the neoconservative critique of education and particularly its emphasis on parental choice among programs; behind the Mobile dynamic lay the competitive market model for improving the schools. The question remains: Was the shift in problem and policy brought about by changing empirical conditions, activists' rhetoric and agitation, media coverage of the issues, or what?

Objective Conditions

Performance indicators for Mobile were ambiguous and invited partisan interpretation by "liberal" and "conservative" community activists in ways that stimulated redefinition of the "race problem" and appropriate policy. For instance, if the racial gap in learning or employment narrowed over time, conservatives could argue that the liberals' redistributive policies were no longer necessary. If the gap was still wide after twenty-five years, conservatives could say that liberal policies had failed. Either way, they deemed new approaches to be necessary.

Demographics Census data for Mobile County show significant changes in recent decades in terms of racial inequality. In 1950, 45 percent of the white population had a high school education or better; only 11 percent of African Americans did so. By 1990 the figures had changed: 82 percent of whites and 61 percent of blacks had at least a high school diploma. The ratio of inequality moved from 4:1 to 1.3:1. The gap closed significantly in college education as well. In 1950, 5.6 percent of whites and 1.5 percent of blacks had completed at least four years of college. By 1990 the figures were 27 and 10.7 percent, respectively. The ratio had narrowed from 3.7:1 to 2.5:1. Occupational data show a more revealing change. In 1950, 26.7 percent of whites and 5.6 percent of blacks were employed in managerial and professional occupations. The figures were 34.3 and 17 percent, respectively, by 1990. The ratio had narrowed from 4.8:1 to 2.0:1.[22]

Ideological activists construed empirical conditions in different ways. The data show marked improvement in educational and occupational status for many blacks but not for some others. Relative to whites, the inequality narrowed sharply but did not disappear altogether. Liberals, both black and white, argued that more should be done, while conservatives, again of each race, asserted that after so much redistributionist effort, any remaining inequality was the result of failed individual discipline (often brought about by inadequate subcultural socialization).

Interracial Exposure Social scientists have sought to measure the amount of interracial exposure in school systems caused by desegregation.[23] The principal measure used for this purpose is called the index of dissimilarity, and this is its formula:

$$D = \frac{1}{2} \sum \left| \frac{W_i}{W} - \frac{B_i}{B} \right|$$

where W_i is the number of whites in each school and W is the number of whites in the whole school system; where B_i is the number of blacks in each school and B is the number of African Americans in the school system. The result of the calculation is the proportion of blacks who would have to be reassigned to white schools, if no whites were moved, in order to have the same proportion of blacks in each school as in the system as a whole. The values range from 00.0, perfect racial balance in the schools, to 1.00, a situation where 100 percent of the black students would have to be reassigned in order to reach racial balance.

As figure 2 shows, Mobile was highly segregated in 1968. When busing began in 1971, Mobile, as elsewhere across the South, made a strong move

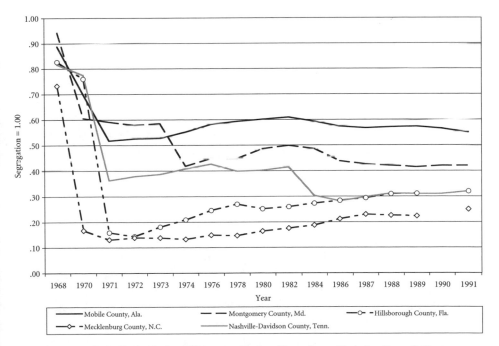

Figure 2. Dissimilarity Index: Whites vs. Blacks. (Data from Christine Rossell, Boston University)

toward racial balance in schools. Charlotte–Mecklenburg County, North Carolina, and Tampa–Hillsborough County, Florida, achieved a condition of near-perfect racial balance. In Mobile, however, racial balance was not nearly so well achieved; Mobile County public schools were the most racially unbalanced of the five systems discussed here. At any point from 1971 through 1991 more than half of Mobile's black students would have had to have been reassigned, largely through busing, in order to achieve perfect racial balance in the schools. As I have shown, throughout the 1970s, 1980s, and 1990s the community rejected this approach.

In *The Carrot or the Stick for School Desegregation Policy,* Christine Rossell argues that the index of dissimilarity can be misleading. The index of dissimilarity measures racial balance but not interracial exposure. The dissimilarity index does not take into account white flight. Rossell advanced an index of racial exposure that takes into account both racial balance and white flight. The index of racial exposure measures the percentage of whites in the average black student's school and is calculated thus:

$$S_{mw} = \frac{\sum_{k=1} N_{km} P_{kw}}{\sum_{k=1} N_{km}}$$

where k represents each school and N_{km} is the number (N) of minorities (m) in a particular school (k) and where P_{kw} is the proportion (P) white (w) in the same school (k). Figure 3 shows the results of this calculation for five representative school systems.

Mobile County shows the lowest interracial exposure. The average black child is part of a student body that is 30 percent white. The index is relatively flat, indicating relatively little white flight beyond the level associated with the initial shock in 1971. Other school systems, most notably Charlotte–Mecklenburg County, North Carolina, and Hillsborough County, Florida, have had far higher rates of interracial exposure, but that exposure has lessened significantly over the years as the white population in the public schools has decreased.

Indeed, the data show a slow departure over the decades from the notion of racial balance and interracial exposure in all five of the representative southern school systems. The process of racial separation proceeded even further in the 1990s, according to Gary Orfield and Susan Eaton in *Dismantling Desegregation: The Quiet Reversal of Brown v. Board of Education.*[24] In the South and all across the country, races separate still more as school sys-

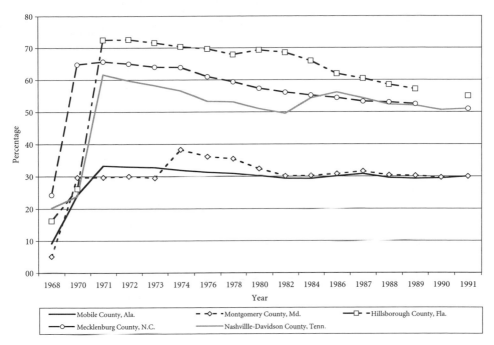

Figure 3. Percentage White in Average Black Child's School (Data from Christine Rossell, Boston University)

tems have moved out from under court orders. Only time will tell the full extent of separation in Mobile as elsewhere.

Other objective data regarding public schools were also mixed.

Test Scores Until recently, the Mobile school system maintained no identification of individuals' achievement test scores by race, so research about a racial achievement gap historically is not possible. Nevertheless, it is safe to assume that when busing began, whites and blacks had different levels of academic achievement. By equalizing opportunity, busing was to reduce the achievement gap. Recent state-mandated achievement test data show that the racial gap remains wide. In Mobile County systemwide averages of achievement scores by race are 45.18 and 25.8 for whites and blacks, respectively—a ratio of 1:0.57. The systemwide average for all races is 36.13 from 1991 to 1994, well below the national norm of 50.

Special Education Programs The gap remained wide in other areas too. Two types of special education programs illustrate racial data over time (see figure

4). Mobile high schools offered honors programs for especially motivated and able students. Analysis shows that the percentage of white students receiving honors diplomas at high school graduation increased incrementally from less than 4 percent to almost 7 percent between 1983 and 1994; the black increase was similar but at a lower rate, varying from less than 1 percent to more than 3 percent. Those at the other end of the academic spectrum—those who attended school but could not perform well enough academically to get a high school diploma because they were intellectually or emotionally handicapped—received a certificate of attendance (or education). See figure 5. Analysis shows the percentage varied over time, but the gap between whites and blacks was relatively constant and the trends roughly parallel.

Suspensions   Another racially sensitive indicator of system stress is the number of youngsters suspended from school. When charted over time (see figure 6), the rate for blacks increases steadily, from just over 7 percent in 1987 to 16 percent in 1994. After a lag the white rate increases sharply, from 6 to 10 percent in two years. School officials and parents, worried about the growth of gang-related activity, took a "tough" line.

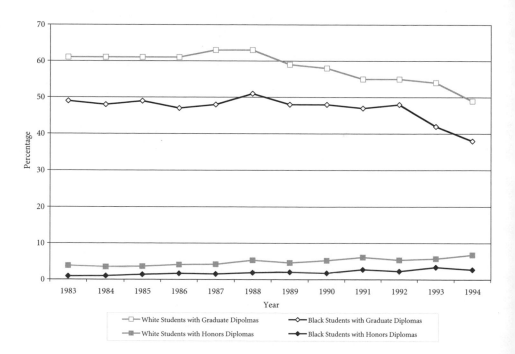

Figure 4. Types of Diplomas, by Race (Data from author's files)

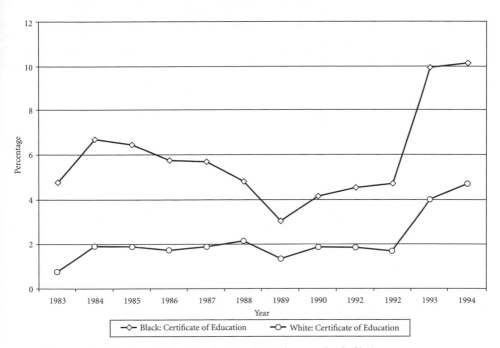

Figure 5. Certificates of Education, by Race (Data from author's files)

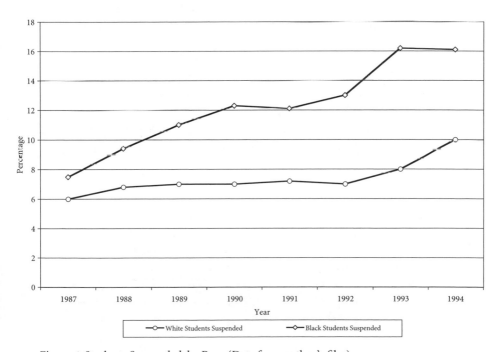

Figure 6. Students Suspended, by Race (Data from author's files)

Dropout Rate The high school dropout rate increased along with the suspension rate; perhaps the rates were functionally related. In 1988, 40 percent of ninth graders did not graduate four years later, and that percentage became almost 50 percent by 1994, but the decline in graduation rates affected both races. Blacks were less likely to graduate than whites, but the two trends varied together.

Altogether, the objective indicators of system performance give mixed signals, and, like the broader social indicators, the school data invite interpretation by media and community activists. The achievement test scores were not good and arguably have not improved. Achievement gaps between the races remain wide on all academic indicators. Suspensions and dropout rates have increased for both races. More positively, on the other hand, more high school graduates received honors diplomas, and more went on to college.

Ironically, the civil rights movement's emphasis on white discrimination as the cause of black disadvantage implied that when segregation was ended, most racial differences would soon end. When the differences did not end—in test scores, graduation rates, and the like—even after years of school desegregation, some blacks and many whites came to believe that the whole effort was wasted and sought to end busing for racial balance.

It is important to note, however, that the objective trend data could have been interpreted to support a white-discrimination explanation for racial inequality. The gap between blacks and whites was wide and persistent. One could argue that the gap was evidence that blacks still bore the burden of their historical inequality; indeed, senior African American school district officials made this claim. The number of blacks assigned to special education classes dropped significantly when a black assistant superintendent made that her priority. But changing the rules for special education also caused fewer whites to be assigned to special education classes; in the end the racial gap remained about the same. Arguably, still more effective affirmative action could be required to remove the historical burden.[25]

Alternatively, the indicators about trends in performance could be the focus of investigation. If so, one could emphasize that the parallel trends show that programs and policies affected each race similarly and that the persistent gap between the races only proves that blacks simply did not work hard enough to succeed even when equal opportunity was there.

It is crucial to note that local conditions did not interpret themselves; Mobile residents did. And Dan Alexander and Robert Gilliard certainly did their part to construe the facts in different ways.

Media and Race

Mobile experienced a significant cultural shift: The white population redefined the race problem and its associated public policy—busing—despite or, more likely, because of the ambiguity of objective local conditions. The next question is, "Was the shift a result of lived experience or media construction?"

For this book I analyzed network television news programs and a local newspaper, the *Mobile Register,* to find patterns of coverage that dovetailed with the changes in public opinion. Figure 7 graphs the number of stories on the network evening news shows between 1970 and 1995 that had as their focus one of three issues—busing for school desegregation, crime, and social welfare—that touch race directly or indirectly. Several points are worth noting. First, the media hugely emphasized school desegregation in the early 1970s, and the number of stories decreased greatly in the later 1980s; indeed, busing almost disappeared as a televised national issue by 1984. During the years of the greatest shift in white Mobile residents' attitudes about the problem of racial inequality and the policy of busing, the national media paid little or no attention. Second, coverage of the social welfare system

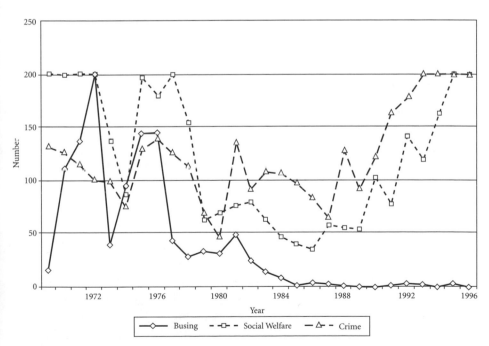

Figure 7. Television News Coverage of Three Issues. Note that the number of stories has been truncated for $n > 200$. (Data from author's files)

and crime peaked twice—once in the early 1970s, during the Nixon administration, again in the late 1980s, during the Reagan-Bush years and continuing into the 1990s. Conservative administrations wanted to preserve order.

During the 1980s commentators argued that a conservative sociopolitical
movement was attacking established liberal federal policies by using racially
"coded" language.[26] "Welfare queens" and "street crime" were colored black.[27]
Subtle language racialized white resentment against taxes and regulations,
and the movement justified alternative conservative approaches in terms of
increasing both personal freedom and individual responsibility—fundamental tenets of mythic American culture. As Edsall and Edsall note: "The GOP
would stand as a bulwark against, and an adversary of, all costs imposed by
the liberal agenda of race, rights, and taxes . . . [it sought] to end racial preferences, to end affirmative action, to take the government out of the business of enforcing racial integration, and to define 'reverse discrimination' as
the symbol of liberalism run amok."[28]

I will attempt here no detailed analysis of the racial bias of television
news—it is unnecessary, given the scholarly literature.[29] Nevertheless, certain
conclusions are warranted. Nationally, news programs ignored school desegregation after the early 1980s; therefore, network news could not have caused
Mobile's attitude changes on busing policy. Television news did give considerable attention to crime and welfare, and surely this prompted people to talk
among themselves. Once individuals knew the "codes," they could make
racial interpretations of overtly nonracial stories.[30]

Locally, I examined the *Mobile Register,* a daily newspaper, to see whether
its coverage stimulated the changes in public opinion. I examined a sample
of 390 days between 1980 and 1994; table 7 reports the distribution of relative emphasis.

Clearly, partisan politics dominated the newspaper; 60 percent of the edi-
tions carried news stories about political struggle. Almost 8 in 10 had op-ed
columns also devoted to partisan conflict. The paper also gave heavy play to
crime, war and relations among foreign states, and human interest stories.
Issues about social welfare and education received little emphasis, however.

One percent of the op-ed columns mentioned desegregation itself; I found
no front-page news stories, no editorials, and no letters to the editor about
desegregation. This otherwise stunning finding was not entirely surprising.
Interviews that I conducted made clear that the paper's publisher and senior
staff decided to play down education news, because busing and racialized
school board politics had raised racial conflict to dramatic heights during the
1960s and 1970s. When the senior staff of the newspaper was replaced in 1994,
the paper immediately began to cover education, including its racial aspects.

Table 7. Types of Mobile Daily Newspaper Coverage Based on a Sample of 390 Days, 1980–94

	News	Editorial	Columns	Letters
Economic problems	31%	36%	43%	37%
Noneconomic problems				
Politics; partisan	60	33	77	27
Courts; justice system	16	11	8	8
Media; press; journalism	1	4	9	10
Dissatisfaction with government	1	13	4	15
Crime; violence	40	7	9	10
War; threat of war	26	3	5	3
International relations	38	11	36	4
Foreign domestic politics (including domestic insurrections)	20	5	9	1
Military weapons	9	5	5	3
Terrorist attack (not hostage situation)	4	1	—	0
Space-related issues	4	—	—	1
Human interest	36	13	38	33
Weather	18	1	1	1
Non-natural disaster	13	—	1	0
Traffic/roads	8	6	3	7
Sports	5	3	4	2
Health	7	4	4	6
Social welfare	1	—	1	1
Social Security; age-related issues	2	2	1	2
Poverty; homelessness	—	—	—	—
Environment, including nuclear power	9	6	3	9
Education	8	7	4	8
Desegregation	—	—	1	—
Achievement testing	1	—	—	0
Ethics; moral decline	11	3	4	5
Abortion	2	—	1	1
Cultural conflict; ideology; values (patriotism, prayer in school, textbooks)	3	6	17	14
Racism; race relations	6	—	7	3
Immigration	1	1	1	0
Sexual harassment	—	1	3	1

Source: Data from author's files.

I examined in detail items dealing with crime, welfare, and education to determine whether they were racialized, either implicitly or explicitly in newspaper content. Those results appear in table 8.

Most items paid little overt attention to race. Only nine of the 390 days sampled had stories about education, and of those stories, only 30 percent

Table 8. Racial Emphasis in Mobile Daily Newspaper Items about Education, Social Welfare, and Crime Based on a Sample of 390 Days, 1980–94

	Education	Social Welfare	Crime
News stories			
Number of days topic covered	9	3	28
Percentage emphasizing race	30	0	18
Editorials			
Number of days topic covered	2	2	11
Percentage emphasizing race	7	0	0
Columns			
Number of days topic covered	2	29	5
Percentage emphasizing race	12	0	0
Letters			
Number of days topic covered	3	2	25
Percentage emphasizing race	10	0	0

Source: Data from author's files.

mentioned race. Twenty-eight days had stories about crime; only 18 percent of these mentioned race. Otherwise, editorials, columns, and letters-to-the-editor about education, social welfare, and crime made no mention of racial aspects. The newspaper's policy of staying away from education, pointed to by elite respondents, is confirmed by content analysis.

Neither the local newspaper nor the national television news programs emphasized busing, so the significant changes in the views of white Mobile residents regarding busing must have begun and accelerated by word of mouth around dinner tables and across fences. Interpretations of local conditions were doubtless conditioned by the new understanding of racial inequality sponsored by conservative activists in Mobile. As figure 7 shows, other issue-arenas said to be embedded in racial discourse—namely, welfare and crime—were emphasized in the national television news programs, and particularly after Vice President George H. W. Bush played the "race card" by using the Willie Horton campaign ploy in 1988. Whites in Mobile were accustomed to making racialized interpretations of seemingly benign trends and events.

If political activists construct meaning by using "coded language" contained within media portrayals of social issues, the shift in opinions among white Mobile residents would be similar regardless of personal experience with the schools and desegregation generally, and that is what I found. Overall, whites moved as a group toward new positions on both the cause of racial inequality and the policy needed to address the problem.

Discussion

The evidence I have presented in this chapter suggests that a significant re-definition of the problem of racial inequality occurred in Mobile and prob-ably in other places. Whites increasingly attributed the notion that African Americans are able to obtain and enjoy fewer of the good things than whites to the failure of blacks to work themselves out of their deficiency; other ex-planations once had more support. The shift in the explanation for racial inequality occurred at each age level, but it was most dramatic among youn-ger whites between 1986 and 1994. Younger whites joined older whites in say-ing blacks did not work hard enough.

In Mobile views on busing for racial balance also changed over time among whites. White respondents agreed less and less that black children learned more because of busing and that busing helped reduce prejudice. A consen-sus increasingly came to judge busing as a failure on its own terms. Addition-ally, a large plurality of whites remained steadfast in the belief that busing hurt white children's educational achievement.

Across all three surveys more whites preferred "better programs" than the "nearest school." Quite possibly, the rhetoric of parental (public school) choice lay behind this. The surveys also showed that increasingly whites were no longer opposed to blacks' making up 50 percent of a school, a figure that approximated the then-current racial ratio in the schools. Where once whites preferred fewer blacks (say, 20 percent of a school's population) in order for a school to qualify as "fully desegregated," by 1994 a narrow plurality of whites said they would accept racial balance in schools. This change implies great-er willingness to enter into an interracial setting, if that setting had stronger programmatic characteristics devoted to individuals with different interests and aptitudes.

These shifts represent significant cultural change because they are gener-al phenomena; whites in different age and experience groupings moved in the same direction. Since the national and local media gave education, and especially busing, so little coverage, media operatives themselves did not construct the new views directly.

Nor can local objective conditions explain the transformations. The per-formance data are mixed. And while education and occupation inequalities had narrowed in recent decades, a substantial gap between the races re-mained. The glass could be half full or half empty.

The Mobile results show converging construction: contemporaneous lo-cal and national events stimulated activists' reframing of others' worldviews. In Mobile local school board members and movement activists prepared the ground in the 1977 "testing" and 1982 "busing" confrontations. When national conservatives, including the Reagan-Bush administrations, and especially the 1988 Republican presidential campaign, attacked liberal policies in education, social welfare, and crime as promoting wasteful dependence, their racialized appeals merged with and legitimized the rhetoric of local white community activists.

In Mobile the argument that blacks were innately inferior once secured sep-arate-but-*un*equal social policy, including public education; that rationale and policy prevailed until the civil rights movement overturned both in the 1960s. The civil rights movement's definition of the problem of racial inequality— the burden of past discrimination—and its concomitant public policy, affir-mative action, seem themselves to have been overthrown in the late 1980s by the conservative movement's emphasis on the unfairness, inefficacy, and waste of liberal policies. Conservatives applied mythic themes, like individual self-reliance, to cast the problem of racial inequality into a new frame.[31]

During the triumph of liberal perspectives and policies in the 1960s, the critical community of intellectuals at think tanks and writing in *Commen-tary* and *Public Interest* developed both a critique of liberal notions and an alternative conservative approach. Conservative social and political activists, both local and national, used the new intellectual critique to mobilize white resentments into a force for a major political counterthrust. In Mobile no particular "critical event" stimulated the cultural shift between 1986 and 1994; instead a series of smaller occasions prompted incremental adjustments in the popular mind. Because I found no evidence that the media directly forced the cultural change in Mobile, it is much more likely that new meaning and rhetoric were fashioned and expressed face-to-face in lived lives.

Conclusion

Both Mobile and the South changed significantly from the 1950s to 1990s. Formal institutions of racial hierarchy were beaten down. Dixie was Americanized. These changes did not come easily or inevitably, and it is well that we learn two important lessons from the historical dynamic. First, we need to understand that public narratives animated political life and shaped government decisions. Therefore we must regard public storytellers, men like John LeFlore, Bill Westbrook, and Dan Alexander, as significant political actors, not merely as cardboard cutouts giving voice to historical forces. They influenced the way others saw the world. Second, from Mobile's example we must realize that whatever seems empirically and morally certain in the moment is neither inevitable nor permanent. Although a plurality of whites now claim that any remaining racial inequality is the result of the failure of individual African Americans to take advantage of opportunity, that explanation is not fixed forever. Other explanations can emerge and become dominant over time because storytellers are always shifting their rhetoric for tactical advantage. Attentive citizens must pay attention to the stories being offered today by the newer generations of Dan Alexanders, Bill Westbrooks, and John LeFlores among us, even as we remember the past. All the metanarratives of race remain open for use.

Reprise

The crises of the Civil War and Reconstruction provoked southern whites to confront both their racial sentiments and social institutions, and three sociopolitical mentalities constructed different answers to the problem of racial inequality. White racial radicals believed that inequality was natural and probably fashioned by God. As a result, radicals claimed, public laws that kept the races separate and that treated blacks differently were prudent, given the nature of black aptitudes and appetites. On the other hand, bourbon conservatives, white people with established bases of socioeconomic status in the South, generally considered blacks naturally deficient and appropriated many of the stories told by racial radicals. But unlike the white radicals, conservatives wanted no ugly displays of racial intolerance. They preferred firm paternal guidance to the harsh measures so often put forward by radicals to keep blacks in their place at the bottom of the social ladder. Liberals, on the other hand, took the view that blacks and whites were inherently no different, that whites had held blacks back, and that government policies and programs could move blacks into their rightful place of full equality in American life. Because liberals held a view of assimilation that gave priority to the cultural values and practices of middle-class whites, liberals not-so-secretly wanted black people to be just like themselves.

The second reconstruction of the American South was an effort by the federal government, at the demand of African Americans and white liberals, North and South, to change public practices that discriminated against black people. School desegregation and voting rights were two principal instruments used to make the assault. And, indeed, the hierarchical culture of the Jim Crow South did change between 1954, when the national government initiated its intense pressure through the *Brown v. Board of Education* decision, and 1997, when the federal court finally withdrew its control over Mobile's schools. In Mobile at century's end African Americans sat on the school board, and the school system's policies encouraged individuals, not races, to be judged and rewarded. Nevertheless, federal law was the occasion for change and not the proximate cause. The federal government, through court decisions and executive policies, could compel some public actions, but it could not change people's minds. Court decisions and other critical events required interpretation, and therefore the cultural transformation of the American South, signaled by Mobile's example, required the actions of committed souls as much as it did federal power.

Stories, both lived and told, and the course of Southern history have an intimate connection. When the upper-class matron Dorothy Danner DaPonte told stories about the intellectual achievements of her black foster daughter, she implicitly challenged the myth of the genetic inferiority of black people so long and so deeply rooted in the South. Indeed, DaPonte's very life was a reproach to the prevailing culture, and she knew it.

John LeFlore, letter carrier and black civil rights leader, had no doubt that whites were racists, but he told and lived a story of hope and faith—hope in the future of black people in the United States and faith in the law's capacity to make things right. He insisted. He prodded. He shamed. And he sued. Both his story and his actions showed that the reasonable enforcement of fundamental rights under U.S. law could change white men.

If DaPonte's and LeFlore's stories and their very lives were political acts, so too were their opponents'. The legal case that the school board's attorneys presented in federal court in 1963 argued that scientific evidence supported the claim that black children could not be schooled with more advanced whites. The legal briefs and expert testimony were not stories per se, but both forms of discourse depended on earlier cultural and causal narratives about biology and God's will to give them relevance and force.

Between the 1950s and 1990s the socioeconomic gap between blacks and whites narrowed considerably. Regional economic development had something to do with these striking changes, of course, but other factors were just as significant in bringing about cultural change.[1] New interpretations of events changed people's perceptions of social life in ways that made state-mandated racial inequality illegitimate but that also rationalized any continuing inequality as lack of individual effort by blacks.

Critical Events

During school desegregation in Mobile five critical events, or strings of events, occasioned public narratives by the contending liberal, conservative, and radical mentalities: The breach of the color line in 1963, when the federal courts finally compelled desegregation of the schools; the end of freedom of choice in school enrollment in 1968; the coming of busing in 1970–71; the issue of competence testing from 1977 to 1980; and the decision to return to community-identified schooling, first implicitly in 1982, when busing for racial balance was blunted, and then again in 1988, when the full implications of the end of busing were spelled out. The first three were imposed upon Mobile and the South, but the latter two were indigenous.

These critical events were eruptions in the real world. And to each the attentive citizen responded, "What does it all mean?" Supplying meaning to others is the first political act in a stream of discourse that often leads people to define their many individual frustrations as a common problem, one that compels the use of government to fashion a suitable remedy.

The Narrative Contest

Among whites, the hierarchy of metanarratives underlying "the race problem" shifted in unknown increments throughout the same decades that the demographics of black life changed. In the 1950s many white people believed, and said publicly, that blacks were genetically inferior, and many more said that the black culture was so debased that white children would be contaminated if put into proximity with it. The civil rights movement, on the other hand, proclaimed that white people had held blacks down through systematic abuse and neglect.

Generally speaking, four factors significantly influence the success or failure of stories offered by movement spokesmen in the contest to shape the meanings attached to significant events. First, fidelity to established facts: Lived experience is filtered through earlier stories, but some things really do happen, and successful stories cannot ignore the real world. Second, successful prediction: If, for example, one forecasts disaster and it does not come, the story and the storyteller are diminished. Third, coherence: Stories that have integrity are grounded in fundamental cultural values that reconcile contemporary issues. Fourth, repetition: Stories that are repeated, regardless of other factors, undergird or change cultures.

In Mobile each of these factors came into play as political activists advanced their interpretations. Some stories were impeached when they failed to account for established facts, predicted future happenings incorrectly, became attached to peripheral rather than core values, or were not repeated often enough. A brief summary illustrates this dynamic in table 9.

1955–63

When blacks first threatened the color line in the 1950s, a rich white woman challenged the segregation of schools in Mobile, and her simple request caused liberal, conservative, and radical white narratives to come into intense, public conflict.

Dorothy Danner DaPonte provided her black foster daughter with all the advantages of the white upper class, including schooling in Europe. I related their personal stories in *The Confession of Dorothy Danner*, but the pair's public story was most clearly marked by the letter that Dorothy DaPonte sent to the president of the school board in 1955. She said she had raised Caroline properly and that she would cause no trouble in "white" schools. Moreover, "such acceptance of her would give the Negro race an opportunity to show what their development can be under favorable circumstances." Dorothy DaPonte lived

Table 9. Summary of Public Narratives

Liberals	Conservatives	Radicals
1955–63: Breaking the color line with freedom of choice		
White discrimination caused inequality. Blacks can improve their performance if their environment is improved.	National government forces change unfairly and thereby provokes instability; North is morally hypocritical. Go slow, or people will revolt.	Communists and other outsiders foment black rebellion against otherwise tranquil South. Whites and blacks who break the norm are crazy or defiant and will be lynched. Blacks are biologically inferior—brains are too small to succeed in competition with whites.
1968: Forced desegregation begins		
Blacks are made invisible in textbooks and that diminishes both their self-image and respect by whites. The real sources of community disruption are the unequal buildings, books, and resources given to black students over time. Blacks can be made civilized by the schools if they are fully integrated.	The federal government is arrogant, and the North is hypocritical, but patience is called for. Desegregation "experts" are nothing more than outside agitators who don't know anything about the community. Constitutionally protected freedom of association supports freedom of choice in schooling.	NOW is secretly a black urban terrorist group. Black neighborhoods are like jungles; forcing white children to attend black schools threatens their health and safety. Desegregation actually undermines the black community.
1970–71: Busing for racial balance		
Integration does not damage black students' legitimate pride; it challenges and aids them. It is good for individual whites and for America when whites show respect for blacks.	Black communities have pride in their schools, and busing destroys the linkage between school and community. White are victims too: Middle-class whites are sacrificed to aid lower-class blacks.	Busing will destroy black communities just like it will white communities. White children are thrust into disease and violence when bused into black communities. Black culture will infect white children with its moral decay.
1978: Competency testing		
Dan Alexander is a racist just like George Wallace. Competency tests are racially biased, and their use will unfairly hold blacks down.		Social promotions and incompetent teachers are unfair to all students, especially those from less privileged backgrounds. Alexander is a martyr: Federal court control of school board is illegitimate use of government power.
1986–98: Community schools		
	What was once a fight for integration evolved into a battle for "equity" as black plaintiffs shifted from improving the racial balance at schools to improving their own neighborhood schools.	

out and publicly expressed the liberal model: If the environment were altered, the performance of blacks would improve. She directly challenged the implicit genetic view of racial inequality. She sought to make Caroline and later Caroline's son, Alfred, into role models for black improvement.

Pointedly, if quietly, the conservative bourbon mentality denied her request and noted the failure of DaPonte's experiment when it could. To wit: Caroline became pregnant in high school and soon abandoned her infant son, first to her real maternal grandmother and later to DaPonte. DaPonte's socially prominent first cousin, Mary Bacon Barney, noted with feeling one incident that seemed to her to encapsulate the whole public spectacle: "If you had seen Dorothy coming into concerts and things with Alfred dressed up like a little baboon. He was so tacky looking, you couldn't believe it. He wasn't dressed like a nice little [white] boy. He would have on a funny hat with a feather, and he just looked awful. Dorothy would walk down the aisle, sit on the front row, practically, so everybody would see her come in with this little black boy. . . . It was pitiful really."[2]

Publicly, the Klan responded to DaPonte's challenge by burning a cross in her driveway; it acted out an old and powerful public story about what would happen if she persisted. Radical whites also told private stories about DaPonte's effort—that the black child was hers, not the maid's, and that her husband had committed suicide when he found out.[3]

Not much happened in Mobile after the DaPonte episode. Her efforts at school desegregation were stillborn. Both radical and conservative whites portrayed her as a crazy woman. The old stories of southern hierarchy seemed to have won out again. Subsequent efforts by the federal government to desegregate buses, public accommodations, and schools were seen against a background of northern oppression of the South during the first Reconstruction. Only crazy people or Yankees wanted change.

In 1963, eight years after DaPonte first tried to desegregate the schools through Caroline, John LeFlore sought to break the color line by enrolling black students at Murphy High School. The story that John LeFlore brought to the school board was simple: The federal courts had required desegregation in 1954, 1955, and still again in 1958, and other southern cities had moved forward, but Mobile had not. Surely, good and truthful men on the board would desegregate Mobile now. It was the right thing to do. In short, LeFlore's public narrative was a challenge to the honor of these good southern gentlemen. Failing that, he implied, he would go to federal court, where the school board's policies and practices would surely be declared outside the law.

As conservatives, school board members used the tactic of delay, and they complained that they were being asked to move too soon because people would rebel if pushed too fast. Gov. George Wallace, the seeming radical, was always in this camp: Resist but do so without violence. For him the issue was always the illegitimate use of federal power and how that might be thwarted. When blacks showed up at Murphy High School, Governor Wallace had them met by the state police, not a mob of white separatists. Wallace's order denying access claimed that integration would totally destroy the educational process.

Others too had their say. White radicals' accounts featured stories of the cultural and genetic inferiority of blacks but noted that inferior people could not rise up unaided. Therefore radical whites emphasized the threat to order posed by subversive outsiders. Right after LeFlore appeared before the school board to request school integration in 1963, its members discussed the threat of communism and the need to counter that threat by teaching American-ism in classrooms. That fall, 1963, after the court ordered Mobile's schools to admit blacks across the board, Arthur Hanes told a large crowd of apprehen-sive whites that communists were infiltrating black churches and fomenting race war. "The South," the former Birmingham mayor stated, "is the last bas-tion of race pride and it is the stronghold of true nationalistic feeling. Accord-ingly, it is the target of left-wing abuse. They say the Civil War was fought one hundred years ago, but I tell you that the Civil War is just starting."[4]

The radicals' claims were undercut when whites did not vigorously, per-sistently, and publicly rebel. Admittedly, some protested when the schools were desegregated, but these protests did not last. No race war occurred, then or later. But the notion of illegitimate federal power became fixed in the minds of a great many white southerners.

1968

From 1963 to 1968, while desegregation in Mobile was based on freedom of choice, little changed in the racial makeup of schools, but the rhetorical bat-tle continued apace. Indeed, during the next major crisis, in 1968, the radi-cal mentality stood out with its stories of outside agitators, alien ideas, and the cultural inferiority of blacks.

Radicals were buttressed when a police official claimed in court that a black organization called NOW (Neighborhood Organized Workers) was really a terrorist-training cadre. Radicals told another story more widely. That was the story of the danger to white children if they were assigned to black neigh-borhood schools. White children would be in moral as well as physical dan-ger if compelled to go to schools in black areas because black culture was so deficient. Recall P. D. Betancourt, who told stories of hearing gunfire, police sirens, and screams of agony from the Maysville area on many weekend nights. It was incredible, he told white crowds, that anyone would assign white students there.

The real innovation in rhetoric, however, was the white radicals' claim that desegregation hurt black communities, and over time this story became increasingly coherent and predicted well. In Mobile the white radical spokesman Bill Westbrook said that desegregation, particularly the end of freedom of choice, would destroy the black community and that the supposed liberators of black people—the NAACP and federal government—were really its oppressors because they helped to destroy neighborhood schools.

The conservatives never attacked their radical cousins' accounts but instead continually complained about the hypocrisy of the North and the unfairness of federal power directed only at the South. Conservatives shared with radicals the notion that outsiders, whether communists, academic experts, or members of the American Friends Service Committee, were to blame for disruption in their community.

In 1968, just as freedom of choice was ending, liberals began to insist on cultural fusion. Access to facilities was not enough to permit African Americans to gain equality. Liberal leaders, whether black or white, told stories about the invisibility of African Americans in the schools' textbooks and demanded that those U.S. history texts be rewritten to accommodate new and better stories. Racial separation was not the issue any longer; at issue instead were the terms of cultural assimilation. Some black leaders argued that the schools should teach "black culture" and "black self-determination" to blacks and whites in order to strengthen respect for all that black people had achieved.

No widespread white rebellion occurred with the end of freedom of choice, just as no such rebellion had occurred in 1963 when the schools were first desegregated. By and large, individual white families faced the issues of desegregation on their own. In Mobile, Westbrook argued that black communities would suffer as integration became the norm, and that notion resonated with many blacks because they feared the loss of control over their own communities' schools as whites moved into them.

Increasingly, black spokesmen insisted on policies for massive redistribution of resources as well as social status. Recall that David Jacobs, a militant spokesman for black Mobilians, made it plain: "White schools have the money. They have the facilities. They have the equipment. The white folks in the suburbs have the good teachers whether they are black or white. And they rob the black community of their best teachers to put them in white schools. And this is a fact."[5] The U.S. Justice Department and federal courts came to accept that view, and busing for racial balance was the result. Busing, which was on the horizon nationally, was an affirmative action program; it was designed to redistribute resources and respect between the two races. But many white people decried that logic and necessity. Recall the insistence of Westbrook: "Mr. Jacobs remarks that 'Black folks are tired.' I was just wondering why they wouldn't work. I was wondering why they was all on the welfare. And I was also wondering why they all went down to get their food stamps. But I guess they're tired. And I'm certainly glad to know that."[6] In 1968 for white radicals, work, not government largesse, was the solution for inequality.

1971

In 1971, when the federal courts threatened to use busing to achieve racial balance, white radicals continued to insist that black communities, as much as their own, were being seriously damaged by desegregation, and black communities would be hurt still further once busing began. The radicals' seeming respect for the integrity of black communities seemed contrary to their message for whites, to whom they continued to talk about the physical danger to white children if they were bused into black sections of town.

In Mobile conservative spokesmen began to accept the radicals' interpretation, although conservative leaders more often said that white children's values, not their physical safety, were at stake. The use of federal power, through busing, broke the back of traditional conservative leadership, because the conservatives' continued impotence in the face of federal power meant that whites could not trust them to maintain the status quo. Sure enough, the old elite lost control of the school board altogether when busing was implemented.

1977–80

Dan Alexander changed everything. Alexander told story after story about student and teacher incompetence. He said low standards hurt all children but particularly those from limited backgrounds. Social promotions prevented them from meaningful achievement. Poor teachers damaged too many children. The school system needed competency tests to raise the bar for all children and their teachers. This persistent appeal to individual achievement rather than racial discrimination overwhelmed black leaders. Alexander hardly ever mentioned race, yet black leaders knew that black children and black teachers were more likely to score low on the tests. Black leaders like Robert Gilliard and Norman Cox were in a double bind, because they too wanted

higher educational achievement. They chose to attack Dan Alexander's motives by calling him a racist, yet the values that Alexander expressed were core
values of American life: individual achievement in a fair and competitive
market. Black leaders attacked the legitimacy of the tests but implicitly conceded the superiority of Alexander's approach. By attacking Alexander's
motives while he voiced culturally fundamental values, they lost the moral
high ground.

Whites were able to read into Alexander's pronouncements what they liked.
Racial radicals believed that achievement tests would demonstrate the genetic and cultural inferiority of blacks, so they supported Alexander; conservatives especially liked his appeal to individual achievement, because it fit the
competitive free-market principles espoused by the national Republican Party,
to which they had become increasingly loyal. Alexander never claimed the
mantle of racial radicalism, but others often pushed him in that direction.

1984–98

Throughout the 1980s, in the face of a persistent gap in educational attain-
ment by blacks and whites, black spokesmen emerged who told stories of
damage done to black children and communities by busing and by the school
consolidation seemingly required for racial balance. Instead of racial balance
in schools, they wanted community schools rooted in the black cultural experience, so that parents, teachers, and children could work together. These
new stories held sway, and community schools became the hallmark of the
board's plan to end court-ordered desegregation in 1998. Ironically, white
radicals were the first whites (in 1968 and 1971) to offer public narratives about
the damage done to black communities by school desegregation, and by the
1990s a new biracial consensus had emerged: Busing hurts both children and
communities; we can have special programs, tailored to meet the interests
of particular students, who may opt to enroll, and these programs are to be
embedded within a school system made up of community schools.

Analysis

As this summary shows, people told many stories around the issue of school
desegregation and racial inequality over the years in Mobile. Each social
movement, whether liberal, conservative, or radical, favored its own version
of reality.

1. Radicals used stories to generate fear: fear of physical danger, fear of alien
ideas, and fear of contamination by black culture, and they used the fear to

engender hate. Initially, the radicals' narrative looked powerful: If you make us desegregate our schools, putting our children at risk, there will be a white rebellion, even including violence, on a massive scale. This radical story became lame as one crisis led to another and as most whites first complained and then complied with federal law rather than rise up in rebellion. The radicals' prediction of race war and chaos was proved false by major events in 1963, 1968, and 1971, which caused their claim to lose some of its force among whites.

2. The radicals used other stories more successfully. In Mobile white spokesmen publicly stated that desegregation, particularly busing, would destroy black communities, and over time many black leaders publicly articulated that story. When black children failed to achieve academically as quickly as had been hoped, the stresses of school desegregation, including the alleged neglect of black children in desegregated schools in white areas, led blacks to call for a return to black control of black community schools. Repetition of the underlying narrative by both whites and blacks seemed to figure in the success of this story, as did its emphasis on the core belief in the value of community in times of great uncertainty.

3. Dan Alexander told and acted out the story of the oppressive control of the Mobile schools by the federal government. He did not have to say, "just like last time," in order for many people, both black and white, to recall the first Reconstruction of the South. They were conditioned to believe that resistance, patience, and time favored yet another Redemption, when whites would once again gain political power and reestablish a racial hierarchy. So when Alexander began to talk of incompetent teachers and the unjustified "social promotions" of pupils, many people, both black and white, believed that he was offering another form of white Redemption. They regarded test scores and competence as the functional equivalent of the doctrine of separate-but-equal: Both were designed to put blacks back into a subordinate place. That is why Gilliard and Cox fought so hard. They just did not trust the race-neutral language to protect black children and teachers. But the stories of incompetence tapped into the deepest part of American culture. All Americans, black and white, favored the notion that real achievement should secure tangible reward. Anything that compromised individual achievement seemed indefensible in an increasingly competitive world.

4. The radicals' use of fear worked. It was not the fear of physical danger, but it was a kind of cultural fear. Many whites, perhaps most, believed that black cultural patterns, such as illegitimate births, single-parent families, crime, and substance abuse, would undermine white children's discipline and performance. Cultural assimilation might work the other way. Indicators of academic success in Mobile showed that black children achieved more than

they had before desegregation and that whites were not educationally hurt by desegregation, yet many believed otherwise.

5. Alexander introduced the rhetoric of student and teacher competence, touting individual achievement regardless of race. It is especially important to note that all this happened before Ronald Reagan became president. In fact, for Mobile's white population the Reagan administration seems only to have legitimized nationally the underlying public narrative first told by Alexander. Later, of course, Alexander was used by influential national conservatives, men like Richard Viguerie and Paul Weyrich, to mobilize a national movement, but he developed this line first and independently.

Reagan came to power in 1980 and spoke often about criminals and welfare cheats; everyone was aware that the faces of the miscreants were typically painted black. Clear evidence of this cultural shift occurred nationally after 1986 and may have been associated with the George H. W. Bush campaign's playing of the race card in the 1988 presidential election. By the late 1980s, more than any other explanation, people in Mobile and elsewhere came to believe that any continuing racial inequality was the fault of individual black people themselves, that they they simply did not try hard enough to achieve social and economic equality with whites.

6. Public rhetoric changed during these decades, but so did practice. Blacks and whites began to cooperate to achieve educational ends. In the mid-1980s the Mobile school board stopped being defiant and began to negotiate with the lawyer for the parent-plaintiffs in *Birdie Mae Davis* in order to anticipate and accept the complaints of black citizens. The school board agreed to create magnet programs in hard-to-desegregate inner-city schools and to establish in them racially balanced student populations. As a first priority, the board agreed to fund renovations and programs in inner-city schools so that black community schools would be first-rate facilities.

While all the metanarratives about racial inequality were voiced from time to time in the 1980s and 1990s, the notion of individual responsibility took hold. Both black and white leaders increasingly seemed to agree that lingering inequality between the races was the product of poor decisions and inadequate efforts by blacks themselves. Increasingly, though, blacks as well as whites seemed to need community schools as well as greater resources in order to achieve competitive success as individuals.

The Power of Stories

In this book I have argued that stories told in whole or in part, in public or private, are often political gestures with real effect. Thus storytellers are important political actors on the constantly evolving stage of human affairs. They engage people's imagination and stimulate action. In Mobile, clearly, the perceptions, values, and behaviors of many people, black as well as white southerners, changed during the decades that the community wrestled with school desegregation because they came to imagine a new and different world.

Political power has three different dimensions, and all were manifested in Mobile. Clearly, individuals and groups have political power to the extent that they command resources, like money, group size and strength, or knowledge and skills, because A can use these things to get B to do something that B would not otherwise do. Storytellers can help to mobilize resources. Stories told by liberal and radical leaders—men like Jerry Pogue and Bill Westbrook—energized citizens for action. But that is not the only face of power. Agenda setting, the largely unexceptional decision to permit some voices to be heard but not others, is also a kind of power. Without the capacity to express grievances publicly, nothing else is possible. Stories get attention. Those who have been in the political arena for a long time use this second face of power, almost without thought, against those who have yet to get their story heard. In Mobile, after a period of public spectacle in the 1970s, the Board of School Commissioners decided that aggrieved people could speak directly to the board only if they submitted a written statement well in advance of the monthly "delegation" meeting. How many people were unable to overcome this hurdle and were thus denied the public telling of their story? We can never know, because these inarticulate people were marginalized all the more by this exercise of the second face of power.

The third face of political power is the capture of "the other's" imagination, and this is the most powerful, if most subtle, aspect of systematic influence. Typically, in all societies some foundational myth becomes the engine of all life's energies. In the United States the myth of human progress is just such a myth. The notion that we can work hard to conquer nature and reap the benefits animates individuals and whole groups. A corollary myth is individual responsibility for one's success or failure in this land of opportunity. All our lives—our hopes and dreams, our fears and guilts, everything—is affected by these myths about the world.

The power of a public narrative rests on the use of foundation myths, but it is not limited to those alone. Personal stories told around a dinner table or across a back fence, public stories provided by politically active groups and institutions, conceptual stories undergirding the theories of social scientists—these too are filled with power. They too shape human perspectives and through them human destinies.

Stories are not faithful representations of a real world but subjective projections of our imaginations. When someone says that the public schools are no damn good and relates a personal story illustrating their failure, the story is as likely to be a psychological rationalization for personal preferences as an objectively accurate assessment of empirical facts. This is the stuff of life, and it is the way we come to see the world—through others' stories.

Nothing is inevitable about the process of change. Sometimes stories work their magic on our minds, and people come to see the world in a new way. But sometimes we just shake our head at the other's ignorance, ignorance made clear by the story she tells.

The real world disciplines us. The stories we tell cannot be thought credible if they differ too much from what we already know and believe or from what our own senses tell us. Nevertheless, because the empirical world is so often unclear, even to attentive observers, there is a wide latitude for narrative contest.

A focus on narrative politics gives priority to human beings in the process of social and cultural change. Great social forces—urbanization, Internet communications, commercial globalization—all the things that seem to drive the nations of the world are important, but so too are the storytellers, in all places and times.

The Future

By the end of the second reconstruction, Mobile had been refashioned. The distributions of racial attitudes, patterns of social interaction, and public policies were no longer predicated on a castelike racial hierarchy. The school board and others used the language of individualism and community to justify their new plans and programs. White public opinion accepted racial balance in schools as long as special programs were available for those who wanted to work at another pace or subject.

But the new culture masked continuing inequalities between the races in education, employment, health, and welfare. The difference between the Jim Crow South and the New South is the justification given for the continuing inequalities: innate differences versus individual effort.

As we have learned, dominant stories contain the seeds of government policy. At the end of Mobile's school desegregation saga, the conservative mentality regained priority of place largely because conservatism is a residual category. Stability is the hallmark of the conservative mentality, and people wanted stability. The implied terms of the new status quo fashioned out of school politics were these: The school board approved community schools and set up dedicated programs for those with special interests and talents.

Achievement tests certified one's standing for promotion from grade to grade or placement in special academic programs. Busing was no longer an issue as communities reclaimed their schools. Nearly everyone talked instead about the values of individual achievement within a context of cultural pluralism. Inequality can result from the aggregation of individual actions, but that is fair because everyone has a chance to succeed given the options available in the schools.

The liberal mentality in Mobile, and throughout much of the South, became moribund among whites over the years. Affirmative action in jobs and schooling offended many people because it became synonymous with reverse discrimination. Busing for racial balance was an affirmative action policy, and busing was credited with damaging communities and children. For a great many people the federal government, the principal tool of the liberal mind, became a distrusted agent of unwelcome change.

What about the old white radicals? What has become of them? At the end of the century Bill Westbrook had withdrawn into private life, and no one locally spoke from the old stories of innate racial difference. But nationally other voices, voices of white nationalism, continued to make that claim. It is as if Dixie had swept the nation.

Professor Carol Swain is not sanguine about the prospects. She argues that whites, who have become angry at racial double standards in education, employment, and government contracting, feel doubly threatened as they become aware that whites will become a minority ethnic group in the salad bowl that America promises to become sometime during the middle part of the twenty-first century.[7] She credits intellectuals among them—men like Jared Taylor, Michael Levin, and William Pierce—for boldly exercising narrative power in support of racial hierarchy.

According to Jared Taylor, author of *Paved with Good Intentions,* "Affirmative action . . . has come about only because we have a racially mixed society and blacks can't compete on an equal basis. They cannot do it by themselves so they get an extra boost from government. . . . They're biologically different."[8]

Michael Levin, a Jewish intellectual affiliated with the City University of New York, published *Why Race Matters: Racial Differences and What They Mean* (1997).[9] He also argues that blacks are genetically inferior: "There's a fact of discrepancy in outcomes between the races. Whites always do better than blacks in virtually any field of endeavor—whether it's education, making money, life span, you name it, except perhaps in athletics—and this difference in outcome is consistently blamed on white racism and white discrimination. . . . Now my central contention, which I think is pretty well documented by science, is that the reason whites do better than blacks comparatively is simply that they are more intelligent, they have certain traits of temperament which conduce to long-run success, and these differences are genetic in origin."[10]

It is not just these few who peer into the genetic abyss. The researchers Mark Snyderman and Stanley Rothman surveyed a sample of mostly academic experts and found that 53 percent believed that IQ differences between whites and African Americans were genetic; 17 percent attributed the IQ differences to environmental forces, while 28 percent refused to answer.[11]

William Pierce, a former physics professor at the University of Oregon, wrote *The Turner Diaries,* and it has become the bible of the nationalist cause.[12] The *Diaries* give a fictional account of racial apocalypse.

These new storytellers have a common theme: Contemporary white nationalists have a strong belief in the genetic and cultural inequality of the races, and they want to make race a qualification for full membership in the nation. In this way they build upon and subsume the mentality of the old southern white radical.

In Mobile, in the South, and in the United States liberal, conservative, and radical views of racial inequality remain embedded in the minds of citizens, waiting only for new interpretations to be offered, of both new and old events, by new storytellers in the endless struggle over our collective destiny.

Notes

Introduction

1. Charles Grayson Summersell, *Mobile: History of a Seaport Town* (University: University of Alabama Press, 1949).

2. Stevens is quoted in T. Harry Williams, Richard N. Current, and Frank Freidel, *A History of the United States, to 1876* (New York: Alfred A. Knopf, 1959), 655.

3. Tourgee is quoted in T. Harry Williams, Richard N. Current, and Frank Freidel, *A History of the United States, Since 1865* (New York: Alfred A. Knopf, 1959), 28.

4. Joel Williamson, *The Crucible of Race: Black-White Relations in the American South Since Emancipation* (New York: Oxford University Press, 1984), 5–7.

5. Molly Patterson and Kristen Renwick Monroe, "Narrative in Political Science," *Annual Review of Political Science* (Palo Alto, Calif.: Annual Reviews, 1998), 315–31.

6. Ibid., 316.

7. Margaret R. Somers and Gloria D. Gibson, "Reclaiming the Epistemological 'Other': Narrative and the Social Constitution of Identity," in *Social Theory and the Politics of Identity*, ed. Craig J. Calhoun (Oxford: Blackwell, 1994), 35–99.

8. Ibid.; others call these metastories. See Sanford Schram and Philip Neisser, eds., *Tales of the State: Narrative in Contemporary U.S. Politics and Public Policy* (New York: Rowman and Littlefield, 1997), 11.

9. James S. Coleman et al., *Equality of Educational Opportunity* (Washington, D.C.: U.S. Department of Health, Education, and Welfare, 1966).

10. *National Observer,* June 7, 1975; see also David J. Armor, *Forced Justice: School Desegregation and the Law* (New York: Oxford University Press, 1995).

11. H. S. Jennings, et al., *Scientific Aspects of the Race Problem* (New York: Longmans, Green, 1941); August Meier, *Negro Thought in America, 1880–1915: Racial Ideologies in the Age of Booker T. Washington* (Ann Arbor: University of Michigan Press, 1963); Cal M. Logue and Howard Dorgan, eds., *The Oratory of Southern Demagogues* (Baton Rouge: Louisiana State University Press, 1981); Kelly Miller, *Radicals and Conservatives* (New York: Schocken, 1968), first published in 1908 under the title *Race Adjustment;* John LeConte,

The Race Problem in the South (Miami: Mnemosyne, 1969), first published in 1892 by D. Appleton, New York; William Archer, *Through Afro-America* (Westport, Conn.: Negro Universities Press, 1970), originally published in 1910 by Chapman Hall Ltd., London; Edgar Thompson, ed., *Race Relations and the Race Problem: A Definition and Analysis* (Durham, N.C.: Duke University Press, 1939); William H. Tucker, *The Science and Politics of Racial Research* (Urbana: University of Illinois Press, 1994); James B. McKee, *Sociology and the Race Problem: The Failed Perspective* (Urbana: University of Illinois Press, 1993); J. David Smith, *Eugenic Assault on America: Scenes in Red, White, and Black* (Fairfax, Va.: George Mason University Press, 1993); Roy L. Brooks, *Rethinking the American Race Problem* (Berkeley: University of California Press, 1990).

12. Richard Herrnstein and Charles Murray, *The Bell Curve: Intelligence and Social Class in American Life* (New York: Free Press, 1994).

13. *Intelligence: A Multidisciplinary Journal* 24 (1994): 1. The journal is published in Greenwich, Connecticut, by Ablex.

14. Edward Banfield, *The Unheavenly City: The Nature and Future of Our Urban Crisis* (Boston: Little, Brown, 1970).

15. Robert Singh, *The Farrakhan Phenomenon: Race, Reaction, and the Paranoid Style in American Politics* (Washington, D.C.: Georgetown University Press, 1997), 262–65.

16. Thomas Sowell, *Race and Economics* (New York: David McKay, 1975).

17. Charles Murray, *Losing Ground: American Social Policy, 1950–1980* (New York: Basic Books, 1984).

18. Arthur M. Schlesinger Jr., *The Disuniting of America: Reflections on a Multicultural Society* (New York: W. W. Norton, 1992).

19. Patricia A. Turner, *I Heard It Through the Grapevine* (Berkeley: University of California Press, 1993).

20. Andrew Hacker, *Two Nations: Black and White, Separate, Hostile, Unequal* (New York: Ballantine Books, 1995), 218.

21. Michael Thompson, Richard Ellis, and Aaron Wildavsky, *Cultural Theory* (Boulder, Colo.: Westview Press, 1990), 1.

22. Ibid.; see the discussion that begins on p. 5. The interaction of two dimensions of social life defines cultural types. First is a group dimension; it refers to the degree to which an individual is embedded within specific social units. The grid dimension denotes the degree to which individuals are constrained by externally imposed injunctions.

23. Richard J. Ellis, *American Political Cultures* (New York: Oxford University Press, 1993).

24. Richard A. Pride and J. David Woodard, *The Burden of Busing: The Politics of Desegregation in Nashville, Tennessee* (Knoxville: University of Tennessee Press, 1985).

25. Harry Eckstein, "Culturalist Theory of Political Change," *American Political Science Review* 82 (September 1988): 789–804; Steven Chilton, "Defining Political Culture," *Western Political Quarterly* 41 (September 1988): 419–45; John Street, "Review Article: From Civic Culture to Mass Culture," *British Journal of Political Science* 24 (January 1994): 95–114.

26. Frederick M. Dolan and Thomas L. Dumm, eds., *Rhetorical Republic: Governing Representations on American Politics* (Amherst: University of Massachusetts Press, 1993).

27. Donald Schon and Martin Rein, *Frame Reflection: Toward the Resolution of Intrac-*

table Policy Controversies (New York: Basic Books, 1994); Schram and Neisser, *Tales of the State;* Emery Roe, *Narrative Policy Analysis: Theory and Practice* (Durham, N.C.: Duke University Press, 1994).

28. Murray Edelman, *The Symbolic Uses of Politics* (Urbana: University of Illinois Press, 1964).

29. Richard Merelman, *Representing Black Culture: Racial Conflict and Cultural Politics in the United States* (New York: Routledge, 1995), 3.

30. Stanford M. Lyman, "The Contribution of Herbert Blumer," *Symbolic Interaction* 7:1 (Spring 1974): 107–20.

31. Laurel Richardson, "Narrative and Sociology," *Journal of Contemporary Ethnography* 19:1 (April 1990): 116–35; David R. Maines, "Narrative's Moment and Sociology's Phenomena: Toward a Narrative Sociology," *Sociological Quarterly* 34:1 (1993): 17–38; David R. Maines, "Information Pools and Racialized Narrative Structures," *Sociological Quarterly* 40:2 (1999): 317–26; David R. Maines and Jeffrey C. Bridger, "Narratives, Community and Land Use Decisions," *The Social Science Journal* 29:4 (1992): 363–80.

32. David R. Maines, *The Faultline of Consciousness: A View of Interactionism in Sociology* (New York: Aldine de Gruyter, 2001).

33. Ibid., 207.

34. John Gaventa, *Power and Powerlessness: Quiescence and Rebellion in an Appalachian Valley* (Urbana: University of Illinois Press, 1980).

35. Christopher Lasch, *The True and Only Heaven: Progress and Its Critics* (New York: W. W. Norton, 1991).

36. Williamson, *Crucible of Race*, 182.

37. Ibid., 89.

38. Schram and Neisser, *Tales of the State*, 5.

39. Ibid.

40. Walter R. Fisher, *Human Communication as Narration: Toward a Philosophy of Reason, Value, and Action* (Columbia: University of South Carolina Press, 1987).

41. Ibid., foreword.

42. Ibid., 48.

43. Ibid., 48–49.

44. Ibid., ix.

45. Ibid., 23.

46. Ibid., 194.

47. Ibid.

48. Aldon D. Morris and Carol McClurg Mueller, eds., *Frontiers of Social Movement Theory* (New Haven, Conn.: Yale University Press, 1992).

49. Stephen Hilgartner and Charles Bosk, "The Rise and Fall of Social Problems: A Public Arenas Model," *American Journal of Sociology* 94 (1988): 55; Roe, *Narrative Policy Analysis.*

50. Richard A. Pride, "How Activists and Media Frame Social Problems: Critical Events Versus Performance Trends for Schools," *Political Communication* 12:1 (1995): 5–26.

51. L. M. Killian, "Social Movements," in *Handbook of Modern Sociology*, ed. Robert E. L. Faris (Chicago: Rand McNally, 1964), 447–48; Neil J. Smelser, *Theory of Collective Behavior* (New York: Free Press, 1962), 16–17.

52. Suzanne Staggenborg, "Critical Events and the Mobilization of the Pro-Choice Movement," *Research in Political Sociology* 6 (1993): 320; emphasis added.

53. Ibid.

54. Milton Gordon, *Assimilation in American Life* (New York: Oxford University Press, 1964).

55. Schlesinger, *Disuniting of America.*

56. Pride and Woodard, *Burden of Busing.*

57. Carl L. Bankston and Stephen J. Caldas, *A Troubled Dream: The Promise and Failure of School Desegregation in Louisiana* (Nashville, Tenn.: Vanderbilt University Press, 2002).

58. Samuel P. Huntington, *American Politics: The Promise of Disharmony* (Cambridge, Mass.: Harvard University Press, 1981).

59. Ibid.

60. Jennifer L. Hochschild, *Facing Up to the American Dream: Race, Class, and the Soul of the Nation* (Princeton, N.J.: Princeton University Press, 1995).

Chapter 1: Breaking the Color Line

1. Copy in author's possession.

2. Charles S. Bullock III and Charles M. Lamb, *Implementation of Civil Rights Policy* (Monterey, Calif.: Brooks Cole, 1984), 56.

3. 1955 Ala. Acts 492.

4. Dorothy DaPonte, interview by author, Mobile, Alabama, July 5, 1986.

5. *Alabama Journal,* Sept. 15, 1956.

6. Ibid.

7. Copy in author's possession.

8. *Mobile Press,* Sept. 12, 1956.

9. *Mobile Register,* Sept. 18, 1956.

10. *New York Post,* Nov. 11, 1956.

11. Albert S. Foley, S. J., "The Dynamics of School Desegregation in Mobile, Alabama," National Institute of Education Project (Harvard Graduate School of Education, Boston, 1978), 6.

12. Ibid., 8.

13. For more of this story see Richard Pride, *The Confession of Dorothy Danner: Telling a Life* (Nashville, Tenn.: Vanderbilt University Press, 1995).

14. A review of the data shows that other candidates often appeared on the ballot, but they got few votes in the countywide at-large elections that were held then. When I asked informants about this, they said that deference to the elite was considerable and that "word was simply put out" about who should be elected; there was no real campaigning.

15. Copy in author's possession.

16. Taylor Branch, *Parting the Waters: America in the King Years, 1954–63* (New York: Simon and Schuster, 1989), 186–87.

17. 1955 Ala. Acts 492.

18. David J. Garrow, *Bearing the Cross: Martin Luther King, Jr., and the Southern Christian Leadership Conference* (New York: William Morrow, 1986), 11–82.

19. *Mobile Register,* Feb. 12, 1981; on political action and economic vulnerability see Lester Salamon and Stephen Van Evera, "Fear, Apathy, and Discrimination," *American Political Science Review* 67:4 (1973): 1288–1306.

20. Central Office, Mobile County Public Schools, *1962 Workbook,* 166, archived—as are all school records—at the main administration building, Barton Academy, 504 Government Street, Mobile (hereafter Barton Academy archives).

21. Ibid., 33 and 96.

22. Board of School Commissioners, Mobile County Public Schools, Minutes, Nov. 28, 1962, Barton Academy archives.

23. *Mobile Register,* Jan. 17, 1963.

24. *Mobile Register,* Feb. 2, 1963.

25. James U. Blacksher and Gregory B. Stein, "Proposed Findings of Facts and Conclusions of Law," *Birdie Mae Davis et al., Plaintiffs; Joyce Figures Gant et al., Plaintiffs-Intervenors v. Board of School Commissioners et al.,* Civil Action No. 3003-63-H, Apr. 3, 1984, p. 4, from the files of Blacksher and Stein, Mobile; seven of the new schools were to be all black.

26. *Mobile Press* and *Register,* June 26, 1963.

27. The court did permit the school board to postpone desegregation of rural areas of the county until 1964. The board's efforts to have the full Fifth U.S. Circuit Court of Appeals overturn the three-judge panel were rejected. The school board subsequently decided to apply to the U.S. Supreme Court for a stay of the Fifth Circuit's injunction.

28. *Mobile Register,* July 10, 1963.

29. *Mobile Register,* July 18, 1963.

30. Foley, "Dynamics of School Desegregation," 11–12.

31. At an August 12 hearing in U.S. District Court, Thomas ruled that the board's plan had to include only the city of Mobile; desegregating the rural areas of the county could be delayed until September 1964. Both parties had stipulated to the bifurcation of the county between city and rural areas, but the parents had wanted the first stage to include the cities of Prichard and Chickasaw with Mobile in the first stage of desegregation, and Thomas's ruling did not include them. After the hearing Clarence Moses, attorney for the parents, said the NAACP in New York would decide whether to appeal Thomas's ruling.

32. *Board of School Commissioners of Mobile Co. v. Davis,* 84 S. Ct. 11, 11–12 (Black, Circuit Justice, 1963).

33. *Mobile Register,* Aug. 20, 1963.

34. Ibid.

35. *Mobile Register,* Aug. 30, 1963.

36. *Mobile Register,* Sept. 2, 1963.

37. *Mobile Press,* Sept. 11, 1963, and *Mobile Register,* Sept. 11, 1963.

38. Joseph Gusfield, *Symbolic Crusade: Status Politics and the American Temperance Movement* (Urbana: University of Illinois Press, 1986), 16.

39. *Mobile Press,* Sept. 11, 1963, and *Mobile Register,* Sept. 11, 1963.

40. Charles E. McNeil, interview by author, Mobile, July 14, 1986.

41. *Mobile Press,* Sept. 10, 1963, and *Mobile Register,* Sept. 10, 1963.

42. *Mobile Press,* Sept. 11, 1963, and *Mobile Register,* Sept. 11, 1963. These incidents are discussed from Wallace's point of view in Stephan Lesher, *George Wallace: American Populist* (Reading, Mass.: Addison-Wesley, 1994), 237–53.

43. *Mobile Register,* Sept. 11, 1963.

44. Ibid.

45. Ibid.

46. *Mobile Register,* Sept. 12, 1963.

47. *Mobile Press,* Sept. 12, 1963.

48. Foley, "Dynamics of School Desegregation," 16.

49. *Mobile Register,* Sept. 17, 1963.

50. *Mobile Register,* Oct. 3, 1963.

51. Foley, "Dynamics of School Desegregation," 17–18.

Chapter 2: Freedom of Choice, 1963–68

1. *Mobile Press,* Nov. 15, 1963.

2. Transcript, *Birdie Mae Davis et al., Plaintiffs; Joyce Figures Gant et al., Plaintiffs-Intervenors v. Board of School Commissioners et al.,* Civil Action No. 3003-63-H, Nov. 14, 1963, pp. 9–19.

3. Ibid., 19–22.

4. Ibid., 19–27; *Ralph Stell et al. v. Savannah-Chatham County Board of Education, et al.,* 200 F. Supp. 667 (1973). In this case the U.S. District Court had agreed that the school board could use educational grounds for assigning students. The case was on appeal when Thomas heard arguments in *Birdie Mae Davis.*

5. Cranford Burns, interview by author, Mobile, May 26, 1987.

6. Ibid.

7. Ibid.; Charles McNeil, interview by author, July 14, 1986; Bob Williams, interview by author, July 13, 1986; William Crane, interview by author, May 27, 1987.

8. Transcript, *Birdie Mae Davis,* 28–77.

9. Ibid.

10. *Mobile Register,* Nov. 16, 1963.

11. Ibid.

12. Ibid.

13. Ibid.

14. *Armstrong v. Board of Education of the City of Birmingham,* 333 F.2d 47 (5th Cir. 1964).

15. James Blacksher and Gregory Stein, "Proposed Findings of Fact and Conclusions of Law," *Birdie Mae Davis,* Apr. 3, 1984, pp. 6–7, from the files of Blacksher and Stein, Mobile. Thomas held another hearing on the NAACP's motion on February 21, 1965, but on March 31 he once again approved the board's plan with minor modifications.

16. Ibid., 7–8.

17. *Mobile Press,* Sept. 2, 1964, and *Mobile Register,* Sept. 2, 1964.

18. *Mobile Register,* May 14, 1966.

19. *Mobile Register,* Aug. 13, 1966.

20. *Birdie Mae Davis,* 364 F.2d 896 (5th Cir. 1966).

21. *Mobile Register,* Sept. 7, 1966.

22. *U.S. v. Jefferson County Board of Education*, 380 F.2d 385, 389–90 (5th Cir. 1967). On March 30, 1967, the Fifth Circuit, sitting en banc, affirmed the panel's December 30 ruling.

23. *Mobile Press*, June 15, 1967.

24. *Mobile Press*, Sept. 9, 1967.

25. *Mobile Press*, Sept. 2, 1967.

26. *Mobile Register*, Aug. 16, 1967.

27. *Mobile Press*, Oct. 14, 1967.

28. *Mobile Press*, Dec. 5, 1967.

29. *Mobile Press*, Jan. 1, 1968.

30. *Birdie Mae Davis*, 393 F.2d 690 (5th Cir. 1968); *Mobile Register*, Mar. 13, 1968.

31. Blacksher and Stein, "Proposed Findings," 10.

32. Ibid., 11–14.

33. Albert S. Foley, S. J., "The Dynamics of School Desegregation in Mobile, Alabama," National Institute of Education Project, Harvard Graduate School of Education, Boston, 1978, pp. 29–30.

34. Ibid., 30–31.

35. Ibid., 32.

36. Ibid. The American Friends Service Committee appealed the order to the Fifth U.S. Circuit Court of Appeals, which overruled Thomas six months later.

37. *Mobile Register*, May 21, 1968.

38. Ibid.

39. Ibid.

40. *Mobile Register*, May 28, 1968.

41. *Mobile Press*, May 30, 1968.

42. *Mobile Press*, May 27, 1968.

43. *Mobile Register*, May 31, 1968, and *Mobile Press*, May 31, 1968.

44. *Mobile Register*, June 13, 1968.

45. *Mobile Register*, June 25, 1968.

46. Ibid.

47. *Mobile Register*, July 17, 1968.

48. *Mobile Register*, July 19, 1968.

49. *Mobile Register*, July 20, 1968.

50. *Mobile Register*, July 23, 1968.

51. Ibid. Under Lieberman's proposed attendance zones for senior high schools, Williamson, Central, and Blount, the all-black high schools, would become 57 percent, 14 percent, and 25 percent white, respectively. The overwhelmingly white Murphy, Shaw, and Vigor high schools would become 34 percent, 12 percent, and 40 percent black, respectively.

52. *Mobile Register*, July 23, 1968.

53. Ibid.

54. *Mobile Register*, July 25, 1968.

55. Ibid.

56. Ibid.

57. *Mobile Register*, July 26, 1968.

58. Foley, "Dynamics of School Desegregation," 30.

59. *Mobile Register,* July 30, 1968.

60. Blacksher and Stein, "Proposed Findings," 12.

61. *Mobile Press,* July 31, 1968.

62. Foley, "Dynamics of School Desegregation," 28.

Chapter 3: Assimilation

1. Milton Gordon, *Assimilation in American Life* (New York: Oxford University Press, 1964), 85.

2. *Mobile Press,* Sept. 6, 1968.

3. *Mobile Press,* Sept. 9, 1968.

4. *Mobile Press,* Oct. 2, 1968.

5. *Mobile Press,* Sept. 16, 1968.

6. *Mobile Press,* Oct. 1 and 4, 1968.

7. *Mobile Press,* Nov. 27, 1968.

8. *Mobile Register,* Feb. 13, 1969.

9. David L. Jacobs to Cranford Burns, Jan. 20, 1969, in Board of School Commissioners, Mobile County Public Schools, Minutes (hereafter, Board Minutes), Jan. 22, 1969, archived at Barton Academy, 504 Government Street, Mobile.

10. Ibid.

11. W. B. Westbrook to the school board, Jan. 18, 1969, in Board Minutes, Jan. 22, 1969.

12. *Mobile Register,* Feb. 13, 1969.

13. Board Minutes, Apr. 23, 1969, p. 119.

14. Ibid., 120.

15. Ibid.

16. Ibid., 124.

17. Board Minutes, May 28, 1969, p. 159.

18. Ibid., 160.

19. Ibid., 164.

20. Ibid., 162.

21. Ibid., 163.

22. Court order, *Birdie Mae Davis et al., Plaintiffs; Joyce Figures Gant et al., Plaintiffs-Intervenors v. Board of School Commissioners et al.,* Civil Action No. 3003-63-H, Mar. 14, 1969, pp. 1–2.

23. *Mobile Press* and *Register,* Dec. 29, 1968.

24. *Mobile Press,* Apr. 8, 1969.

25. *Davis v. Board of School Commissioners of Mobile County,* 414 F.2d 609, 610–11 (5th Cir. 1969).

26. *Mobile Register,* June 11, 1969.

27. *Mobile Press,* June 6, 1969.

28. The elementary schools were Owens, Stanton Road, Gorgas, Brazier, and Grant.

29. *Mobile Register,* July 11, 1969.

30. The plan called for crosstown busing of 1,260 pupils to the following elementary schools: John Will, 40; Forrest Hill, 355; Austin, 65; Fonde, 225; Shepard, 125; Morningside, 120; Maryvale, 130; Mertz, 125; and Westlawn, 75.

31. *Mobile Register,* July 25, 1969.

32. *Mobile Register,* July 30, 1969.

33. *Mobile Press,* July 12, 1969.

34. *Mobile Press,* July 15, 1969.

35. *Mobile Press,* Aug. 1, 1969, and *Mobile Register,* Aug. 2, 1969.

36. Order, *Birdie Mae Davis,* Aug. 1, 1969; *Mobile Press,* Aug. 1, 1969, and *Mobile Register,* Aug. 2, 1969.

37. *Mobile Press,* Aug. 1, 1969, and *Mobile Register,* Aug. 2, 1969.

38. *Mobile Register,* Aug. 7, 1969.

39. Board Minutes, July 23, 1969, p. 213.

40. Ibid.

41. Ibid., 215.

42. Ibid., 216.

43. Board Minutes, Aug. 27, 1969, pp. 256–57.

44. *Mobile Register,* Sept. 24 and 25, 1969. The headline appeared in the paper of Sept. 25.

45. Board Minutes, Sept. 24, 1969, p. 285.

46. *Mobile Register,* Sept. 24 and 25, 1969.

47. *Mobile Register,* Sept. 26, 1969.

48. *Mobile Press* and *Register,* Oct. 10, 1969.

49. Board Minutes, Oct. 22, 1969, p. 316.

50. Ibid., 317–18.

51. Board Minutes, Nov. 12, 1969, pp. 344–45.

52. *Birdie Mae Davis* was considered with *Singleton v. Jackson,* 419 F.2d 1211, 1220 (5th Cir. 1970) (en banc).

53. *Mobile Register,* Jan. 20 and 27, 1970.

54. Board Minutes, Jan. 28, 1970, p. 21.

55. Ibid., 18–19.

56. Court order, *Birdie Mae Davis,* Jan. 31, 1970, pp. 1–2.

57. The order may be found in James Blacksher and Gregory Stein, "Proposed Findings of Fact and Conclusions of Law Concerning Youngblood Hearing, Submitted by the Plaintiffs Birdie Mae Davis, et al., and Plaintiffs-Intervenors Joyce Figures Gant, et al.," *Birdie Mae Davis,* Oct. 7, 1969, pp. 18–23, from the files of Blacksher and Stein, Mobile.

58. *Mobile Register,* Feb. 1, 1970.

59. Board Minutes, Feb. 25, 1970, p. 59.

60. Ibid., 66.

61. *Mobile Register,* Mar. 6, 1970.

62. *Mobile Register,* Mar. 19, 1970.

63. Ibid.

64. Ibid.

65. *Mobile Register,* Mar. 24, 1970.

66. *Birdie Mae Davis,* 430 F.2d 883, 883–88 (5th Cir. 1970).

67. *Mobile Press,* Aug. 13, 1970; in the July 1970 plan the all-white schools were Chickasaw, Westlawn, Mertz, Forest Hill, and Morningside. The all-black schools would be Robbins and Brazier.

68. *Mobile Press,* July 29, 1970; the STEP plan caused conflict within the black community. See Board Minutes, July 22, 1970, p. 255.

69. Board Minutes, July 22, 1970, pp. 269–70.

70. *Mobile Register,* Aug. 30, 1970.

Chapter 4: Busing

1. *Mobile Register,* Sept. 9, 1970.

2. Albert S. Foley, S. J., "The Dynamics of School Desegregation in Mobile, Alabama," National Institute of Education Project, Harvard Graduate School of Education, Boston, 1978, pp. 39–40.

3. Ibid., 41.

4. *Mobile Register,* Sept. 10, 1970.

5. Ibid.

6. *Mobile Register,* Sept. 11, 1970.

7. *Mobile Register,* Sept. 12, 1970.

8. *Mobile Register,* Sept. 11, 1970.

9. *Mobile Register,* Sept. 12, 1970.

10. *Mobile Press,* Sept. 14, 1970.

11. Foley, "Dynamics of School Desegregation," 43–45.

12. Ibid., 48–49.

13. *Mobile Register,* Oct. 4, 1970.

14. *Mobile Press,* Oct. 8, 1970.

15. *Mobile Press,* Sept. 25, 1970.

16. *Mobile Press,* Oct. 8, 1970. Barton Academy was the first public school in Alabama. In time it became the central office headquarters for the Mobile public schools and a meeting place for the school board.

17. *Mobile Register,* Oct. 14, 1970.

18. *Mobile Press* and *Register,* Jan. 31, 1971.

19. *Mobile Beacon,* Feb. 6, 1971.

20. Ibid.

21. *Mobile Press,* Feb. 23, 1971.

22. *Mobile Register,* Feb. 27, 1971.

23. *Mobile Press,* Feb. 23, 1971.

24. *Mobile Register,* Feb. 26, 1971.

25. *Mobile Press,* Apr. 20, 1971.

26. *Swann v. Charlotte-Mecklenburg Board of Education,* 402 U.S. 1 (1971).

27. *Mobile Press,* Apr. 21, 1971, and *Mobile Register,* Apr. 21, 1971.

28. Ibid.

29. *Mobile Register,* Apr. 24, 1971.

30. Board of School Commissioners, Mobile County Public Schools, Minutes (hereafter, Board Minutes), Apr. 28, 1971, archived at Barton Academy, 504 Government Street, Mobile.

31. Ibid., "Exhibit D."

32. *Mobile Beacon,* July 10, 1971.

33. *Mobile Press,* May 14, 1971.

34. Foley, "Dynamics of School Desegregation," 59.

35. Ibid., 60.

36. *Mobile Register,* July 10, 1971.

37. The schools were Chickasaw, Indian Springs, Eight Mile, Hamilton, Shepard, Mertz, Westlawn, Dickson, Will, Austin, Forest Hill, Fonde, Crichton, Woodcock, Morningside, Adelia Williams, Brookley, Craighead, and Dodge.

38. The schools were Brazier, Owens, Fonvielle, Robbins, and Stanton Road.

39. The schools were Caldwell and Ella Grant.

40. *Mobile Register,* July 10, 1971; Foley, "Dynamics of School Desegregation," 62–64.

41. *Mobile Register,* July 22, 1971.

42. *Mobile Press,* July 16, 1971

43. *Mobile Press,* July 28, 1971.

44. *Mobile Press,* Aug. 2, 1971.

45. Board Minutes, July 28, 1971, p. 126.

46. Ibid., 127.

47. Ibid., 129.

48. *Mobile Press,* Aug. 18, 1971.

49. *Mobile Press,* Aug. 19, 1971.

50. Ibid.

51. Foley, "Dynamics of School Desegregation," 65.

52. *Mobile Register,* Sept. 9, 1971.

53. *Birmingham News,* Sept. 3, 1971.

54. Foley, "Dynamics of School Desegregation," 67. Foley reports that this work was funded by the National Institute of Mental Health.

55. *Mobile Beacon,* May 29, 1971; Foley, "Dynamics of School Desegregation," 66–67.

56. Foley, "Dynamics of School Desegregation," 68–69.

57. *Mobile Register,* Sept. 3, 1971.

58. *Mobile Press,* July 14, 1971.

59. *Mobile Press,* Aug. 27, 1971.

60. Foley, "Dynamics of School Desegregation," 70–71.

61. Ibid., 72.

62. *Mobile Register,* Oct. 2, 1971; *Birmingham News,* Oct. 2, 1971.

63. *Mobile Register,* Oct. 5, 1971.

64. *Mobile Press,* Nov. 23, 1971; *Birmingham News,* Dec. 28, 1971.

65. James Blacksher and Gregory Stein, "Proposed Findings of Fact and Conclusions of Law Concerning Youngblood Hearing, Submitted by Plaintiffs Birdie Mae Davis, et al., and Plaintiffs-Intervenors Joyce Figures Gant, et al.," *Birdie Mae Davis et al., Plaintiffs; Joyce Figures Gant et al., Plaintiffs-Intervenors v. Board of School Commissioners et al.,* Civil Action No. 3003-63-H, Apr. 3, 1984, from the files of Blacksher and Stein, Mobile.

66. Foley, "Dynamics of School Desegregation," 72–73.

Chapter 5: Power Transitions

1. *Mobile Register,* July 5, 1972.

2. *Mobile Press,* Apr. 6, 1973.

3. Albert S. Foley, S. J., "The Dynamics of School Desegregation in Mobile, Alabama,"

National Institute of Education Project, Harvard Graduate School of Education, Boston, 1978, pp. 79–80.

4. Ibid., 74.

5. Ibid., 75–76.

6. Ibid.

7. Ibid., 77.

8. Ibid., 78.

9. U.S. Commission on Civil Rights, *Desegregating the Boston Public Schools: A Crisis of Civic Responsibility,* (Washington, D.C.: U.S. Government Printing Office, 1975), xxiii; see also Judith F. Buncher, ed., *The School Busing Controversy: 1970–75* (New York: Facts on File, 1975), 248.

10. *Mobile Press,* Apr. 13, 1974, and *Mobile Register,* Apr. 13, 1974.

11. Board of School Commissioners, Mobile County Public Schools, Minutes (hereafter, Board Minutes), Feb. 26, 1975.

12. Board Minutes, Mar. 5, 1975.

13. Board Minutes, Mar. 26, 1975, p. 63.

14. Board Minutes, Aug. 13, 1975.

15. Board Minutes, June 25, 1975.

16. Board Minutes, Sept. 10, 1975, pp. 270–73; the Silverstein quote appears on p. 270.

17. Board Minutes, Nov. 12, 1975, pp. 337–40; the pie quote appears on p. 340.

18. Board Minutes, Jan. 7, 1976.

19. *Bolden v. City of Mobile,* Civil Action No. 75-297-P (S.D. Ala.), and *Brown v. Board of School Commissioners of Mobile County,* Civil Action No. 75-298-P (S.D. Ala. 1975).

20. Chandler Davidson, ed., *Minority Vote Dilution* (Washington, D.C.: Howard University Press, 1984); for Mobile see esp. Peyton McCrary, "The Significance of *Bolden v. The City of Mobile,*" 47–63.

21. Board Minutes, Apr. 27, 1977.

22. *U.S. News and World Report,* Feb. 6, 1978, pp. 48–49.

23. *Phi Delta Kappan,* Feb. 1978, p. 398.

24. Board Minutes, Jan. 11, 1978, p. 4.

25. Ibid.

26. Board Minutes, Jan. 16, 1978.

27. Board Minutes, Jan. 25, 1978.

28. Ibid., 41–42. In the discussion staff members mentioned balancing a check book and being able to perform artificial respiration as nonacademic survival skills.

29. These were recommended in addition to the special education diploma, which was already issued to trainable and educable mentally challenged students.

30. Board Minutes, Jan. 25, 1978; at the regular January 25 meeting of the board, other troubles manifested themselves. The system needed about 150 more teachers, because of state-mandated kindergarten, special education, and vocational requirements, as well as the board's effort to reduce the pupil-teacher ratio. In the past, particularly since 1970, the system had been able to place teachers in make-do classrooms in hallways, conference rooms, and closets, but this could no longer be done. The board needed to consider purchasing more portables or going on double session in some schools. During the board's general discussion, it came out that the district had only $30 million for capital improvements but need-

ed $225 million. The district could not build new additions or new schools without the support of the NAACP, which was representing the parent-plaintiffs in the *Birdie Mae Davis* case. Board members wondered aloud whether the NAACP would cooperate.

31. Board Minutes, Feb. 15, 1978.

32. Board Minutes, Feb. 22, 1978.

33. Board Minutes, Mar. 1, 1978.

34. Board Minutes, Mar. 15, 1978.

35. Board Minutes, Mar. 22, 1978.

36. Ibid., p. 112.

37. *Mobile Register,* Mar. 25, 1978.

38. Board Minutes, special meeting, Mar. 29, 1978.

39. Board Minutes, Apr. 12, 1978, p. 125.

40. Ibid.

41. Ibid.

42. Ibid.

43. Board Minutes, May 10, 1978.

44. Board Minutes, May 19, 1978.

45. Board Minutes, May 24, 1978, p. 199.

46. Ibid.

47. Board Minutes, May 29, 1978, p. 236.

48. Board Minutes, June 30, 1978.

49. Board Minutes, July 26, 1978.

50. Board Minutes, Aug. 2, 1978.

Chapter 6: Community School

1. Court order, *Birdie Mae Davis et al., Plaintiffs; Joyce Figures Gant et al., Plaintiffs-Intervenors v. Board of School Commissioners et al.,* Civil Action No. 3003-63-H, Dec. 20, 1968; see Abe Philips to Harold Collins, May 17, 1972, and attachment 177A, archived at Barton Academy, 504 Government Street, Mobile (hereafter, Barton Academy archives).

2. Court order, *Birdie Mae Davis,* Mar. 14, 1969; see Philips to Collins and attachment 179A.

3. The appellate court, as part of the more general review of the Mobile case in which it ruled that freedom of choice was unconstitutional, enjoined construction of Toulminville High School, among other projects on June 3, 1969; see Philips to Collins and attachment 187A-87B.

4. *Singleton v. Jackson,* 419 F.2d 1211, 1218 (5th Cir. 1970), emphasis added.

5. "A Comprehensive Plan for a Unitary School System," July 8, 1971, p. 13, Barton Academy archives.

6. *Mobile Register,* Mar. 9, 1972, and *Mobile Press,* Mar. 9, 1972.

7. *Mobile Beacon,* Mar. 18, 1972.

8. Abe Philips to Harold Collins, May 17, 1972, Barton Academy archives.

9. Court order, *Birdie Mae Davis,* Mar. 28, 1975.

10. See Mobile school board report to U.S. District Court, October 1974, Barton Academy archives.

11. Court order, *Birdie Mae Davis,* Mar. 28, 1975, p. 9, n. 5.

12. Ibid., 8.

13. John L. Devery Jr. to Harold R. Collins, May 7, 1975, Barton Academy archives.

14. Ibid.

15. Abe Philips to Robert R. Williams, president of the Board of School Commissioners, June 13, 1975, Barton Academy archives.

16. The Toulminville-Shaw Pre-Planning Advisory Site Selection Committee included Rev. C. C. Suggs Sr., chair of the Interdenominational Ministerial Alliance; Rev. Richard Rodda, vice chair; George L. Langham, Toulminville faculty; Pollie Jackson, Toulminville PTA; Alice Meadows, Shaw PTA; Christina Popwell, Shaw faculty; Morris Sneed, Shaw community; Rev. C. A. Lett, Mobile Ministerial Association; Leonard Wyatt, Toulminville community; Rev. T. E. Williams, Interdenominational Ministerial Alliance; H. Minge Reed, federal court representative; Carolyn Mitchell, Toulminville student; and Bo Hudson, Shaw student.

17. C. C. Suggs and Richard Rodda to Harold Collins, Nov. 4, 1975, Barton Academy archives.

18. Ibid.

19. Jim Blacksher to Judge Brevard Hand, December 4, 1975; Harold Collins, memo to Lem Taylor and Clardy, senior staff, Dec. 17, 1975, Barton Academy archives.

20. Lemuel Taylor, memo to Harold Collins, Jan. 21, 1976, Barton Academy archives.

21. *Mobile Press,* Feb. 12, 1981, and *Mobile Register,* Feb. 13, 1981.

22. See Board of School Commissioners, "A Proposed Design for the Development of High Schools in the Toulminville-Shaw Areas of the Mobile County Public School System," undated, Barton Academy archives. The quote appears on p. 17.

23. "Response of the United States to Defendants' Proposal for School Construction in the Toulminville-Shaw Area," *Birdie Mae Davis,* May 28, 1976.

24. Abe Pillans to Richard LoDestro, Aug. 13, 1976; Larry Newton, memo to senior staff, Dec. 3, 1976, including draft of NAACP's proposed consent decree; letter and proposed consent decree from J. Stanley Pottinger, assistant attorney general, and Anita Marshall, attorney for the Justice Department, to Abe Philips, Dec. 12, 1976, Barton Academy archives.

25. "Consent Order Concerning Toulminville–Shaw Area New Construction," *Birdie Mae Davis,* Feb. 7, 1977.

26. Board of School Commissioners, Mobile County Public Schools, Minutes (hereafter, Board Minutes), Mar. 15, 1978, pp. 97–98, Barton Academy archives.

27. The nine were the Mount Vernon area, Satsuma, Eight Mile area, Toulminville, Wolf Ridge, Baker, Theodore, St. Elmo, and the south end of the county.

28. In the first cluster would be Mary Montgomery, Blount, Vigor, Eight Mile, and Satsuma. The second cluster would include Toulminville, Wolf Ridge, Shaw, and Baker. Murphy, Williamson, Theodore, Mobile County High School, and Alba would comprise the third cluster.

29. Another complex would be built in the southern section of the county. Alba, Mobile County School, and Theodore would be closed, and overflow from Murphy, Shaw, and Toulminville would also be assigned to the southern complex.

30. Board Minutes, Mar. 15, 1978.

31. Board Minutes, Mar. 22, 1978.

32. Robert Campbell to Brevard Hand, Board Minutes, Sept. 12, 1978, emphasis added.

33. Board Minutes, Aug. 22, 1979; Blount community leaders were formally shown the plan's outlines at a meeting on July 27.

34. Board Minutes, Aug. 22, 1979, p. 412.

35. Ibid., p. 427.

36. Board Minutes, Aug. 29, 1979.

37. Ibid., 434.

38. Ibid., 439.

Chapter 7: Blacks on the Board

1. *Brown v. Moore* 428 F. Supp. 1123 (S. D. Ala. 1976); on appeal by the school board the appellate court affirmed the district court's decision (*Brown v. Moore* 575 F.2d 298 [5th Cir. 1978]). The U.S. Supreme Court vacated that ruling and remanded the case for further proceedings in light of its ruling in *Bolden* 446 U.S. 55 (1980), which required single-district elections in the city. The new proceeding in U.S. District Court is known as *Brown v. Board of School Commissioners of Mobile County* 542 F. Supp. 1078 (S. D. Ala. 1982).

2. Peyton McCrary, "The Significance of *Bolden v. The City of Mobile*," and James Blacksher and Larry Menefee, "At-Large Elections and One Person, One Vote," in *Minority Vote Dilution*, ed. Chandler Davidson, 47–64 and 203–48 (Washington, D.C.: Howard University Press, 1984).

3. Robert Campbell, the school board's lawyer, quoted Pittman during the board meeting of April 16. See Board of School Commissioners, Mobile County Public Schools, Minutes (hereafter, Board Minutes), Apr. 16, 1979, pp. 172–73, archived at Barton Academy, 504 Government Street, Mobile.

4. Board Minutes, Dec. 8, 1978, pp. 617–19.

5. The intention of the state board of education was to mandate that such testing begin the following year, and the Mobile central office staff members thought it worthless to develop and use their own test for one year if the state test was going to supersede it; the effort to develop a local test would have wasted too much time and money.

6. Board Minutes, Dec. 15, 1978, pp. 617–19.

7. Board Minutes, Jan. 10, 1979. The staff said the district had received Dr. Raoul Arreola's confidential report on the various tests available, and it was circulating. The board probably would take it up in two weeks.

8. Board Minutes, Jan. 10, 1979, pp. 19–20.

9. Sanford Lloyd to editor, *Mobile Register,* Jan. 30, 1979.

10. Board Minutes, Jan. 24, 1979, p. 31.

11. Ibid., 43–47

12. Ibid., 47–51

13. *Mobile Register,* Jan. 31, 1979.

14. Board Minutes, Feb. 7, 1979, p. 64.

15. Ibid., 64.

16. Ibid., 67.

17. Ibid., 70–71.

18. Ibid., 78–79.

19. Ibid., 80.

20. Board Minutes, Feb. 21, 1979, p. 88.

21. *Mobile Press,* Mar. 7, 1979.

22. *Mobile Register,* Mar. 15, 1979.

23. Board Minutes, Mar. 7, 1979, p. 114.

24. Ibid., 116.

25. Ibid., 118.

26. Board Minutes, Mar. 14, 1979, p. 139.

27. Board Minutes, Apr. 11, 1979.

28. Board Minutes, Apr. 16, 1979, pp. 172–73.

29. Ibid., 178.

30. Board Minutes, Apr. 17, 1979, p. 204.

31. *Mobile Press,* Apr. 18, 1979.

32. Board Minutes, Apr. 25, 1979.

33. *Birmingham Post-Herald,* Apr. 19, 1979.

Chapter 8: Grandstanding

1. *Mobile Register,* Jan. 6, 1980.

2. *Mobile Register,* Jan. 3, 1980.

3. *Mobile Register,* Jan. 9, 1980.

4. *Mobile Press,* Jan. 17, 1980.

5. *Mobile Register,* Jan. 24, 1980.

6. *Mobile Press* and *Register,* Feb. 17, 1980.

7. *Mobile Press,* Feb. 7, 1980, and *Mobile Register,* Feb. 8, 1980.

8. Dan Alexander, telephone interview by author, Feb. 14, 1999.

9. Ibid.

10. *Mobile Press,* Feb. 12, 1980; *Birmingham News,* Feb. 17, 1980.

11. *Mobile Press,* Feb. 12, 1980; *Mobile Register,* Feb. 14, 1980.

12. *Mobile Press,* Feb. 13, 1980.

13. *Mobile Register,* Mar. 27, 1980.

14. *Mobile Register,* Feb. 21, 1980, Baldwin County sec.

15. *Mobile Register,* Feb. 26, 1980.

16. Board of School Commissioners, Mobile County Public Schools, Minutes (hereafter, Board Minutes), Feb. 27, 1980, archived at Barton Academy, 504 Government Street, Mobile.

17. *Mobile Register,* Mar. 13, 1980.

18. Board Minutes, Mar. 12, 1980.

19. *Mobile Register,* Mar. 27, 1980.

20. *Mobile Register,* Mar. 15, 1980; *Mobile Press* and *Register,* Mar. 27, 1980.

21. *Mobile Register,* Mar. 28, 1980.

22. *Mobile Register* Mar. 27, 1980; as school board president, Alexander had been stripped of voting authority except to break a tie.

23. *Mobile Register,* Mar. 27, 1980.

24. Ibid.

25. *Mobile Register,* Mar. 25, 1980.

26. Ibid.

27. *Mobile Press,* Mar. 28, 1980.

28. *Mobile Register,* Mar. 13, 1980.

29. Ibid.

30. *Mobile Register,* Mar. 17, 1980.

31. *Mobile Press,* Apr. 6, 1980.

32. *Mobile Register,* Apr. 25, 1980.

33. *Mobile Register,* May 10, 1980.

34. *Mobile Register,* June 13, 1980.

35. *Mobile Press* and *Register,* June 15, 1980.

36. *Mobile Register,* November 2, 1981.

37. See Richard K. Scher, Jon L. Mills, and John J. Hotaling, *Voting Rights and Democracy* (Chicago: Nelson Hall, 1997), 62; *Mobile Press,* Apr. 22, 1980.

38. Although Mobile's population in 1980 was 35 percent black, no black had ever been elected as commissioner; see *Mobile Register,* Apr. 27, 1980.

39. *Mobile Register,* Apr. 23, 1980.

40. *Mobile Register,* Apr. 24 and July 10, 1980.

41. *Mobile Register,* Apr. 23, 1980.

42. Ibid.

43. Ibid.

44. Ibid.

45. Ibid.

46. *Birmingham News,* July 9, 1980.

47. *Mobile Register,* November 8, 1980.

48. *Mobile Press,* Apr. 22, 1980; *Mobile Register,* Apr. 23, 1980.

49. Ibid.

50. *Mobile Press,* Apr. 22, 1980.

51. Twelve black residents of Mobile filed *Brown v. Moore* in 1975 as a class-action suit; they contended that the at-large commission system violated their constitutional rights. See *Mobile Press,* Oct. 16, 1980, and *Mobile Register,* Oct. 16, 1980.

52. *Mobile Register,* Apr. 23, 1980.

53. Ibid.

54. *Inner City News,* May 3, 1980.

55. Ibid.

56. *Mobile Press,* May 7, 1980; *Mobile Register,* May 8, 1980.

57. *Mobile Register,* July 26, 1980.

58. *Mobile Register,* July 29, 1980.

59. According to the ruling in *Brown v. Moore,* the two commissioners elected from single-member districts in 1978, Cox and Gilliard, would make the board a six-member panel until November 1980 when a District 5 representative would be sworn in. The terms of both Drago and Alexander would expire in November 1980 (*Mobile Register,* Sept. 25, 1980).

60. Ibid.

61. *Mobile Register,* July 29, 1980.

62. Ibid.

63. Ibid.

64. *Mobile Register,* July 24, 1980.

65. *Mobile Register,* July 15, 1980.

66. *Mobile Press,* July 31, 1980.

67. Ibid.

68. *Inner City News,* Aug. 2, 1980.

69. Ibid.

70. *Mobile Register,* Aug. 1, 1980.

71. *Mobile Register,* Aug. 13, 1980. The apparent confusion on the board was so great that in November the commissioners were even unsure about who chaired some committees. See *Mobile Register,* Nov. 20, 1980.

72. *Mobile Press,* Aug. 26, 1981, and *Mobile Register,* Aug. 26, 1981.

73. *Mobile Register,* Aug. 20, 1980.

74. *Mobile Press,* Aug. 22, 1980.

75. *Azalea City News,* Aug. 28, 1980.

76. *Mobile Register,* Oct. 16, 1980.

77. Ibid.

78. *Mobile Register,* Oct. 22, 1980.

79. Ibid.

80. Raymond Wolters, *Right Turn: William Bradford Reynolds, the Reagan Administration, and Black Civil Rights* (New Brunswick, N.J.: Transaction Books, 1996).

81. Thomas Byrne Edsall and Mary D. Edsall, *Chain Reaction: The Impact of Race, Rights, and Taxes on American Politics* (New York: W. W. Norton, 1991), 173–214.

82. Nicholas Laham, *The Reagan Presidency and the Politics of Race* (Westport, Conn.: Praeger, 1998), 12.

83. *Montgomery Advertiser,* Jan. 11, 1981.

84. Ibid.

85. *Mobile Press,* Jan. 7, 1981.

86. *Mobile Press,* Jan. 8, 1981.

87. In June, for example, the Atlanta school board voted to base layoffs on judgments of competence rather than seniority, outraging teacher unions across Georgia (*Mobile Press,* June 1, 1981).

88. The requirements mandated that the district use a white/black ratio of 60:40 for assigning teachers to each school (*Mobile Press,* Apr. 1, 1981).

89. *Mobile Press,* Jan. 7, 1981.

90. Ibid.

91. *Mobile Register,* Feb. 14, 1981.

92. Ibid.

93. *Mobile Register,* Feb. 21, 1981.

94. Ibid.

95. *Mobile Press,* Apr. 13, 1981.

96. *Mobile Register,* Apr. 14, 1981.

97. *Mobile Register,* Apr. 15, 1981.

98. Ibid.
99. Ibid.
100. Ibid.
101. *Mobile Register,* Apr. 18, 1981.
102. Ibid.
103. *Mobile Press* and *Register,* Apr. 19, 1981.
104. *Mobile Register,* Apr. 14, 1981.
105. *Mobile Register,* Apr. 19, 1981.
106. *Mobile Register,* Apr. 14 and 19, 1981.
107. *Mobile Press,* Apr. 23, 1981.
108. Ibid.
109. *Mobile Press,* Mar. 6, 1980.
110. *Mobile Register,* Dec. 27, 1981.
111. Ibid.
112. *Mobile Register,* May 30, 1981.
113. Ibid.; *Mobile Register,* June 26, 1981.
114. *Mobile Press,* July 24, 1981, and *Mobile Register,* July 22 and 24, 1981.
115. *Mobile Press,* July 24, 1981.
116. *Mobile Press,* July 22, 1981.
117. *Montgomery Advertiser,* July 24, 1981.
118. Ibid.
119. *Mobile Press,* July 24, 1981.
120. *Mobile Register,* Aug. 19, 1981.
121. In addition to Alabama State, the threat to withdraw state accreditation would have applied to Alabama A&M, Huntington College, Jacksonville State University, Mobile College, Talladega College, Troy State University at Dothan, and the Tuskegee Institute (*Mobile Register,* Aug. 19, 1981).
122. *Mobile Register,* Aug. 19, 1981.
123. *Inner City News,* Aug. 29, 1981.
124. *Mobile Register,* Aug. 20, 1981.
125. Ibid.
126. *Montgomery Advisor,* Oct. 22, 1981.
127. *Montgomery Advertiser,* Oct. 22, 1981.
128. *Mobile Press,* Oct. 28, 1981, and *Mobile Register,* Oct. 28, 1981.
129. Ibid.
130. Ibid.
131. *Montgomery Advertiser,* Dec. 23, 1981.
132. *Azalea City News,* Nov. 18, 1981.
133. *Azalea City News,* Dec. 10, 1981.
134. *Birmingham News,* Oct. 1, 1981.
135. *Mobile Register,* Mar. 27, 1982.
136. *Montgomery Advertiser,* Jan. 31, 1982.
137. Ibid.
138. Ibid.
139. *Montgomery Advertiser,* Feb. 13, 1982.

140. *Azalea City News,* Jan. 28, 1982.

141. *Mobile Register,* Apr. 23, 1982.

142. *Azalea City News,* Apr. 22, 1982.

143. *Birmingham News,* Apr. 16, 1982; *New Times,* Apr. 22, 1982.

144. *Mobile Register,* Apr. 17, 1982. The custom was that the local delegation would submit such legislation and the legislature would approve it as a courtesy.

145. *Mobile Register,* Apr. 29, 1982.

146. *Mobile Press,* Apr. 26, 1982, and *Mobile Register,* Apr. 26, 1982.

147. *Azalea City News,* Apr. 22, 1982.

148. Ibid.

149. *Inner City News,* Apr. 24, 1982.

150. Ibid.

151. *Montgomery Advertiser,* Apr. 16, 1982.

152. *Mobile Press,* Apr. 27, 1982, and *Mobile Register,* Apr. 27, 1982.

153. Ibid.; *Register,* Apr. 28, 1982.

154. *New Times,* Apr. 29, 1982.

155. Ibid.

156. Ibid.

157. *Montgomery Advertiser,* May 15, 1982.

158. *Mobile Register,* May 26, 1982.

159. *Mobile Register,* May 28, 1982.

160. *Mobile Register,* May 27, 1982.

161. *Mobile Press* and *Register,* May 30, 1982.

162. *Mobile Register,* June 26, 1982.

163. *Birmingham News,* May 18, 1982; *Mobile Press* and *Register,* May 21, 1982.

164. *Mobile Register,* June 2, 1982.

165. *Mobile County News,* May 27, 1982.

166. *Mobile Register,* Aug. 8, 1982.

167. *Montgomery Advertiser,* May 20, 1982.

168. *Mobile Register,* Aug. 8, 1982.

169. Ibid.

170. *Mobile Press,* Oct. 28, 1982.

171. *Montgomery Advertiser,* May 20, 1982.

172. *New Times,* June 3 and July 23, 1982.

173. *Mobile Register,* June 22, 1982.

174. *Mobile Register,* July 23, 1982.

175. Ibid.

176. *New Times,* Aug. 5, 1982.

177. *Mobile Press,* Nov. 11, 1982.

178. *New Times,* Sept. 30, 1982.

179. *Mobile Press* and *Register,* Aug. 1, 1982.

180. *Mobile Press* and *Register,* Dec. 12, 1982.

181. *Azalea City News,* Jan. 27, 1983.

182. Ibid.

183. *Mobile Press* and *Register,* Feb. 20, 1983. Note that some news reports suggested that

the faculty and staff of at least one Prichard school—Blount High School—were *not* opposed to relocating the school. See also *Mobile Press* and *Register,* Feb. 27, 1983.

184. *Mobile Press* and *Register,* Feb. 20, 1983.

185. *Mobile Press* and *Register,* Feb. 20, 1983, and *Mobile Register,* Feb. 25, 1983.

186. *Inner City News,* Feb. 26, 1983.

187. *Inner City News,* Jan. 29, 1983.

188. *Inner City News,* Feb. 26, 1983.

189. *Mobile Register,* Mar. 18, 1983. The final tally was 41 in favor, 41 against, with one abstention.

190. Ibid.

191. *Mobile County News,* Feb. 10, 1983.

192. *Mobile Register,* Mar. 27, 1983.

193. *Mobile Register,* Mar. 24, 1983.

194. Ibid.

195. *Mobile Register,* May 13, 1983.

196. *Mobile Register,* June 1, 1983.

197. Ibid.

198. *Mobile Register,* June 2, 1983.

199. *Mobile Press* and *Register,* May 29, 1983.

200. Ibid.

201. *Mobile Register,* July 15, 1983.

202. *Mobile Press,* July 14, 1983.

203. *Mobile Press,* July 22, 1983.

204. *Mobile Press,* July 29, 1983.

205. *Mobile Register,* July 30, 1983.

206. *Mobile Register,* Aug. 5, 1983.

207. *Mobile Register,* Sept. 10, 1983.

208. *Mobile Register,* Oct. 27, 1983.

209. *Mobile Register,* July 17, 1983.

210. *New Times,* Aug. 11, 1983.

211. *Mobile Press,* July 22, 1983; *Mobile Beacon,* June 18, 1983; *Mobile Press* and *Register,* Sept. 12, 1983.

212. See *Mobile Register,* Oct. 27, 1983.

213. *Mobile Press,* July 19, 1983, and *Mobile Register,* Aug. 20, 1983.

214. *Mobile Register,* June 8, 1983, and *Mobile Press* and *Register,* Aug. 14, 1983.

215. *Mobile Register,* Sept. 17, 1983.

216. *Mobile Register,* Sept. 1, 1983.

217. Ibid.

218. *Mobile Press,* Sept. 29, 1983, and *Mobile Register,* Sept. 29, 1983.

219. Ibid.

220. Certification of Drago's 1980 election in "old District 5" was still pending. By court order Bosarge could not run for reelection until 1986, the year of the District 5 election. See *Mobile Press,* Nov. 9, 1983, and *Mobile Register,* Nov. 9, 1983.

221. *Azalea City News,* Sept. 27, 1983.

222. *Mobile Register,* Nov. 17, 1983.

223. *New Times,* Oct. 20, 1983.

224. Ibid.

225. *Mobile Register,* Dec. 24, 1983.

226. *Mobile Register,* Sept. 1, 1983.

227. Ibid.

228. *Mobile Register,* Oct. 8, 1983.

229. *Mobile Register,* Aug. 12, 1983.

230. *Mobile Register,* Aug. 13, 1983.

231. *Mobile Register,* Sept. 20, 1983.

Chapter 9: Narrative Closure

1. Raymond Wolters, *Right Turn: William Bradford Reynolds, the Reagan Administration, and Black Civil Rights* (New Brunswick, N.J.: Transaction Books, 1996), 343.

2. Ibid., 305.

3. Ibid., 363.

4. Agreement, *Birdie Mae Davis et al., Plaintiffs; Joyce Figures Gant et al., Plaintiffs-Intervenors v. Board of School Commissioners et al.,* Civil Action No. 3003-63-H, Nov. 22, 1988.

5. Ibid., 12.

6. Ibid., 17, 18.

7. Ibid., 20.

8. *Mobile Register,* June 6, 1996.

9. *Mobile Register,* Jan. 8, 1996.

10. The Supreme Court rulings were *Board of Education of Oklahoma City Public Schools v. Dowell,* 498 U.S. 437 (1991), and *Freeman v. Pitts* 503 U.S. 467 (1992); Stipulation and Order of Dismissal, and Agreement, *Birdie Mae Davis et al.,* Mar. 27, 1997.

11. *Mobile Register,* Jan. 7, 1996.

12. Ibid.

13. Ibid.

14. Ibid.

15. Ibid.

16. Ibid.

17. *Mobile Register,* Mar. 3, 1997.

18. *Mobile Register,* Jan. 7, 1996.

19. *Mobile Register,* Mar. 12, 1996.

20. *Mobile Register,* Apr. 26, 1996.

21. *Mobile Register,* Jan. 22, 1997.

22. Stipulation and Order of Dismissal, and Agreement, *Birdie Mae Davis et al.,* Mar. 27, 1997.

23. *Mobile Register,* Mar. 6, 1997.

24. *Mobile Register,* Jan. 22, 1997.

25. Ibid.

26. *Mobile Register,* Mar. 2, 1997.

27. *Mobile Register,* Apr. 10, 1997.

28. *Mobile Register,* May 15, 1997.

29. *Mobile Register,* Mar. 1, 1997.

30. *Mobile Register,* Jan. 8, 1996.

31. Ibid.

Chapter 10: Redefining the Problem of Racial Inequality

1. Richard A. Pride, "How Activists and Media Frame Social Problems: Critical Events Versus Performance Trends for Schools," *Political Communication* 12:1 (1995): 5–26; Suzanne Staggenborg, "Critical Events and the Mobilization of the Pro-Choice Movement," *Research in Political Sociology* 6 (1993): 319–45.

2. David R. Maines, "Narrative's Moment and Sociology's Phenomena: Toward a Narrative Sociology," *Sociological Quarterly* 34 (1993): 17–38.

3. Thomas Rochon, *Ideas in Movement: Critical Communities and Movements as Forces for Cultural Change* (Princeton, N.J.: Princeton University Press, 1998), 23.

4. Ibid., 31.

5. Pride, "How Activists and Media Frame Social Problems"; Murray Edelman, *Constructing the Political Spectacle* (Chicago: University of Chicago Press, 1988); Dan Nimmo and J. E. Combs, *Mediated Political Realities* (New York: Longman, 1983).

6. Rochon, *Ideas in Movement,* 36.

7. Erving Goffman, *Frame Analysis: An Essay on the Organization of Experience* (New York: Harper and Row, 1974), 21; see also Todd Gitlin, *The Whole World Is Watching: Mass Media and the Making and Unmaking of the New Left* (Berkeley: University of California Press, 1980), and W. A. Gamson and A. Modigliani, "The Changing Culture of Affirmative Action," *Research in Sociology* 3 (1987): 137–77.

8. Gaye Tuchman, *Making News: A Study in the Construction of Reality* (New York: Free Press, 1978); Doris Graber, *Processing the News* (New York: Longman, 1988); S. M. Livingstone, *Making Sense of Television: The Psychology of Audience Interpretation* (Elmsford, N.Y.: Pergamon Press, 1990); and W. A. Gamson, *Talking Politics* (New York: Cambridge University Press, 1992).

9. Anthony Downs, "Up and Down with Ecology—The Issue Attention Cycle," *Public Interest* 28 (1972): 38–50; Stephen Hilgartner and Charles Bosk, "The Rise and Fall of Social Problems: A Public Arenas Model," *American Journal of Sociology* 94 (1988): 53–78; David A. Snow and Robert D. Benford, "Master Frames and Cycles of Protest," in *Frontiers of Social Movement Theory,* ed. Aldon Morris and Carol McClurg Mueller (New Haven, Conn.: Yale University Press, 1992), 133–55; and Zhongdang Pan and Gerald M. Kosicki, "Framing Analysis: An Approach to News Discourse," *Political Communication* 10 (1993): 55–75.

10. Paul Sniderman and Michael G. Hagen, *Race and Inequality: A Study in American Values* (Chatham, N.J.: Chatham House, 1985).

11. Howard Schuman, Charlotte Steeh, Lawrence Bobo, and Maria Krysan, *Racial Attitudes in America: Trends and Interpretations* (Cambridge, Mass.: Harvard University Press, 1997).

12. This chapter originally appeared as Richard Pride, "Redefining the Problem of Racial Inequality," *Political Communication* 16 (1999): 147–67.

13. Willis Hawley, *Strategies for Effective Desegregation: Lessons from Research* (Lexington, Mass.: Lexington Books, 1983).

14. David J. Armor, *Forced Justice: School Desegregation and the Law* (New York: Oxford University Press, 1995); Gary Orfield, *Must We Bus?* (Washington, D.C.: Brookings Institution, 1978); Gary Orfield, "Public Opinion and School Desegregation," *Teachers College Record* 96 (1995): 654–69; Richard A. Pride and J. David Woodard, *The Burden of Busing: The Politics of Desegregation in Nashville, Tennessee* (Knoxville: University of Tennessee Press, 1985); and Christine Rossell and David Armor, "The Effectiveness of School Desegregation Plans, 1968–1991," *American Politics Quarterly* 24 (1995): 267–302.

15. Mark Gerson, *The Neoconservative Vision* (New York: Madison Books, 1996).

16. Sara Diamond, *Roads to Dominion: Right-Wing Movements and Political Power in the United States* (New York: Guilford Press, 1995), 185.

17. Gerson, *Neoconservative Vision*, 85–86.

18. Diamond, *Roads to Dominion*, 205.

19. Schuman et al., *Racial Attitudes in America;* William G. Mayer, *The Changing American Mind: How and Why American Public Opinion Changed Between 1960 and 1988* (Ann Arbor: University of Michigan Press, 1992), 365–74.

20. Orfield, "Public Opinion and School Desegregation."

21. Michael Thompson, Richard Ellis, and Aaron Wildavsky, *Cultural Theory* (Boulder, Colo.: Westview Press, 1990); Richard J. Ellis, *American Political Cultures* (New York: Oxford University Press, 1993).

22. The calculations are based on data from U.S. Census Bureau, *U.S. Census of Population: 1950*, vol. 2: *Characteristics of the Population, Part 2, Alabama* (Washington, D.C.: U.S. Government Printing Office, 1952), 87, and *1990 U.S. Census of Population, Social and Economic Characteristics, Alabama* (U.S. Government Printing Office, 1993), 229, 250.

23. Christine Rossell, *The Carrot or the Stick for Desegregation Policy? Magnet Schools or Forced Busing* (Philadelphia: Temple University Press, 1990), 33–39.

24. Gary Orfield and Susan Eaton, *Dismantling Desegregation: The Quiet Reversal of "Brown v. Board of Education"* (New York: New Press, 1996).

25. Stephen Steinberg, *Turning Back: The Retreat from Racial Justice in American Thought and Policy* (Boston: Beacon Press, 1995).

26. Thomas Byrne Edsall and Mary D. Edsall, *Chain Reaction: The Impact of Race, Rights, and Taxes on American Politics* (New York: W. W. Norton, 1991); Carl Rowan, *The Coming Race War in America: A Wake-Up Call* (New York: Little, Brown, 1997).

27. Christopher Campbell, *Race, Myth, and the News* (Thousand Oaks, Calif.: Sage, 1995).

28. Edsall and Edsall, *Chain Reaction*, 178.

29. Jannette L. Dates and William Barlow, *Split Image: African Americans in the Mass Media* (Washington, D.C.: Howard University Press, 1990); Robert M. Entman and Andrew Rojecki, *The Black Image in the White Mind: Media and Race in America* (Chicago: University of Chicago Press, 2000); Martin Gilens, *Why Americans Hate Welfare: Race, Media, and the Politics of Antipoverty* (Chicago: University of Chicago Press, 1999); Ronald Jacobs, *Race, Media, and the Crisis of Civil Society: From Watts to Rodney King* (New York: Cambridge University Press, 2000); and Robert Entman, "Blacks in the News: Television, Modern Racism, and Cultural Change," *Journalism Quarterly* 69:2 (1990): 341–61.

30. Campbell, *Race, Myth, and the News*.

31. Gerson, *Neoconservative Vision;* David Frum, *Dead Right* (New York: Basic Books, 1996).

Conclusion

1. Earl Black and Merle Black, *Politics and Society in the South* (Cambridge, Mass.: Harvard University Press, 1987), 23–72.

2. Richard A. Pride, *The Confession of Dorothy Danner: Telling a Life* (Nashville, Tenn.: Vanderbilt University Press, 1995), 206–207.

3. Ibid., 256.

4. *Mobile Register,* Aug. 30, 1963. See also Carol Swain, *The New White Nationalism in America: Its Challenge to Integration* (New York: Cambridge University Press, 2002).

5. Board of School Commissioners, Mobile County Public Schools, Minutes (hereafter, Board Minutes), Apr. 23, 1969, p. 120.

6. Board Minutes, May 28, 1969, p. 159.

7. Carol Swain, "Affirmative Action, White Nationalism, and the Politics of Race on College Campuses," unpublished paper, 2000, p. 2.

8. Jared Taylor, interview quoted in Swain, "Affirmative Action," p. 14; see also Jared Taylor, *Paved with Good Intentions* (New York: Carrol and Graf, 1992).

9. Michael Levin, *Why Race Matters: Racial Differences and What They Mean* (New York: Greenwood Press, 1997).

10. Levin, interview quoted in Swain, "Affirmative Action," p. 15.

11. Barry Mehler, "Race and 'Reason': Academic Ideas a Pillar of Racist Thought," *Intelligence Report* (Winter 1999): 27, quoted in Swain, "Affirmative Action," p. 24.

12. William Pierce [Andrew Macdonald, pseud.], *The Turner Diaries,* 2d ed. (Hillsboro, W. Va.: National Vanguard Books, 1995).

Index

RICHARD A. PRIDE is an associate professor of political science at Vanderbilt University. He is the author of *Origins of Democracy: A Cross-National Study of Mobilization, Party Systems, and Democratic Stability* (1970) and *The Confession of Dorothy Danner* (1995), coauthor of *The Burden of Busing: The Politics of Desegregation in Nashville, Tennessee* (1985), and coeditor of *Cross-National Micro-Analysis: Procedures and Problems* (1972).

The University of Illinois Press
is a founding member of the
Association of American University Presses.

———————————————————————————

Composed in 10.5/13 Minion
with Minion display
by Jim Proefrock
at the University of Illinois Press
Manufactured by Thomson-Shore, Inc.

University of Illinois Press
1325 South Oak Street
Champaign, IL 61820-6903
www.press.uillinois.edu